Working Relationships

Working Relationships

CREATING CAREER OPPORTUNITIES FOR JOB SEEKERS WITH DISABILITIES THROUGH EMPLOYER PARTNERSHIPS

Richard G. Luecking, Ed.D.
TransCen, Inc.
Rockville, Maryland

Ellen S. Fabian, Ph.D.
University of Maryland
College Park, Maryland

George P. Tilson, Ed.D.
TransCen, Inc.
Rockville, Maryland

with Mark Donovan,
Jo Ann Hutchinson, Debra Martin Luecking,
Sara Murphy, and J. Erin Riehle

·P·A·U·L·H·
BROOKES
PUBLISHING CO.®

Baltimore • London • Sydney

Paul H. Brookes Publishing Co.
Post Office Box 10624
Baltimore, MD 21285-0624

www.brookespublishing.com

Typeset by Barton Matheson Willse & Worthington, Baltimore, Maryland.
Manufactured in the United States of America by
IBT Global, Troy, New York.

All case studies in this book are based on the authors' actual experiences. In all
instances, names have been changed; in some instances, identifying features
have been altered to further protect confidentiality.

A previous edition of this book was published under the title *A Working
Relationship: The Job Development Specialist's Guide to Successful Partnerships with
Business.*

Second printing, February 2010.

Library of Congress Cataloging-in-Publication Data

Luecking, Richard G.
     Working relationships: creating career opportunities for job seekers with
disabilities through employer partnerships/ by Richard G. Luecking, Ellen S.
Fabian, and George P. Tilson.
          p.   cm.
     Rev. ed. of: A working relationship / Ellen S. Fabian. c1994.
     Includes bibliographical references and index.
     ISBN-13: 978-1-55766-709-0
     ISBN-10: 1-55766-709-8
     1. People with disabilities—Employment—United States.   2. Employees—
Recruiting—United States.   3. Employment agencies—United States.
I. Fabian, Ellen S.   II. Tilson, George P.   III. Fabian, Ellen S. Working
relationship.   IV. Title.
HD7256.U5L843   2004
658.3'0087—dc22
                                                                                      2003061128

British Library Cataloguing in Publication data are available from the British Library.

Contents

About the Authors

Richard G. Luecking, Ed.D., is President of TransCen. Prior to this affiliation, Dr. Luecking held professional and administrative positions in the fields of rehabilitation, special education, and nonprofit management. He has devoted most of his career to initiatives that link government-sponsored career and workforce development programs with businesses and employers. He has actively promoted these partnerships through program development, training, publications, and leadership in various professional, business, and community organizations.

Ellen S. Fabian, Ph.D., is Associate Professor in the Department of Counseling and Personnel Services (CAPS) at the University of Maryland, College Park. Dr. Fabian's career includes program development and evaluation in job development and supported employment, as well as research, training, and teaching in these and related areas. She has served in a number of leadership positions and maintains a strong interest in psychiatric rehabilitation, career development, and rehabilitation counseling.

George P. Tilson, Ed.D., is Senior Vice President of TransCen. Since 1975, his career has centered on vocational preparation, employment, and independent living of people with disabilities. He has worked as a special educator, job placement specialist, program manager, and human resources consultant and trainer. His current specialization is translating theory into practice in the areas of job development and placement.

TransCen, located in Rockville, Maryland, is dedicated to the improvement of educational and employment outcomes for individuals with disabilities. Its name was chosen to illustrate its role as a transition center. The authors and their colleagues at TransCen have developed, implemented, and researched numerous innovations regarding workforce and career development. Established in 1986, TransCen, a nonprofit organization, has been at the forefront of systems change efforts—working with school districts, human service organizations, business, government agencies, families, advocacy groups, and job seekers. As a result, TransCen has developed a host of targeted training and technical assistance offerings, both independently and in concert with broad initiatives and national consortiums. For more information, visit TransCen at its Bobby Approved™ web site, www.transcen.org.

About the Collaborators

Mark Donovan, Vice Chairman of the Marriott Foundation for People with Disabilities, was the organization's inaugural Executive Director and served in that role for 12 years. Prior to his tenure with the foundation, he worked for 10 years in operations management and 7 years in human resources. Mr. Donovan is a 1972 graduate of Earlham College.

Jo Ann Hutchinson, M.Ed., Rh.D., is Research Associate Professor at the University of Maryland's Rehabilitation Counseling Program. She received her master's degree in rehabilitation counseling from Coppin State College and her doctoral degree in rehabilitation administration from Southern Illinois University. In addition to teaching courses in rehabilitation counseling, Dr. Hutchinson serves as Director of the Region III Community Rehabilitation Providers Rehabilitation Continuing Education Program.

Debra Martin Luecking, M.A., Ed.D., is Director of the Center on Disability and Employment at The University of Tennessee. She received her master's degree in education administration from California State University, Northridge, and her doctoral degree in vocational education from The University of Tennessee. She has focused her 25-year career as a teacher, consultant, manager of direct services, administrator, and developer in advancing the learning of the workforce and community members toward general inclusion of people with disabilities.

Sara Murphy, M.S.Ed., is Director of Worklink, TransCen's San Francisco–based employment services office. Since the mid-1980s, she has been involved in establishing fully integrated transition and employment services for people with significant disabilities. She has been instrumental in creating innovative employment programs that are exclusively community-based and provide individualized, career-oriented employment assistance for job seekers with intensive support needs.

J. Erin Riehle, M.S.N., R.N., is Co-Director of Project SEARCH and Director of the Division of Disability Services at the Convalescent Hospital for Children, an affiliate of Cincinnati Children's Hospital Medical Center. She launched a national and local award-winning collaboration in 1995 among the Division of Disability Services, Great Oaks Institute of Career Development, and the Hamilton County Board of Mental Retardation/ Developmental Disabilities to provide employment opportunities in a health care setting for individual with disabilities, which has since been extended to include unemployed people, underemployed people, and those on public assistance.

Foreword

I gladly wrote the foreword to the authors' 1994 edition of this book, *A Working Relationship: The Job Development Specialist's Guide to Successful Partnerships with Business,* because I endorsed what they did and how they did it. The Marriott Foundation has partnered with Rich Luecking, George Tilson, and their organization, TransCen, since the late 1980s because we are attracted to their application of basic business principles to partnerships with business. When my family established the Marriott Foundation for People with Disabilities and its signature program, *Bridges...from school to work,* in 1989, we had no idea what it would become in the years ahead. What was clear as we rolled out the initial pilot was that TransCen would be an important partner in turning the concept of *Bridges* into reality for what are now thousands of young people with disabilities.

For the same reasons, I am honored to provide the foreword for this new book, *Working Relationships: Creating Career Opportunities for Job Seekers with Disabilities Through Employer Partnerships.* Its proven strategies for linking job seekers with employers reflects the two purposes of our *Bridges* program: to help young people with disabilities identify and gain access to avenues to a future that includes productive and fulfilling employment, and to help guide employers to a rich and largely untapped applicant pool. The authors know how this works and they do it well. TransCen has consistently demonstrated both its technical expertise and its commitment to our shared vision in matching the aspirations and talent of job seekers with the human resources needs of business.

Marriott's business success, starting with the nine-seat root beer stand my father opened in 1927 and continuing through its current international business presence, has been the result of a strong commitment to customer service, flexibility in responding to the ever-changing marketplace, and relationships that are based on trust and mutual return on investment. This book contains contemporary approaches rooted in these same principles—principles that have reliably powered business success and growth.

The experience of the Marriott companies is that a corporation's bottom line and the employment of individuals with disabilities are not incompatible. This book explains why. My regard for the authors' approach to linking job seekers and employers remains as high now as it was in 1994. I encourage anyone interested in promoting the employment of people with disabilities to seriously take into account the vision, perspective, and expertise contained herein.

Richard E. Marriott

Chairman, Host Marriott Corporation
Chairman, Marriott Foundation for People with Disabilities

Preface

When you come to a fork in the road, take it.

YOGI BERRA

It would be an incredible understatement to say that the world has changed a bit since we published our first book on business partnerships, *A Working Relationship: The Job Development Specialist's Guide to Successful Partnerships with Business,* in 1994. The field of disability employment services has seen the evolution of several new policy and legislative directions. At the same time, the business world has had to react to rapid changes in both the economy and in the way human resources are managed. An adventurous spirit, as implied in Yogi Berra's malapropism, has never been more necessary if we are to successfully navigate these changes.

Each successive year since *A Working Relationship* was published has taught us that there is no single or effortless path to develop partnerships between employers and employment specialists and employment organizations. Many effective alternatives will get us to the same place; however, some ways are better than others. Much of what we wrote about in the first book concerning service competence, customer satisfaction, mutual return on investment in partnerships, and excellence in human resources management is still very relevant. These issues are covered in this new edition, *Working Relationships: Creating Career Opportunities for Job Seekers with Disabilities Through Employer Partnerships,* but with significantly expanded information to support the relevant strategies.

Mostly, though, we have included new information that we have learned through experience and from the experiences of many colleagues around the country. We are encouraged by the many new, innovative, effective employment approaches that hold significant promise for improving employment outcomes for people with disabilities. We have included what we have learned from these experiences to bolster knowledge in this area. In turn, we have also added a theoretical and conceptual framework that supports the strategies we recommend and that may also provide a framework for future practice and research in the important task of job development for people with disabilities.

We are discouraged, however, that too many employment specialists still rely on a "beg, place, and pray" approach to job development. This approach not only relies on charitable responses from employers but also reflects an unfortunate underlying lack of conviction that people with disabilities can offer important contributions to employers' enterprises. Thus, this book was written for two reasons. First, a need still exists to show that there is a job for everyone who wants to work, regardless of the nature or circumstance of disability and regardless of the economic vitality of the communities in which they live. Every employment service agency should adopt a mission based on the premise that every individual can become a contributing member of the workforce. Second, there is still a need to elevate and professionalize interactions between disability employment specialists and those entities that provide the jobs—businesses and employers. The concept of excellent customer service that drives the success of many prominent businesses is equally relevant to job development initiatives. As we discuss throughout the book, the elevation of job developer–employer interaction improves considerably when employers are regarded and treated as the valuable customers they are. Thus, the spirit and basic philosophy of our first book remain.

In addition to paraphrasing what we said in our first book on employer partnerships, we add considerations about assisting individuals in pursuing a truly self-directed job search. Employment professionals and employment agencies must consider the following in order to truly effect a change in the way they do business with employers and link them to job seekers:

1. Actively address employer concerns and misperceptions about people with disabilities by first recognizing the talents and capabilities of individual job seekers.

2. Make sure the job search is driven by the uniqueness of every job seeker and every employer.

3. Refocus on job development and employer relationships as the *most* important concerns within organizations representing job seekers with disabilities.

4. Operate proactively, not reactively, in the business world: You cannot afford to wait for employers to seek you out. Launch yourself into the business market and demonstrate the value of your service.

5. Examine from the inside out all perceptions regarding services and commitment to delivering high-quality services. Without quality, professionals and service organizations should not be in the service business.

In writing this book, as with the last, we have watched how these fundamental activities can affect the development of successful business partnerships and ultimately jobs and careers for people with disabilities. In every sense this book is about value-driven partnerships that reshape the way we go about the business of opening up the workplace for people with disabilities. The contemporary and ever-changing business climate and new policy directions emanating from federal and state venues necessitate a continual re-examination of how we go about our work. There will always be forks in the road. We hope to arm readers with tools that will help them pick the right one—or at least do the right thing, no matter which fork is chosen.

Acknowledgments

As has been the case many times over the past 15 years, we are again indebted to Richard E. Marriott for his vision and support of efforts that link employers and job seekers with disabilities. We are honored that he has graciously agreed to provide the foreword to another of our books. We have learned so much from all of the Marriott folks about employer expectations and about customer service.

Several of our colleagues at TransCen deserve mention for not only their ability to develop working relationships with employers but also, in some cases, for contributing editorial assistance in compiling much of the background material and many of the case studies that eventually went into this book. They are Sara Murphy, Meredith Gramlich, Amy Dwyre, Kelli Crane, Marianne Mooney, Maggie Leedy, LaVerne Buchanan, Lisa Cuozzo, Sharon Bryant, Suellen Farrington, Marian Vessels, Fay Mays-Bester, Laura Ritterbush, Christy Stuart, Deborah Muir, and Walter Glaser. Theresa Johnson also deserves special mention for her exemplary competence and important contributions that support our efforts. To other present and past TransCen colleagues and associates, thank you for creating and nurturing the hundreds of working relationships that make this work successful.

Finally, thanks go to all of the employers and job seekers with whom we and our colleagues have worked. They continually show that the career development of people with disabilities can and should be well matched with effective business/employer operations.

Introduction

Working Relationships: Creating Career Opportunities for Job Seekers with Disabilities Through Employer Partnerships is about how people with disabilities and employers can be linked. This linking is often done through the intercession and assistance of professionals and organizations whose mission is to help make these links. Acting as intermediaries (i.e., agents who form partnerships and develop relationships in order to connect and facilitate communication among different parties), these professionals and organizations have been at the core of disability employment initiatives for decades.

Professionals who perform these intermediary roles have many different titles, such as rehabilitation counselor, vocational counselor, job developer, job coach, and employment specialist. To simplify matters, we have chosen to use the term *employment specialist* throughout the book to refer to any individual or professional who simultaneously assists people with disabilities to obtain jobs and careers and assists employers to hire and accommodate people with disabilities.

Similarly, many types of organizations and entities have missions related to assisting people with disabilities with career development and linking them with prospective employers. Some of these organizations assist people with a wide range of disabilities, and others serve people who have specific disabilities, who have certain life circumstances, or who want a particular kind of program. Still others serve a broad range of job seekers with other barriers to employment, only a fraction of whom have disabilities. Some of these organizations are government operated. Some are private, nonprofit organizations. Others are private, for-profit. In this book, we use the term *disability employment service agency* or *program* or simply *employment program* interchangeably to mean any of these organizations. They all act as intermediary linking mechanisms between job seekers and employers. Thus, the issues, principles, and strategies discussed in this book are pertinent to any of these organizations, regardless of the specific population they may serve or how they are organized and operated.

Although *Working Relationships* is primarily for employment specialists and disability employment programs, it has several potential secondary audiences: Essentially, anyone interested in the theory, policy, or practice related to employment of people with disabilities will find something relevant here. This includes teachers and trainers of job development personnel, researchers on employment of people with disabilities, administrators of employment service programs, all manner of employment specialists, funders of employment service programs, employment policy makers, and job seekers and their families. However, the primary intent of this book is to provide both theoretical and practical information to professionals within intermediary organizations who strive to assist people with disabilities to identify their career goals, capitalize on their strengths, develop new essential skills, and connect with employers in such a way that everyone benefits.

HOW THE BOOK IS ORGANIZED

We have organized this book into three sections. The first section sets the stage for partnership development that undergirds all links between job seekers and employers. It offers a theoretical and operational framework for job development, describes career development theories as they apply to job development for people with disabilities, explores how employers think about disability and disability employment services, describes how the concept of networking applies to business partnerships and the job search process, provides case studies of partnerships at work, and addresses fundamental skills that employment specialists need. The chapters all provide strategies that employment specialists and disability employment agencies can adopt almost immediately to experience more success in representing job seekers to prospective and current employer customers.

The final section explores new trends and directions that may influence partnership development with businesses and employers in the years to come, including evolving roles for employment specialists, developing organization development strategies that restructure disability employment programs so that they are more business friendly, new focuses on job retention and career growth, and a view of issues and trends that will affect the future employment of people with disabilities.

Two notes on editorial prerogative. First, we are wary of using specific disability labels when referring to individuals in the case studies. Unless there is a compelling reason to name the disability for case study clarity, we do not. It is our belief that too often assumptions are made about individuals' circumstances based on disability label. It is important, of course, to factor in accommodations that particular people need to succeed in the workplace, but even within particular disability categories, the range and type of accommodations are broad and depend mostly on each individual's circumstance. Thus, in general discussion, we almost always refer to people with disabilities simply as *job seekers.* The reader should be able to apply the concepts discussed here to any job seeker, regardless of the nature of job seekers' disability, need for support, or label.

Second, we recognize that employers also come in all sizes and descriptions: private sector, for-profit entities; local, state, and federal government entities; and nonprofit and civic entities. Some employers have a handful of employees; others hire thousands. A host of industry sectors exist under which these various entities could be classified. To simplify matters, in general discussion we use the terms *employer, business,* and *company* interchangeably to refer to any entity—public or private, large or small—that employs job seekers. Again, the issues and strategies related to forming relationships apply to almost any employer. The linking of individual job seekers with individual employers ultimately defines our work, no matter what we call them.

A FINAL NOTE

Studies of employer views of people with disabilities indicate employers have not yet widely embraced the notion of bringing people with disabilities into their workplaces. This is due less to any inherent objection to the idea of employment of people with disabilities than to the fact that employers simply have a hard time finding out about programs and services that serve job seekers with disabilities. When employers do find out, they have trouble understanding what these programs and services are all about. The language and the culture of disability employment services for the most part have not jibed with those of the business world.

It could be argued, then, that part of the reason for continuing high unemployment rates for people with disabilities is that there is still a very basic lack of appreciation or understanding of employer views and circumstances. If not enough people with disabilities are getting jobs and not enough employers are getting connected to sources of workers with disabilities, then more refined approaches and broader perspectives need to be considered. Fortunately, along with the bad news of disappointing employment outcomes for people with disabilities is the good news that the methodology exists to change this trend. This book intends to help professionals augment successful job search approaches with contemporary employer partnership development so that employment of people with disabilities is the rule rather than the exception.

I

Foundations for Partnership

1

Job Development and Placement

TOWARD A NEW EMPHASIS ON OUTCOMES

One society is "better" than another if a greater number of its people have access to experiences that are aligned with their goals.

MIHALY CSIKSZENTMIHALYI, PSYCHOLOGIST AND AUTHOR

The issue of jobs for people with disabilities has become a central focus of disability policy in America. This goal has influenced social policy in part because of the general desire to support opportunity and fairness in our society, as exemplified in the Americans with Disabilities Act (ADA) of 1990 (PL 101-336). An equally compelling reason is the rising cost of disability entitlement programs in America and the desire to promote employment for those individuals with disabilities who want to work. Whatever the reasons for promoting this policy, there is agreement that work is an essential cultural ingredient in America and represents the major path to achieving high quality of life.

Although the goodness of work has been an accepted value underlying social policy in postindustrial America, the data on employment and labor force participation of people with disabilities are not consistent with this value. For example, analysis of employment data (Houtenville, 2001a) showed an employment rate of men with disabilities to be only 34%, compared with a 95% rate of employment for men without disabilities. Similarly, women with disabilities had an employment rate of only 29.5%, compared with 80.8% for women without disabilities. The income gap between workers with disabilities and their nondisabled counterparts is also large (Houtenville, 2001b). The average house-

3

hold income of men with disabilities was only about $12,000, compared with more than $28,000 for men without disabilities. Despite decades of policy emphasizing the financial and social benefits of employment, having a disability in America remains associated with unemployment and lower wages.

This chapter provides an overview of historical barriers to employment for people with disabilities, reviews applicable legislation and social policy that have affected employment of people with disabilities, and introduces a theoretical structure for building networks and developing partnerships with employers that will help generate employment outcomes that are consistent with societal values and policy intent.

BARRIERS TO EMPLOYMENT

Many reasons are offered to explain the persisting poor employment data for individuals with disabilities. Essentially three major barriers to employment participation have been identified in the literature: the disincentives of the Social Security benefits programs, misinformed attitudes toward individuals with disabilities, and lack of access to appropriate rehabilitation and employment search interventions that result in paid employment.

Policy Disincentives

One major barrier frequently mentioned in the literature is the impact of public support programs, particularly those administered by the Social Security Administration (SSA) (LaPlante, Kennedy, Kaye, & Wenger, 1996; Noble, 1998). Supplemental Security Income (SSI) and Social Security Disability Income (SSDI) not only provide monthly income support for eligible beneficiaries, but also health insurance coverage through one of the federal programs, Medicaid or Medicare.

SSA benefits may operate as employment disincentives, a fact made clear by the numbers. For example, fewer than 1% of SSDI and SSI beneficiaries leave the rolls each year as a result of obtaining paid employment. Of those who do leave, about one third return within 3 years (*The Ticket to Work and Self-Sufficiency Program,* 2001). Furthermore, studies by the SSA have pointed to a programmatic correlation between growth of the beneficiary programs and lowered labor force participation rates for individuals with disabilities (Muller, 1992). Smaller studies focusing on the effect of compensation on employment outcomes have found that resistance to seeking competitive employment is greater among individuals who were receiving Social Security benefits (Nichols, 1989) and that the availability of income compensation programs corresponds to withdrawal from the labor force

(Drew et al., 2001). However, it is important to note that periodic surveys of beneficiaries with disabilities indicate an expressed desire to work (LaPlante et al., 1996), suggesting that it is not the *availability* of the compensatory benefits that discourages employment but the fear of losing associated health benefits. The Ticket to Work and Work Incentives Improvement Act of 1999 (PL 106-170), a major revision of social security law, is designed to ease the transition from benefits to employment by providing continuing access to federal health insurance programs. The effect of this law on employment outcomes remains unknown, and its provisions are discussed later in this chapter.

Employer and Societal Attitudes

Another barrier is employer attitudes toward and perceptions about individuals with disabilities. When Congress passed the ADA, it acknowledged that employer attitudes toward individuals with disabilities have historically had a negative impact on employment, stating that the intention of the act was to "eliminate discrimination against individuals with disabilities" (Section 12101[B][1]). The recognition of discrimination was based on various sources of evidence, including the historically poor performance of employers in providing workplace opportunity to individuals with disabilities and surveys of employer attitudes toward job seekers with disabilities (Unger, 2002a). Employer attitudinal surveys have consistently found that employers report the same stereotypical attitudes and myths about workers with disabilities as did the general population. For example, employers tend to have the most negative attitudes toward job seekers with emotional or mental disabilities (Drehmer, 1985; Johnson, Greenwood, & Schriner, 1988) and express general concern regarding work performance and quality of workers with disabilities (Blanck, 1998; Minskoff, Sautter, Hoffmann, & Hawks, 1987). Although some surveys of employer willingness to hire individuals with disabilities reflect more positive attitudes (Hernandez, 2000; Levy, Jessop, Rimmerman, Francis, & Levy, 1993), negative stereotypes toward some individuals with disabilities persist as barriers to workplace opportunity (Cook & Razzano, 1994; Unger, 2002a). Thus, passage of the ADA with the stated intention of ending discrimination was an important effort in reducing attitudinal barriers. The extent to which the ADA is succeeding in this effort is discussed later in the chapter.

Access to Employment Assistance

The third barrier to labor force participation is the lack of effective employment programs. One source of vocational rehabilitation (VR) for individuals with disabilities in America is the public or federal VR program system. This system, existing in all states and U.S. territories, was founded in 1917 and is the only program designed to provide a variety of

VR services to adults with disabilities in order to prepare them to enter or re-enter the workplace (Rubin & Roessler, 1995). The public VR system is distinguished by its ability to offer an array of service options tailored to individual job seeker needs. However, unlike special education services, the public VR system is not an entitlement program, and its funding reflects its limited capacity. For example, in the fiscal year (FY) 1999, about 1.3 million individuals were served nationally in the system. An estimated 60% were identified as successfully rehabilitated, and those cases were closed. This is only a fraction of working-age adults with disabilities who are eligible for VR services (Research Triangle International, 2003).

Other public entities, such as state mental health and developmental disability administrations, also fund services for individuals with disabilities, particularly those with the most severe cognitive and emotional impairments. Historically, state funds have been used to support facility-based programs, such as sheltered workshops for people with significant disabilities, including mental illness and mental retardation (Polloway, Smith, Patton, & Smith, 1996). Since the 1990s, supported employment programs began to feature rapid entry into competitive employment and long-term employment supports, and consumers, families, and professionals have come to prefer this service option (Podmostko, 2000). Again, supported employment programs have inadequate public funding, which has limited their availability. For example, Mank, O'Neill, and Jensen's national study (1998) estimated that for every person who received supported employment services, as many as seven or eight people who could have benefited from these services did not receive them. Thus, even when effective employment intervention programs are available, inadequate public funding of these programs has limited the programs' capacity to help those who need and want their services.

LEGAL AND SOCIAL ISSUES RELEVANT TO EMPLOYMENT

The barriers to getting and keeping a job for people with disabilities have resulted in low labor force participation rates. Changes in federal policy and legislation have addressed many of these barriers. This section reviews the history of these legislative changes.

The Rehabilitation Acts

Early rehabilitation legislation, beginning in 1917, was primarily concerned with building a national system of services and programs that would assist people with disabilities to enter or re-enter the labor market. Services included guidance and counseling, vocational evaluation, work adjustment, job placement, and postemployment support. These laws established the public or state–federal VR programs. Through continuous reauthorization, the Rehabilitation Act (originally passed in 1973 as PL 93-112) has maintained this system of VR programs. These programs annually provide funding and services for more than 1.2 million individuals with disabilities and expend more than $135,000,000 in funding for individuals in authorized supported employment programs (Research Triangle International, 2003).

Disability policy studies have described much of the legislation that guided the U.S. VR system during its first 50 years as based on a prevailing medical model of disability, meaning that problems the individual experienced in entering or re-entering the labor market were believed to reside within the person (e.g., Hahn, 1985). This functional-deficit approach relied on trying to change the person through medical intervention or psychological and vocational therapies in order to prepare him or her to work. Consistent with this perception of disability, many early VR programs focused their efforts on pre-vocational training (i.e., getting people ready for competitive employment by having them work in sheltered workshops), with the prevailing notion being that people couldn't work until they were somehow cured or rehabilitated. Studies of consumer outcomes in sheltered workshops, however, demonstrated that few workshop employees ever entered competitive employment (Parent, Hill, & Wehman, 1989). This circumstance led to the philosophy and development of supported employment approaches, through which people with disabilities are assigned jobs and then trained (Wehman & Kregel, 1985).

Through the 1980s, the process of job development was still viewed as selling the idea of hiring an individual with a disability to a potential employer who might, from charitable or sympathetic motives, give that person a job. In other words, altering the method of job training did not change the perception of disability as being a deficiency or deficit within the person.

The Rehabilitation Act of 1973 was the first that incorporated what became known as the civil rights model of disability, a shift in the perception of disability as deficit to disability as a result of environmental, attitudinal, and physical barriers (Silverstein, 2000). As Harlan Hahn (1985), a noted disability advocate, indicated, "The effects of disability can be attributed to a disabling environment rather than to personal deficiencies." The Rehabilitation Act of 1973 was the first legislation to include mandates protecting individuals with disabilities from job discrimination on the basis of employers' beliefs (myths and stereotypes) about what people with disabilities could not do. Despite its good intentions, the Rehabilitation Act had several flaws and became the catalyst for more encompassing legislation. First, only federal agencies and contractors were prohibited from hiring discrimination based on disability, not all private employers. Second, there was little general knowledge at that time about the need for equal employment of people with disabilities. Third, the act's enforcement mechanisms were ineffective. These problems led to the passage of the Americans with Disabilities Act in 1990.

The Americans with Disabilities Act

The Americans with Disabilities Act (ADA) of 1990 (PL 101-336) has been compared with the Civil Rights Act of 1964 (PL 88-352) in terms of protections for people with disabilities (Blanck, 1998). The ADA was rooted in the civil rights model of disability and declared that discriminatory policies and practices led to the problems and challenges people with disabilities faced in entering the labor market. It outlawed a number of practices that were felt to impede the entry of people with disabilities into jobs by prohibiting discrimination against a "qualified individual with a disability" in hiring, promoting, firing, compensating, and other terms and conditions of employment. Congress clearly intended the ADA to pull people into the labor market by changing policies, practices, and attitudes that had excluded them. Although the ADA has promoted more positive attitudes about people with disabilities, its actual effect on improving labor market entry and jobs remains unknown. The impact of the law on employment also relates to some of the more ambiguous aspects of the law, such as determining who is a qualified person with a disability, that remain to be sorted out in courts (Schwochau & Blanck, 1999). However, the ADA increased the visibility of disability and promoted fairness in access throughout American society (Unger, 2002a). It is an important vehicle in job development and placement activities.

The ADA serves as an important job development tool in several ways. First, it is designed to remove barriers to the workplace by prohibiting discrimination against qualified individuals with disabilities. *Individual with a disability* is defined in the ADA as anyone with a physical, mental, or emotional impairment that substantially limits him or her from performing a major life activity; a person with a record of such an impairment; or a person who is regarded as having such an impairment. Thus, the ADA casts a broad net in order to adhere to the congressional intention of removing barriers to work for all individuals who experience discrimination or bias as a result of a perceived disability.

Another way the ADA assists in job development is that it requires employers to provide reasonable accommodations to qualified individuals with disabilities that would enable them to perform the essential functions of a job. Reasonable accommodations can be physical, policy, or procedural modifications to the environment, such as adding ramps, enlarging doorways, changing desk heights, allowing more breaks, or flexible scheduling. These accommodations allow job seekers with disabilities who disclose their disabilities to employers to ask for the kinds of alterations in the work environment that would enhance their capacity to perform the work, and so expand job options.

The ADA has also improved job development for people with disabilities more indirectly. It induces employers to hire individuals with disabilities because it has improved the visibility of people with disabilities and thus has provided direct evidence of their capabilities. It also indirectly compels employers to hire individuals with disabilities because of employers' own perceptions of the requirements of the law, which, it is important to note, does not require affirmative action in hiring. Despite the advantages of the ADA as a vehicle for improving the employment of people with disabilities, laws cannot directly change institutionalized negative attitudes or address discriminatory practices in a comprehensive manner (Schwochau & Blanck, 1999). Subtle practices exist that effectively discourage individuals with disabilities, particularly those with highly stigmatized disabilities such as psychiatric illnesses, from entering the workplace but that are not obvious or concrete enough to actually be acted on. Moreover, people with disabilities may not want to disclose their conditions to employers, a basic prerequisite for receiving the protections of the law.

To date, the effect of the ADA on employment participation by people with disabilities remains equivocal. Studies comparing labor force participation of individuals with disabilities before and after passage of the ADA have produced some contradictory data: some groups, particularly qualified applicants who are women, may have benefited from the passage, yet the employment yields for other groups remain ambiguous (Schwochau & Blanck, 1999). Studies of labor force participation rates of individuals with significant disabilities, however, have shown increases in employment after passage of the ADA (McNeil, 1997), a factor that might also be attributed to the act's effect on improving employer receptivity and attitudes toward individuals with disabilities.

Social Security Laws

Although the laws that authorize the federal social security program are not directly related to job development activities, they certainly affect the decision of people with disabilities to seek employment and even the types of jobs they eventually secure. Certainly the growth of the SSA's various disability support programs have been the subject of much debate. The two programs that have received the most attention in terms of disability policy are the SSDI program, which authorizes federal disability insurance benefits for workers who contributed to the Social Security Trust Fund prior to becoming disabled, and the SSI program, which provides cash assistance for individuals who are aged, blind, or have disabilities and meet a financial needs test.

Generally, individuals with disabilities qualify for these programs when they can document that their disability presents a total incapacity to work. In the language of the law, they must prove that they are unable to engage in any "substantial gainful activity" or lose not only their income support benefits but also their health insurance provided through either Medicare or Medicaid. Although initially intended as a safety net for those Americans with disabilities who were unable to provide economically for themselves, the programs grew tremendously throughout the 1990s. Today, more than 8 million beneficiaries draw annual benefits, which amount to more than $75 billion. Although the SSA provides various incentives to assist beneficiaries with disabilities to return to work, reports indicate that fewer than 1% of these beneficiaries leave the disability rolls each year because of employment (*The Ticket to Work,* 2001).

Decisions regarding employment and social security benefits are particularly salient for individuals with severe disabilities, the target population of the public VR system, because of their need to weigh the benefits of employment against the potential costs of losing health care and other guarantees under the social security programs. The SSA, through authorizing legislation known as the Ticket to Work and Work Incentives Improvement Act of 1999 (PL 106-170), codified new approaches to expanding the options available for beneficiaries to gain access to employment services in order to work. The new regulations may affect the incentives for beneficiaries with disabilities who want to work because they offer new mechanisms for seeking employment search assistance. These beneficiaries have the ability to use a voucher to buy employment search assistance from qualified vendors. This option, coupled with liberalized retention of certain SSA benefits, was intended to push more people with disabilities into the workforce.

Individuals with Disabilities Education Act

In 1975, children with disabilities became entitled to publicly supported education with the passage of the Education for All Handicapped Children Act (PL 94-142). Subsequently reauthorized as the Individuals with Disabilities Education Act (IDEA) of 1990 (PL 101-476) and amended in 1997, this legislation requires states to provide free appropriate public education for students with disabilities and mandates the development of an individualized education program (IEP) for each child requiring services, which outlines special education and related services that school districts will provide. More than 6.5 million children receive special education services under IDEA (American Youth Policy Forum & Center on Education Policy, 2001).

One major aspect of IDEA is the idea of transition planning, requiring that the IEP set forth a coordinated set of activities that supports the student's movement to adult living, learning, and employment; however, one of the major impediments for youth with disabilities who exit special education programs is the loss of the universal support structure provided to them during their school years. Youth who require adult services to get or remain employed typically encounter a universe of multiple, unconnected services for which they then must meet eligibility requirements (Johnson, Stodden, Emanuel, Luecking, & Mack, 2002). Moreover, many adult services are developed around specific target populations, such as people with developmental disabilities or mental health issues, so that children with other types of disorders, such as learning disabilities, frequently have no specific state system of services with which to connect (Wittenburg & Stapleton, 2000).

The result of this uneven system is that youth with disabilities exiting public schools have poor postschool outcomes, a frequently cited issue. For example, the National Longitudinal Study on Transition (NLST), the largest study to date, found that although about 65% of special education students worked 3–5 years after leaving school, their jobs were typically low-wage, part-time employment (Blackorby & Wagner, 1996). Moreover, almost 30% of youth with disabilities had been arrested at one point during the 3–5 years after leaving school, and only one third live independently. A number of studies have examined the factors that are associated with postschool success for special education students, and one major consensus is that having a job prior to exiting school was the best predictor of positive postschool employment outcomes (Benz, Doren, & Yavanoff, 1998; Colley & Jamison, 1998; Luecking & Fabian, 2000).

Workforce Investment Act

The Workforce Investment Act (WIA) of 1998 (PL 105-220) authorizes funds and sets operational parameters for the nation's system of helping job seekers with barriers to employment become trained and ready to enter or re-enter the workforce. Its intent is also to broaden employers' access to a better prepared workforce, and it has specific provisions for employer leadership in the development and delivery of job training programs in local areas. The WIA replaced previous national workforce development legislation, called the Job Training and Partnership Act (JTPA) of 1992 (PL 97-300). The WIA represents an attempt at significant reform of the delivery of employment and training services by consolidating separate and disconnected services previously organized according to categories of service recipients (e.g., welfare recipients, criminal offenders, veterans, people with disabilities).

To this end, the WIA funds a full range of training, career development, and job placement services for diverse customers in convenient locations, called One-Stop Career Centers. These centers house career development and job placement entities, some of which are partners whose participation is mandated by WIA and some of which are voluntary, nonmandated partners. State VR programs are mandated to participate in One-Stop Career Centers, and most often assign a counselor to maintain a presence at the centers so that disability employment expertise and assistance for people with disabilities is available. In fact, the reauthorization of the Rehabilitation Act was embedded in the WIA, although the funds for state VR services remain separate from those earmarked for the One-Stop Career Centers. Still, the WIA has statutory mandates to include people with disabilities in One-Stop Career Center services, and its general operational principles include individualized service and universal access. Thus, it offers the promise of inclusion of people with disabilities into general job training and placement activities, considerably expanding potential job search resources.

Prior to the WIA, the system of employment services to people with disabilities had operated separately from other employment and training services. Thus, broad access to general employment services by people with disabilities will likely take some time. In the previous JTPA system, only about 9% of the recipients of employment and training services were people with disabilities. Even in the years after the enactment of the WIA, there is still uneven use of the One-Stops by people with disabilities, confusion about how to include and accommodate them, and reluctance of disability employment service providers to form substantive partnerships with One-Stop Career Centers (Hoff, 2003). Several local demonstration grants and national technical assistance centers have been established by the U.S. Department of Labor to provide incentives and expertise to make One-Stop Career Centers more accessible to consumers with disabilities. Although the employment and training system under the WIA is still evolving, in the main it represents another avenue for assisting people with disabilities to obtain employment.

JOB DEVELOPMENT AND PLACEMENT APPROACHES

The field of job development and placement has been almost entirely atheoretical, meaning that it is based on descriptions of strategies and practices that might be derived from business but that have no explanatory potential (Granovetter, 1979; Vandergoot, 1987). For example, some job development and placement strategies use marketing descriptions, and others use labor market terms, such as supply and demand. The lack of a theory relegates a set of practices, such as job development and placement, to lower status among disability or rehabilitation services, as outcomes are seen as more related to chance, luck, or the personality of the individual involved in the activity. As Granovetter (1979) pointed out, it makes job development activities equivalent to sales, a low-prestige occupation in which outcomes appear to rest on the force of the sales person's personality.

The other more important disadvantage of an atheoretical approach is that there are few empirical studies of placement strategies, as compared with counseling or coaching strategies. This paucity makes it difficult to identify what strategies are most effective for whom and how to improve practices. This section briefly reviews the history of job development and placement as it fits with different perceptions of disability and then describes a theoretical model for the job development and placement practices that are featured in this book.

History

The history of job development and placement activities is related to social and political attitudes regarding disability. For example, during the first part of the twentieth century, when disability was viewed as being a problem in the person, job development and placement approaches were based on charitable appeals to employers to hire the handicapped.

The medical model of disability was based on the assumption that removing employment barriers meant either changing the person by ameliorating the condition to the extent possible or when not possible, compensating for the disability by training the person to function in an alternate way (Hahn, 1993). Job development and placement approaches that were based on selling the individual with a disability to the employer were therefore unconscious expressions of the lack of confidence in the capability of people with disabilities to work. In effect, this approach communicated that neither the job development professional nor the employer believed the individual was capable of doing the work.

Further complicating this scenario for the job development professional and the job seeker with a disability was the central paradox of disability policy in America: In order to qualify for federal health insurance benefits from the SSA, individuals with disabilities had to be found totally incapacitated and unable to work. However, people with disabilities who wanted the kind of jobs that provided for health insurance benefits needed to demonstrate and believe in their capability to perform the job. The job seeker with a disability, therefore, was stuck in a system in which none of the participants in the job search—the job seeker, the job development specialist, or the employer—believed that he or she could perform the job. It is small wonder that job placement practices during this time were not very effective, as evidenced by the few sheltered workshop employees who made the transition to competitive work (Greenleigh & Associates, 1975; Wehman & Kregel, 1985).

Generally, job placement approaches based on selling the abilities of the individual with a disability to employers are rooted in a matching process: identifying specific demands of the work setting and then matching those to the skills and interests of the job seeker. The implicit theoretical framework for this approach was one derived from market theory, which stipulates that job seekers have a commodity to sell—human capital—and employers a motive to buy. As human capital consists of an individual's economic value, the implicit assumption regarding job seekers with disabilities would be that work entry problems arise from deficiencies in the job seeker (Rosenbaum, Kariya, Settersten, & Maier, 1990). That is, the individual does not have the necessary skills, aptitudes, or training sufficient for the demands of the job.

Several problems within this market theory framework as an explanation for hiring practices have been identified. First, the information regarding the qualities of the job applicant are not objective; thus, employers cannot measure these characteristics as they would if they are purchasing commodities such as computers or other equipment. Not only is the information not quantifiable in the case of human beings, but the cost of obtaining the information is much higher to the employer, in terms of the time, effort, and money that must be expended (Granovetter, 1985). Second, for the buyer of human capital to be confident that he or she had sufficient information on which to base a decision regarding the best applicant, he or she would have to launch an extensive search that would be prohibitively expensive in terms of the time and effort required to screen and evaluate all applicants who might be considered.

For people with disabilities, job development approaches based on selling human capital have other hidden problems. One is that in a market economy, in order to purchase the best product, the buyer wants simultaneously to extend the search as wide as possible and to identify screening criteria that will make the search manageable. So, for example, employers might specify that only individuals with high school diplomas are eligible to apply for certain positions, even though the high school education itself has little applicability to the tasks required to perform the specific job. Establishing screening criteria, however, allows the employer to limit the scope of the search, thus making it more efficient and less expensive. Employers can use other screening devices to narrow the scope of their employment searches, thus effectively eliminating job seekers with disabilities from even being considered in the pool of applicants (Bissonnette, 1994). In this way, employers cannot legally require individuals to be without disabilities in order to perform a particular job, but they can establish screening criteria based on credentials or experience that effectively limit the opportunity for many job seekers with disabilities.

Establishing these screening criteria is probably not the result of deep-seated prejudices toward individuals with disabilities but simply a method for lowering information costs associated with finding qualified workers. The more selective the criteria are, the less information the employer will need to acquire from and about the job applicant. Conducting widespread educational campaigns aimed at improving employer attitudes toward hiring people with disabilities may not be effective because the screening criteria that disqualifies some people with disabilities are not designed to do so. The effect is incidental, not purposeful. This is a hidden problem with the job placement method that cannot be easily addressed by the method itself. In the 1990s, a new set of practices emerged for helping connect employers and people with disabilities.

Job Development as Networking

Since the 1990s, job development and placement practices have shifted from pushing the individual into a job to pulling individuals with disabilities into the labor market by changing the nature of the work environment, both socially and physically. Gilbride and Stensrud (1999) called this approach "demand side job development," meaning that the job developer's role is to act as a consultant to employers. By assisting employers to modify physical and social barriers to employment of people with disabilities, job developers will, in turn, promote more positive attitudes and expectations. This approach requires that the job development specialists have 1) specific knowledge about the ADA, 2) the human relations skills necessary to be able to effectively market themselves as workplace consultants to employers, and 3) enough contacts so that their services are in sufficient demand.

An implicit, and perhaps most important, consideration in job development approaches based on pulling people into the labor market is the need to develop business contacts that are based on relationships of trust and mutuality (Fabian, Luecking, & Tilson, 1994). This relationship-building approach is consistent with networking theories of economic markets. Network theories suggest that markets—whether they are economic or human—often "depend on the nature of personal relations and the network of relations between and within firms" (Granovetter, 1985, p. 502). Network theories speculate that transactions, such as those that occur in the job placement process, are embedded in personal relationships and that employers prefer to get their information from sources with whom they have dealt before and whom they trust. The underlying assumption within these models is that because information is expensive to obtain, the cheapest, most effective way to find out about job candidates is through referrals from sources who know the potential applicant. This applies whether the individual is referred for a job by a coworker, a business partner, a social or business acquaintance, or an employment agency.

Relationships based on trust have been demonstrated to be key factors in developing the types of networks that lead to job offers (Granovetter, 1973, 1985). Generally, the closer the source of information is to the employer, the greater the degree of confidence the employer will have in the information, particularly if past information provided by that source has been reliable. This premise necessarily leads to two important considerations for job development and placement specialists: expanding their contact networks and ensuring that they are regarded as reliable sources of information. The general reputation of the placement specialist, or his or her agency, is critical. Thus, the practical framework and specific activities of job development and placement described in this book are rooted in network and partnership development and give little weight to traditional approaches based on selling human capital.

SUMMARY

The main purpose of this chapter is to review the background of social and legal policy regarding job placement and people with disabilities and to describe a theoretical framework for understanding how to improve job development and placement practices through relationship building. Rooting job development and placement practices in theory gives more credibility to the practices and strengthens the validity of the strategies by explaining why and how they work. Any good theory also gives rise to research studies as a way of proving theoretical concepts and suggesting new directions and practices. The employment process for people with disabilities is no different than the job search process for other job seekers, as the next chapter describes. Establishing employer relationships is a key ingredient to assisting job seekers in the job search.

2

The Employment Process

A CONCEPTUAL FRAMEWORK

We can never exceed our own expectations.

LAO-TZU

*If you are a counselor or a parent or a sister
or a brother or a friend of a person with a disability, **help them**
find work—and **expect** them to keep working at finding work that they love.*

DALE BROWN

The times and circumstances that influence job development and employment service delivery are in constant flux. As we have seen in the previous chapter, employment services and job development approaches have evolved along with legislative, policy, research, and practice activity. Fluctuating environmental contexts continually influence how partnerships with businesses and employers are formed for job development for individuals with disabilities. An infinite array of variables influences individual job seekers' behavior, the operation of employment service programs, and the places where people work. How do these contexts and variables affect the whole employment process? How do they affect the way in which partnerships are developed and maintained between employment organizations, specialists, and employers? This chapter illustrates a conceptual framework with which to address these questions.

THE BIG PICTURE

The employment process—how people secure work and how employers secure a work force—is greatly affected by the trends of our time (Morris, 1997). The same holds true for other important aspects of our lives, such as education and training. For example, calls for reform and for achieving higher standards of learning have been ongoing and oscillating. This emphasis certainly affects the way teachers are prepared, how they teach and evaluate, what they teach and evaluate, how students learn, and what students ultimately do with the knowledge and skills they have acquired. In another example, each shift of the economy has permanent ramifications. The booming economy of the 1990s created unprecedented job growth, new categories of jobs, and dramatic shifts in clusters of industries. This boom, of course, did not last; however, new cycles of recovery are likely to occur. The ever-changing state of the economy affects every other aspect of our lives, not just what jobs are available.

In turn, a multitude of current events affect the economy (Murnane & Levy, 1996; Olson, 1997). International relations, both political and economic, shift continuously and affect the government's spending priorities. This necessitates dramatic policy shifts in other areas, reprioritizing of funding, and reallocation of resources, from the federal government down to the local level. Such radical adjustments have far-reaching implications for every other facet of our lives: education, employment, financial security, mental and physical health, ethical and spiritual beliefs, and even our diverse cultural traditions.

Considering the employment process in a vacuum would be just as counterproductive as addressing the education process, the economy, health care, or the law in a vacuum. All of these components of our lives are mutually dependent, and a tremendous number of partnerships are required to bolster them. Thus, the context in which employment occurs is constantly shifting (Fox, 1994). As Bolles pointed out, the workplace itself "is always changing, always in turmoil, always in flux" (2003, p. 10).

Any discussion of partnerships among job seekers, employment service organizations, and employers should seek to answer questions such as "Why are partnerships necessary?" and "How can these partnerships affect, or be affected by, the environmental contexts of our times and by variables within individuals and workplaces?" We need a big picture from which to conceptualize our responses to these questions. One framework for considering the way people get jobs is the employment process. It is an interaction between 1) job seeker characteristics, circumstances, and life variables; 2) the needs of employers and the variables in the workplace; and 3) the availability and effectiveness of employment intermediaries. Figure 2.1 depicts this interaction.

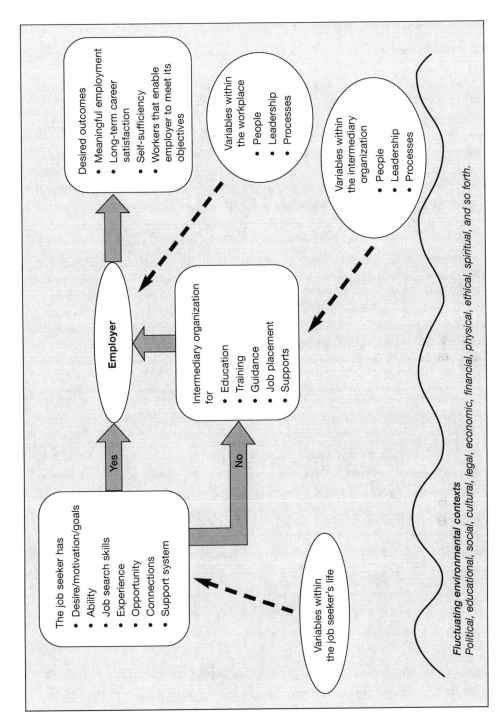

Figure 2.1. The employment process.

Intermediaries in the Employment Process

An intermediary can be a person, such as a family member, friend, or employment professional associated with an organization that specializes in employment services. An intermediary can also be an organization or program. Examples of intermediary organizations include
government-sponsored entities such as state vocational rehabilitation agencies, One-Stop
Career Centers, and employment and training services and programs. Schools and school
programs can also serve as intermediaries when teachers or educational personnel make
contact with employers for the purposes of finding work experiences and jobs for students
when such jobs are an integral part of or an adjunct to a prescribed course of study. Private
rehabilitation companies also often fulfill intermediary roles for job seekers with disabilities.

The largest category of intermediary organizations, however, includes those that are
community-based, such as nonprofit employment organizations. These community-based
organizations might be designated to serve specific categories of job seekers, such as youth,
those who need ongoing support through a supported employment program, or those who
require or desire specific kinds of training or education. Frequently, these intermediary entities
are established to serve individuals with specific disabilities, such as United Cerebral Palsy
organizations, local Arcs serving people with mental retardation, transition programs serving
people with long-term mental illness, or placement services for people with sensory disabilities. It is the whole array of intermediary people and organizations on which this book
is focused.

A job seeker with certain characteristics connects with an employer who needs those
characteristics, and the result is employment for the job seeker and labor for the employer.
Ideally, both benefit from this employment arrangement. If a job seeker lacks certain characteristics or opportunities, he or she may need help from an intermediary—an individual or organization—to acquire those essential characteristics or gain an opportunity to do
so. Just as important, many people with disabilities face the daunting barriers of public
misperception, stigmatizing stereotypes, and even fear. Employers who hold such views—
whether they realize it or not—are likely to overlook qualified workers. As discussed in
Chapter 4, this certainly has less to do with outright hostility toward people with disabilities and more to do with lack of exposure and information. Therefore, intermediaries
can play a critical role in helping employers overcome such misperceptions by addressing
their concerns head on and creating links to employers for job seekers and links for employers to job seekers who can benefit their enterprises. Throughout this book, we most
frequently identify an individual intermediary as an *employment specialist* and an organizational entity that provides intermediary connections as an *employment program* or *employment
agency*. However, by using these terms, we are referring to anyone or any organization that
may have a role in assisting people with disabilities to achieve jobs and careers.

For the moment, let's say that a job seeker received assistance from an intermediary.
The job seeker may then either connect directly to employers, advocating for him- or her-

self, or the job seeker might make connections through the intermediary's network. Once he or she has been hired, an intermediary might provide subsequent supportive services to the new employee and to his or her employer.

As depicted in Figure 2.1, a current runs under the employment process, consisting of the fluctuating environmental contexts within our society. These include such elements as the political, economic, legal, educational, social, cultural, physical, geographic, ethical, and spiritual. Just as an earthquake can radically change a landscape, the landscape of employment is significantly affected by the fluctuating undercurrent of these many societal contexts. The implications for job seekers, employers, and intermediaries are tremendous. We discuss each component of Figure 2.1 in later sections in this chapter. But first let's reflect on work itself and why people work.

WHAT IS WORK AND WHY DO WE DO IT?

Perhaps from the beginning of human interaction, people have worked for other people. An individual has a set of skills, a talent, experience, or sheer brawn. Another individual or group has a desire to accomplish a task, receive a service, or obtain a product using the attributes of that first individual. This might be called the talent-to-task connection. In the most simplistic of explanations, if the individual performing the task or creating the product pleases the individual retaining her or his services, the talent-to-task connection has occurred successfully (Morris, 1997). The other side to the talent-to-task equation is how satisfied the worker is with the worker–employer relationship. By humanitarian standards, this relationship should be mutually beneficial (Boldt, 1999).

The employment process is the focus of this chapter. By using the word *process,* we seem to imply a structure or series of steps, or even a formula. Certainly, procedures must be followed to bring employees and employers together. Employers use strategies to recruit workers, and job seekers must follow some techniques to be considered for employment (Kleiman, 2002). These essentials of the employment process are discussed in subsequent chapters. Here we describe the big picture and set a context for those later discussions. Let's take a look at each of the primary components within the employment process.

Job Seeker Variables

Every human being is unique. Each of us comes to life's table fashioned with characteristics unlike anyone else on the planet. As individuals, we are composed of our genetics, environments, and experiences. Two people might be brilliant musicians, or highly acclaimed nuclear physicists, or talented auto mechanics, or meticulous housekeepers, but they may be as different as night and day (Armstrong, 1993; Fletcher, 1993; Goleman, 1998; Zander & Zander, 2000; Zufelt, 2002). In the context of employment—meaning lifetime careers as well as jobs—job seekers must look at a number of key factors (Sharf, 1997). To what extent do they

1. Know themselves and know what kind of work they want to do? (self-knowledge)
2. Know what kinds of opportunities exist? (exposure to opportunities)
3. Have the desire, motivation, and energy to look for, obtain, and retain a job? (motivation)
4. Have specific talents, acquired skills, knowledge, and qualifications necessary to perform the types of work they want to do? (talent and skill)
5. Have previous work or life experiences that relate to the requirements of their desired work? (previous experience)
6. Have the skills to even search for work? (job search skills)
7. Have a personal and professional network and community connections? (networks and connections)
8. Have a personal support system? (support system)
9. Have the temperament, work values, and habits demanded by employers? (attitudes and work habits)
10. Strive to continually acquire and apply new knowledge and skills? (capacity for growth and learning)

Let's briefly look at each of these factors.

Self-Knowledge   It is extremely difficult for workers to secure and be successful in a job or career if they do not know what it is they want to do. This calls for a certain degree of self-reflection and self-evaluation, which is extremely difficult for some people (Gilley & Boughton, 1996). The sentiments "I just don't know what I want to do" or "Beats me what my career goals are" are common, but they are major impediments to successful employment and career building. We discuss this further in Chapters 3 and 8.

Exposure to Opportunities   Closely tied to the first factor is the second: often people are perplexed about what they want to achieve job- and career-wise because they are not aware of the opportunities that exist for them (Maxwell, 2002). The next chapter explores career development theories. Regardless of the theoretical construct, one thing is certain: exposure precedes interest. Look at any employed person's position and the career field or occupational category of that job. How did the professional photographer, the veteran truck driver, the kindergarten teacher, the data entry clerk, the basketball coach, or the manicurist even get into their careers? While some people happen upon their jobs or take the first job that comes along out of sheer desperation or practical necessity, those with some type of career path (in which a thread of intention connects the various jobs they have held) will likely tell you that at some point in their lives, they were exposed to other people who did similar jobs (Sharf, 1997). How did they come to see others doing these jobs? Perhaps a relative, neighbor, or friend had a similar job. Or maybe they saw a television show or had a teacher or counselor tell them about various jobs. They may even have observed, by sheer happenstance, someone performing the job. In all cases, something about the job they observed resonated within them. Something grabbed their attention and captured their interest. Exposure precedes interest (Fabian, Luecking, & Tilson, 1994).

It would be naïve to suggest that all people work in jobs that really interest them and give them personal gratification. In communities where economic opportunities are few and where people do not have the resources or capability of relocating, people may indeed have to settle for what is available. And in many cases, strong cultural and familial traditions dictate a person's career.

Motivation   Now, look at the factors of desire, motivation, and energy to work. Some workers epitomize high energy and enthusiasm. Others are lethargic and blasé. The rest fall somewhere along the continuum (Zufelt, 2002). The principle that exposure precedes interest can be taken two steps further: interest spurs motivation and motivation fuels action. Several common expressions are illustrative here: "I have an interest at stake," "It's not in my best interest," and "I have a vested interest." One person cannot motivate another because motivation is an internal phenomenon. However, one person can definitely influence another person's motivation level by exposing that person to things that capture his or her interest.

Once again, this is stated very simplistically. Many people are just as motivated to do something because of dire straits or immediate necessity, and this will certainly play a critical part in their ultimate job or career choices. But because this book promotes healthy partnerships—whether between employers and employees, or businesses and human service agencies—we want to make a pitch for the ideal: that individuals do all they can to find employment opportunities that fit their personal goals, temperament, energy level, talents, and skills.

Talent and Skill   It is easy to cite examples in which someone is clearly unsuited for the job or career in which he or she is working. It is not uncommon for workers to experience such unpleasantness when they discover the hard way that they are poorly matched to their jobs. Although many variables can create an ill fit between a worker and a job, we'll focus for a moment on the variables of talent and skill.

Talents may be thought of as those abilities that just seem to come naturally to a person, such as those of the natural athlete, the math whiz, the charmer, the class clown, the born mechanic, the daredevil, the composer prodigy, the orator, the natural entrepreneur, or the nurturer/caregiver, to name a few. Each person may even be considered by others to have such innate natural gifts (Tieger & Barron-Tieger, 2001). This doesn't mean that people don't have to work extremely hard to hone their talents—in fact, most highly successful people can describe years of exertion that allowed them to turn a talent into a marketable craft or into a livelihood (Banks, 2000). And in many cases, people with a natural talent opt to express that talent through an avocation or leisure-time activity, rather than through paid work. Many well-regarded career counselors concur that most people have some type of innate gifts or propensities. The degree to which these talents are recognized or nurtured by each individual or others is another matter (Bell, 2002; Gilley & Broughton, 1996; Goleman, 1998).

Acquired skills are learned. A person is in a learning mode throughout his or her life, from birth to death. Whether through formal education or training or simply by observing and doing, no one can avoid the acquisition of skills, from learning how to walk or read, to calculating distances between planets, to raising children. The questions become how do people become skilled, where do they apply those skills, and where are those skills needed? In terms of the employment process (and the talent-to-task equation), the extent to which a person has the skills, proficiencies, knowledge, and qualifications to perform tasks that have value to an employer will have tremendous impact on hiring and retention outcomes. Obviously, there is a caveat: Many skilled people have been overlooked by employers or have lost jobs for which they were highly competent due to circumstances beyond their control, such as a company going out of business or economic downturns. These employment process variables that exist outside of the individual are discussed in more depth later in this chapter.

Previous Experience   Another important variable is that of experience. Why do employers make such a big deal about a person's prior work experiences? Through previous experiences, a worker acquires many skills, demonstrates competency, and builds a record of performance (Kleiman, 2002). A record of personal and professional experiences often provides evidence of skill enhancement. The basic skills a worker has acquired in an educational or training environment have been honed through practical application. Then, presumably, subsequent opportunities to apply those skills have given the worker a level of expertise that is a commodity to the workplace. Much has been written about obsolete skills (skills that are out of date and no longer applicable in the current economy). Technology is the primary culprit. Even those with a modicum of computer skill know that a person's abilities today can be quickly outpaced by technological advances tomorrow.

To say this has implications for all would-be and current workers is embarrassingly understated but devastatingly real, particularly for those individuals and groups who lack even the most rudimentary of skills or who have limits on acquisition of or opportunities for lifelong learning. It is not uncommon to hear someone lament, "To get the job I want, they say I have to have previous experience. But how will I ever get experience if no one will hire me?" This is a conundrum indeed; however, it needn't be an impassable roadblock. The chapters in Section II introduce myriad strategies to address this issue.

Job Search Skills   We've been talking about concrete skills, such as using tools, writing, inventing, creating, researching, and teaching. Is it possible that a person can have very strong skills and have trouble finding, getting, and keeping a satisfying job? Unfortunately, the answer is clearly yes. The act of navigating the rocky terrain of the job search process demands a set of skills that can be daunting even for the most highly educated and skilled person precisely because this skill set is rarely taught. It's almost as if people are expected to gain the skills required in job seeking through osmosis. Nothing could be further from reality. What do we mean by job searching skills? These skills include exploring available employment options, identifying possibilities, preparing and disseminating the right kind of résumé, following procedures for making job applications (which vary tremendously in scope and depth, depending on the employer), handling an interview effectively, conducting the appropriate follow-up activities, negotiating a job offer, and using a personal and professional network. When it comes to the job search process, there are as many effective and creative strategies out there as there are myths and missteps. It is a serious mistake to discount the education, training, and support needed to help people acquire and use effective job search skills. All people, with perhaps the exception of those who are independently wealthy or those who do not plan to work, need to know how to do a job search (Bolles & Brown, 2001).

Networks and Connections   Building and capitalizing on a strong network of contacts is so critical that we have devoted Chapter 5 to this topic. Making connections with potential employers is heavily dependent on social networking and communication (Misner & Morgan, 2000; Naisbitt, 2000). Imagine how this affects individuals or certain marginalized groups, who may lack access to the social networks that hold the keys to employment and career opportunities or who simply do not have the communication or social skills required to navigate those networks. These people—many people with disabilities, youth, minorities, non–English speakers, former inmates, older citizens, women, and displaced homemakers—must receive the training and supports needed to acquire and apply job searching skills. Intermediary assistance is therefore often needed to make the right connections.

Personal Support Systems   In addition, people need to have an adequate support system (Bandura, 1986; Gilley & Boughton, 1996; Maxwell, 2002; Zander & Zander,

2000). Life presents many obstacles, and a person's ability to handle these challenges depends on not simply his or her innate ability but also support from others. Consider how difficult it would be, for example, to conduct a job search without access to transportation, appropriate clothing for an interview, or an ability to be punctual because of child care problems. These kinds of challenges often require help from others. Some people have remarkable support systems, people in their lives who help them out, who encourage them, and who help them maintain a sense of humor and perspective. Sadly, though, too many individuals are unsuccessful in finding and securing satisfying employment, regardless of their talents, skills, and desires, because they lack a positive cheering section and have no one to turn to for moral and practical support. Again, this is where intermediary organizations and individual advocates can play an extraordinary and major role.

Attitudes and Work Habits   Of course, qualities such as self-knowledge, relevant talents and skills, previous experience, and a strong support system will not help an individual if he or she is incapable of meeting an employer's expectations for appropriate work values and habits. Some sources describe appropriate work values and habits as "soft skills," "employability skills," "job readiness skills," or "social/interpersonal skills." Employers want their workers to show up according to agreed-upon schedules, perform specified tasks efficiently and effectively, get along with co-workers and customers, communicate clearly, display honesty, and—to varying degrees—solve problems. In short, employers expect work to get done in a manner that creates value for customers, which translates to money for the company. A worker who will not show up when expected, treat others with respect, communicate clearly, or try to solve problems is a liability to an employer (Bloch, 2002; Brown, 2000; Kleiman, 2002). Workers who steal, drag their feet on assignments, do not call in when they will be late or absent, and refuse to show any initiative cost an employer money. When this happens, the relationship between the employer and employee is damaged and may be severed.

For a lively discussion, ask a diverse group of people whether they think work habits and values can be learned, as one learns to repair an airplane engine or to read. Another question sure to generate animated discussion: Is having a good attitude a skill? From our perspective, these are skills—whether the person learns them from home, in places of worship, at school, or from other places. The term *attitude* is fraught with emotion, and no one can argue that emotions drive, or at least strongly influence, a person's attitude at any given time. An upper-level manager at Marriott International once told us,

> You bet attitude is a skill! It is observed through a person's behavior, and it can either positively affect the workplace and the person's potential for promotion, or it can contribute to a lousy working environment and jeopardize customer service. There's something I call "chronic negativity" and in my book, chronic negativity will get you fired!

To have a successful career, a worker must have these critical work skills. If a job seeker does not have them, he or she needs to get them.

Capacity for Growth and Learning   A final variable within the individual—capacity for growth and learning—can affect the ultimate outcome of a person's job or career. What is the individual's capacity for continued growth and learning? To what extent can the individual make adaptations as job tasks change? The degree to which an individual can leave one job and secure another is likely to hinge on this factor. Promotions and advancement within an organization are typically contingent on the individual's proven ability to acquire new skills or to apply existing skills in new ways. This is particularly critical for certain marginalized individuals and groups. Often, job placement agencies may help a person find an initial job but are unable or unwilling to help him or her find subsequent jobs or make career changes. People often discover that the skills that made them a good fit for one job are not the skills they need for another, and they need assistance in gaining access to and benefiting from education and training opportunities.

Employer Variables

The term *employer* is used frequently and casually. However, depending on context, it can mean vastly different things, which have important implications for job seekers and those who assist them. Take, for example, Marriott International. As a very large global corporation, Marriott is an employer. Likewise, all of the hotel properties and other business groups it operates are employers. The company's many divisions are employers. In this sense, the term *employer* refers to an entity, not a person. And within each entity, there are variables: people, leadership, and processes. One particular large resort hotel run by Marriott has different departments, including human resources, marketing, public relations, procurement, housekeeping, accounting, catering services, event planning, food service, building maintenance, laundry operations, security, and so forth. Each of these departments has a unique function, yet all are obviously interdependent. Each department might also be considered an employer, and within each of these units, there are variables: the individuals that comprise the workforce (people), decision makers and managers (leadership), and processes. To focus even further, the security department is likely to have a hierarchy of personnel including a director, managers, security guards, administrative support staff, and technicians. Any of those individuals who supervise others may be considered employers. But again, each department, as an entity, has the variables of people, leadership, and processes. Contrast Marriott International with a small, independently owned and operated inn. For people working at this inn, the employer is both the entity (the inn) and the boss (the owner).

There is a reason for making the distinction between an entity as an employer and a person as an employer. At a macroeconomic level, it is more useful to refer to an entity as an employer, as in "Hewlett-Packard has joined the ranks of other employers in considering a merger with corporate giant Compaq." At the employment process level, where individual job seekers are linked with jobs, the individual variables within the worksite are what is important: the people who work there, the leadership structure, and the operational processes followed by that worksite. From now on, when we refer to an employer, we mean the people within the organization and, most often, those individuals with whom the worker may come into contact.

What do job seekers and employers have in common? They are human beings. And just as job seekers have many variables affecting their lives, so do individual employer contacts. However, employer contacts are also very much affected by the leadership, structure, and processes within their own organization. For example, the small inn may need to hire a cook. The owner puts up a sign in her yard and a job seeker applies. The structure and processes are simple. Contrast that with the leadership, structure, and processes within a large corporation.

Once again, it may be useful to refer to Figure 2.1. We've talked about job seekers and employers. The goal is for a job seeker to navigate the employment process in a manner that allows him or her to be considered and then hired by an employer. Ideally, certain desired outcomes are then met for both parties:

1. The employee gets the job he or she sought and achieves acceptable compensation and job satisfaction.
2. The employer finds the talent that allows the organization to get its goods and services to the consumer in a manner that meets the organization's objectives.

But what happens when, for myriad reasons, a job seeker is unsuccessful in linking with an employer and achieving employment success? As we have noted, this is where intermediaries figure into the employment equation.

Intermediary Variables

Some individuals may in fact not have the experience or opportunity to successfully navigate the employment process by themselves. There may be many different reasons for this, including a lack of marketable skills, job search skills, work habits, career goals, career awareness, experience, connections, support system, accommodations, or other factors. Many of these job seekers may have a history of being discriminated against in employment, due to false perceptions about them, limited opportunities to gain skills, poor or nonexistent work histories, and so forth (Brown, 2000). Organizations or individuals that specialize in serving job seekers with barriers can be tremendously useful in providing such services as education, training, career guidance, job placement, and a wide variety of other supports. Intermediaries, like the job seekers and the employers, present important variables related to people, leadership, and processes.

Individual Intermediaries: The People   How well trained, prepared, supported, and motivated are the employment specialists who work for the intermediary? Consequently, how skilled and successful are they in linking individual job seekers with jobs and careers? A great deal of the success of the employment process rides on the competence and commitment of the people who represent job seekers. Hence, a high level of skill and professionalism needs to be nurtured in these individuals. Regardless of the job seeker's level of motivation, skill, experience, attitude, and support system, his or her ability to get a job will often depend on the effectiveness of employment specialists. Simply stated, if they are good, job seekers get jobs. If they are not, the barriers to employment for job seekers can become insurmountable. It is our hope that this book will be one tool to nurture and elevate the motivation and effectiveness of these professionals who are so key to the employment process. Chapter 7 discusses the fundamental competencies that are necessary for effective employment specialists.

Intermediary Leadership   Does the leadership of intermediary organizations see the big picture? Do leaders have vision and values consistent with employment acquisition? Do leaders support and train the organization's people? Are the leaders committed to and skilled at partnership development? Do they know how to make their organizations business friendly so that employers find their organizations to be credible partners (see Chapter 14)? The importance of visionary leaders in intermediary organizations cannot be overstated. Without good, solid, supportive leadership, individual employment specialists in the organizations are left to their own devices to assist job seekers. These employment specialists may still be effective, but they usually could be even more so with guidance and vision from the organization's leadership. Individual job seekers—who unfortunately often have little experience or even opportunity to pick an intermediary organization—will be the ultimate beneficiaries of service from intermediary organizations. Whether that service is good or bad will be largely influenced by the quality and commitment of that organization's leadership.

Organizational Processes   How quickly do things get done? How do bureaucratic requirements affect the activities of the intermediary's staff? Are staff rewarded for activity or for outcomes? What influences do funding agencies and accreditation bodies have on the process of helping people find employment? All of these questions are relevant to the success of the employment process. How they are answered will ultimately determine whether an intermediary is going to really get the job done. Again, individual employment specialists and job seeker variables may overcome poorly conceived operational processes. But well-designed processes that emphasize performance and outcome over mere activity can significantly improve the likelihood that job seekers will achieve employment success. Given the importance of this variable, we have devoted Chapter 14 to how organizations can alter and enhance operational activity and performance to establish the kind of relationships with employers that lead to mutually beneficial partnerships that are central to how people get jobs.

Additional Supports   As depicted in Figure 2.1, intermediaries may provide any or all of the following: education, training, guidance, job placement, and an array of other supports such as medical intervention, housing and transportation assistance, therapies, counseling, financial and legal support, and social and recreational outlets, among others. Although the focus of this book is on those intermediaries that provide job development, placement, and employment-related follow-up services, we certainly recognize the important roles that certain intermediaries play in other aspects of job seekers' lives, which have an impact on employment outcomes for those individuals. The intermediary's ability to connect job seekers with the other types of ancillary supports mentioned above often makes the difference in the effectiveness of the employment process.

SUMMARY

Figure 2.1 depicts the three primary components in the employment equation: job seekers, employers, and intermediaries. Yet this equation becomes increasingly complex as additional variables are added. Certainly each individual job seeker has a multitude of intrinsic characteristics and external circumstances that will affect him or her throughout the employment process (Fabian, Luecking, & Tilson, 1994; Szymanski & Parker, 1996). An employment specialist must be willing and able to know the job seeker he or she represents, as thoroughly as possible.

Likewise, there are many variables within a workplace. Each organization that hires workers has its own unique culture. The configurations, variables, and factors that characterize individual places of business (whether public, private, not-for-profit, governmental, multinational, or mom-and-pop) are endless. In addition, there are the following variables: the people within the employer organization, the leadership, the processes that occur in that business, and the policies that govern the organization.

Similarly, individuals and organizations that serve as intermediaries (including schools, colleges, training agencies, human service providers, One-Stop Career Centers, and community-based organizations) are also tremendously diverse and function uniquely from one another, in terms of the people who work for the organization, leadership, and the way they operate. Within an intermediary organization itself, there are a host of variables in the equation. Just as with employers, these include people, leadership, processes, and policies. An individual working for an intermediary organization does not work in isolation. He or she is affected by the unique culture and the variables, within the intermediary organization.

All of these players are affected by the fluctuating currents and tides of the global and local economy, politics, current events, and social phenomena (Alea & Mullins, 1998). The ramifications for job seekers—and those who assist them—seem staggering. Yet an intermediary must be able to navigate this sea of variables within the workplace.

If successful partnerships are founded on mutual understanding, respect, and benefit, intermediary organizations and individual employment specialists must be highly adept at responding and managing all aspects of the equation depicted in Figure 2.1. For the job seeker, employer, and intermediary, this may be tantamount to threading a needle while riding a roller coaster. It makes the entire employment process a daunting one, unless there are clear and effective strategies. This book sorts out the pieces and provides the reader with food for thought and tangible, do-able strategies.

3

Setting the Stage

CAREER DEVELOPMENT STRATEGIES

Jo Ann Hutchinson

We know what we are, but know not what we may be.

WILLIAM SHAKESPEARE

The world of work is not stagnant. Employer demands and expectations change with the economy and its influence. Employers are always interested in hiring people who have the skills and abilities needed to competently complete assigned tasks. People seeking employment in today's workforce, therefore, need to systematically and comprehensively develop goals and strategies that will not only make their employment dreams come true but will also satisfy the ever-evolving skill requirements of employers.

Nearly everyone experiences the challenges involved in looking for and finding employment. The job-seeking process is even more of a challenge if individuals with disabilities are to find the right job, rather than just any job. This distinction plays an enormous part in adding to a sense of fulfillment and enjoyment in an individual's life. Thus, job-seeking activities for people with disabilities should give primary consideration to the job seeker's overall career plan.

The job should involve work that will give the person the experience that he or she needs to begin or continue a progression toward longer-term career goals. Employment specialists are thus faced with the task of helping individuals obtain employment about which they feel passionate and are willing to make the ultimate commitment to succeed.

This chapter discusses the evolution of career development theory to its contemporary application and the integration of theory and the related practical career development strategies into the job development process for individuals with disabilities.

CAREER VERSUS JOB

In the United States, employment is considered among the most important functions of our lives. In fact, people often define themselves by what they do or, in essence, by their jobs. A *job* is defined as a regular activity performed in exchange for payment. It is the position in which a person is employed. *Career,* at one time, was more synonymous with *job.* Over time, however, the concept of career has evolved to mean more than just a job. It is now considered to include a dynamic developmental process intertwined with the roles an individual has in life.

Contemporary definitions of *career* incorporate the development of the whole person throughout a lifespan and his or her interactions with the environment. This phenomenon is evident in Super's (1976) definition of *career* as a course of events that constitutes a life. He further defined *career* as the sequence of occupations and other life roles that combine to express a person's commitment to work in a total pattern of self-development. McDaniels (1984) followed Super's interpretation by defining *career* as the totality of one's work and leisure over a lifespan. Liptak (1992) later suggested that a career is each person's attempt to implement a particular lifestyle made up of work, leisure, and learning.

Helping an individual proceed in and navigate through the various phases of career development requires that employment specialists gain insight into the career issues, concerns, and desires of each individual job seeker. They can accomplish this by implementing specific strategies that lead to identification of each job seeker's values and personal beliefs. To get started, however, employment specialists must have a broad understanding of career development, career development theory, and career development and counseling interventions in order to enhance the potential for success of individuals with disabilities in meaningful, high-quality employment.

The National Career Development Association (2001) defined *career counseling* as the counseling of individuals or groups of individuals about occupations, careers, life/career roles and responsibilities, career decision making, career planning, leisure planning, career pathing, and other career development activities and opportunities (e.g., résumé preparation, interviewing and job search techniques, work trials), together with the issues or conflicts that individuals confront regarding their careers. In essence, then, employment specialists who assist job seekers with disabilities are career counselors.

CAREER DEVELOPMENT THEORIES

Career development is an interpersonal process that involves the total person. It concerns the person's needs, wants, capacity and potential, preferences, and personal insights. In addition, career development is dynamic. As such, it concerns the constantly changing aspects of a person's life. It denotes a lifelong sequence and pattern of an individual's work-related behavior, including any and all work-related experiences and activities before and after someone becomes formally employed. These experiences primarily focus on seeking, obtaining, and processing significant information about oneself, one's occupational and educational alternatives, lifestyles, and role options in order for someone to make informed decisions about work and its relationship to one's other life roles (Hansen, 1976). This section discusses four of the most prominent career development theories used by career counselors. A section that integrates these theories into the job development process for individuals with disabilities follows.

Super's Theory of Vocational Development

Donald Super, an early vocational theorist, proposed a comprehensive, developmental theory of careers (1990) that centered on a person's evolving a self-concept during five "vocational development" stages throughout his or her life span. His vocational development theory had a revolutionary impact on the field. It shifted the focus of research and practice from simply matching an individual's traits to the requirements of a job to recognizing a developmental sequence or progress through career stages (Dawis, 1996). According to Super's theory, an individual's vocational self-concept develops as he or she progresses through five developmental stages over a lifetime:

1. Physical and psychological growth occurs from birth to age 14, when a person's self-concept develops, personal needs dominate, and the activities a person engages in and the aspirations he or she pursues are based on personal interests. As the person's abilities become evident, he or she begins to consider the requirements of specific careers.

2. Exploration occurs from ages 15 to 24. During these years, an individual begins a process of self-examination, role experimentation, and occupational exploration within jobs, leisure, and school activities. This phase includes a strengthening of the self-concept, leading to key decisions related to coursework, hobbies, fantasy, volunteering, and job/career choice.

3. Establishment in an occupation happens from ages 25 to 44. These years are characterized by commitment to a particular occupation and stabilization and advancement within the work world.

4. Maintenance of work situation occurs during ages 45 to 65. During this phase, the person is most concerned with holding onto his or her job. Emphasis is placed on maintaining the satisfactory aspects of work, while making changes to any unsatisfying aspects.

5. Disengagement from work occurs after age 65. Between the ages of 65 and 70, the person's pace at work lessens and his or her duties may be shifted or altered. At this point, many people are employed part time, followed by retirement and an increased use of leisure time and other life activities.

Super's theory contributed to the concepts of career as a progression through life stages and vocational self-concept. It contributed to career counseling practices in terms of designing developmental interventions and associated tasks needed for the individual to progressively build a vocational identity. Super's theory also contributed to career practice by illuminating the role that careers and work represent in an individual's life and the ways in which the career role may take on greater or less importance to the individual during various life stages.

Holland's Personality Theory

Holland's theory (1973) focuses on the concept of matching an individual's personality to the characteristics of a work environment. He proposed that vocational choice was strongly influenced by personality type, and he described six personality types and the corresponding work environments that matched those types. Holland emphasized that career satisfaction was highest for people whose careers were pursued in environments that matched their personality types (Dawis, 1996). Holland's type categories are:

1. Realistic: People in this category value concrete, ordered, systematic, and physical tasks. They prefer working with objects rather than with people or data.

2. Investigative: People in this category are creative and like solving intellectual, scientific, and mathematical problems. Their preference is for working with data and objects.

3. Artistic: People in this category prefer unsystematic tasks, creativity, and artistic projects that might be vague and unstructured. People in this category like to work with objects and people.

4. Social: People in this category prefer educational, religious, and helping careers. They prefer to be involved in activities that inform, train, develop, cure, or enlighten others. They like to work with people.

5. Enterprising: People in this category value political and economic achievement, supervision, and leadership. They have a need for control and accomplishment. They pre-

fer jobs that organize others to accomplish goals and attain gains. They prefer to work with people and data.

6. Conventional: People in this category prefer orderly, highly structured, systematic, and concrete tasks. They prefer working with data and objects.

Holland's theory of careers had the strongest influence on career counseling and career practice. The concept of matching an individual's personality to the characteristics of a work environment has enormous intuitive appeal and has generated a number of career interest inventories, as well as a great deal of research (Hackett & Lent, 1992). Holland's theory and particularly some of the instruments that have been developed within it, such as the Self Directed Search, have proven particularly useful in career counseling for individuals with disabilities.

Social Learning Theories

Krumboltz's social learning theory (1991) suggests that people make sense of what they observe in life by developing beliefs, which they in turn use to guide their own behavior. When their beliefs are correct and constructive in nature, people act in ways that promote or enhance the achievement of their career goals. When, however, their beliefs are inaccurate or are formulated on the basis of limited experiences, people react in ways that make sense to them but that may hinder or interfere with their own personal career goals (Enright, 1996; Krumboltz, 1991; Mitchell & Krumboltz, 1990). Krumboltz further postulated that a person's interests develop as a consequence of learning and that learning, not interests or abilities, is what leads people to certain occupations. In addition, he believed that changes in what a person has learned produce changes in interests and occupational preferences.

Applying some of the concepts of Krumboltz's social learning theory to career development, Lent, Brown, and Hackett (1994) developed the social-cognitive career theory (SCCT), which focused on the importance of understanding career choice and career-related behavior from a person/environment perspective. This theory emphasized that it is equally important to consider how environmental factors shape career choices and vocational performance as it is to understand how certain person characteristics, such as intelligence, do. According to this theory, environmental factors consist of community, family, educational, social, and even geographic experiences that an individual may have. Within this theory, three of the most important career-related individual attributes that are influenced by the environment include self-efficacy beliefs, outcome expectations, and goals.

1. *Self-efficacy* is defined as people's beliefs about their ability to organize and carry out courses of action required to attain selected types of performances. Self-efficacy beliefs develop from and are shaped by actual performance, vicarious experiences, verbal per-

suasion, and physiological cues. Self-efficacy beliefs are among the strongest determinants of personal goals, in that they reflect an individual's belief in his or her ability to perform or accomplish.

2. *Outcome expectations* are defined as personal beliefs about the outcomes of performing particular behaviors. For example, a young woman may decide to enter law school because she has the positive expectation that this course of action will result in a valuable career for herself. Her confidence in her ability to complete law school reflects her self-efficacy beliefs.

3. *Personal goals* are defined as the determination to engage in a particular activity or to have an effect on future outcomes. Goals strongly influence choice and performance, in that people are more apt to accomplish particular tasks that are articulated in well-defined goals.

The constructs that emerge from SCCT, particularly self-efficacy and outcome expectancies, may have particular relevance for understanding the career process for individuals with disabilities, and developing strategies and practices that can assist them to achieve career goals (Fabian, 2000).

Work Adjustment Theories

Not to be confused with the traditional category of vocational rehabilitation service of the same name, work adjustment theories were developed around the assumption that career development does not end when an individual enters an occupation or job. These theories focus on work adjustment, the interactions between the individual and the work environment. Their primary emphasis is on how the individual adapts to the demands of the work environment and how the work environment adapts to the individual (Bolton, 1982). Several models of work adjustment dating back to 1953 are mentioned in the literature. Two of them are discussed here.

The first, the Minnesota theory of work adjustment, assumes that individuals seek to achieve and maintain a harmonious and suitable relationship with their environment. Tenure, or length of sustained employment that is determined by job satisfaction and job satisfactoriness, is the ultimate indicator of vocational adjustment. Satisfaction reflects the degree to which the individual's work needs are satisfied by reinforcers in the work environment. In turn, satisfactoriness is a function of the harmony and suitability between the individual's skill level and the essential duties of the job (Bolton, 1982). Satisfaction with the job contributes to satisfactoriness and vice versa.

The second work adjustment theory is Hershenson's model (Bolton, 1982; Hershenson, 1996). This model examined the development and interactions of an individual's work personality, work competencies, and work goals and their interaction with behavioral expectations, skill requirements, and rewards opportunities of the work setting. According to Hershenson, these interactions result in work adjustment, defined as the individual's work role, task performance, and satisfaction. The model focuses on three factors: the person, the work setting, and work adjustment.

1. The person: Includes three domains developing over time, each in relation to the individual's environment (e.g., culture, family, school, and peer/reference group). They are work personality (including self-concept, work motivation, work-related needs and values competencies, and goals), work competencies (which involve work habits, physical and mental skills that apply to jobs, and interpersonal skills in the work setting), and work goals.
2. The work setting: Includes behavioral expectations, skill requirements, and rewards and opportunities
3. Work adjustment: Includes work role behavior (the work personality of the person), task performance (related to the quantity and quality of one's output—competencies and skill requirements), and worker satisfaction (gratification resulting from one's work)

These models of work adjustment share several common assumptions and beliefs. The three main elements implied as essential in each of the models are as follows:

1. Work personality is central to successful vocational adjustment and includes an emphasis on work motivation, abilities, habits, attitudes, and values.
2. It is important to prepare or adjust the individual to the requirements of the work environment.
3. In-depth assessment of an individual's work personality is a necessary foundation for appropriate service planning and ultimate job placement.

CAREER DEVELOPMENT THEORY
AND JOB SEEKERS WITH DISABILITIES

People with disabilities face the same career challenges and needs as do any other individuals. In fact, people with disabilities display the same enormous heterogeneity of skills, abilities, personalities, and challenges as does any other group of individuals seeking to enter a job or career. As such, each of the career development theories described in this chapter contribute to the ability to assist people with disabilities to make good career choices, even though only Hershenson's theory was developed to specifically apply to people with disabilities. One generalization that cuts across these theories is that career development is determined by the dynamic interaction of the individual and his or her environment (Szymanski, Hershenson, Enright, & Ettinger, 1996). In order to be successful, regardless of the theory used, individual career interventions for people with disabilities must be determined on the basis of understanding the individual and how he or she is influenced by the environment during the career development process. This section discusses the application of each of these theories to the career development process for people with disabilities.

The underlying assumption of Super's theory is a natural progression through the five phases at strategic times within someone's life. To a degree, this theory can be applied effectively when working with people with disabilities; however, when considering the passage through Super's life stages by people with disabilities, employment specialists must understand their unique circumstances. For example, some individuals, for reasons of limited life experiences or cognition, may not experience the progression of the stages during the time periods suggested by Super. Someone who acquires a disability later in life may experience an interruption or even a backward progression in the sequence of developmental stages. Super's theory has practical but limited value.

According to Holland's theory, individuals function best in environments that most fit their personality types. Today, Holland's hexagon of personality types is used widely by vocational counselors and job development professionals to categorize occupations and job seekers during the career development process (Dawis, 1996). This procedure can be successfully used with anyone who has the ability to identify personal preferences.

Both of the social learning theories have practical application to individuals with disabilities as well. Krumboltz (1991) emphasized the relationship between belief development and consequent behavior. You might conclude that a disability could create difficulties in career selection by increasing the likelihood that a person will form inaccurate career beliefs based on limited opportunity to receive positive reinforcement regarding his or her abilities and skills. The theory does not, however, suggest that the presence of a disability alone will complicate career choice. What is relevant is the impact that the disability has on the job seeker's task approach skills and learning experiences (Enright, 1996). Thus employment specialists must strive to assess how a disability may have affected an individual's self-efficacy beliefs, particularly in relation to career goals. In this area, the job development specialist should assist job seekers through counseling to become aware of beliefs that may hinder their pursuit of a career decision and effectively change maladaptive beliefs (Enright, 1996). Social cognitive career theory (Lent et al., 1994), as well, can be effective in career counseling for a person with a disability, who may benefit from positive learning experiences that enhance his or her self-efficacy beliefs. In addition, having successful work experiences can contribute to increasing the person's expectations regarding work and career.

All of these theories have general application to the job-seeking process. The issues involved in adjusting to work once employed, however, have received little attention in career counseling and career development theory, except as they relate to the career be-havior of individuals with disabilities (Hershenson, 1996). Hershenson suggested that vo-cational adjustment involves a dynamic balance between the onset of the disability, the consequent effect on work skills, and the degree to which the disability must be accom-modated. Vocational adjustment theorists emphasize adjustment to one's job as the cor-nerstone of the employment process. These theories provide a conceptual framework for thinking about the vocational adjustment of people with significant disabilities. They indicate which characteristics and response capabilities should be the focus of individual assessment programs. In addition, they suggest what the most effective interventions might be and provide guidelines for the planning and provision of services (Bolton, 1982).

GENERAL CAREER PRINCIPLES
AND THEIR RELATIONSHIP TO PEOPLE WITH DISABILITIES

Given the complexity of the relationship between disability and career development, em-ployment specialists face the challenge of identifying the factors that have the greatest im-pact on the decisions job seekers will make (Enright, 1996). Following is a list of some of the general principles of career development and some key factors that may relate to an in-dividual with a disability, including age of onset of the disability, the formation of one's self-concept, one's feelings of self-efficacy, functional capacity, cultural background, gen-der, and environmental factors (Szymanski & Hanley-Maxwell, 1996).

1. The career development process may begin as early as a child's preschool years and is influenced by early school experiences. A young child begins to form a vocational identity or vocational self-concept that includes work personalities, abilities, and com-petencies. For people with disabilities, this developmental process may be delayed or interrupted as they experience education, and it may be affected by the nature of ed-ucational experiences, such as inclusive or segregated instruction.

2. Career development is influenced by a person's environment, including family, ed-ucation, and socioeconomic status. Thus, people with developmental disabilities and those who acquire disabilities early in life may have more constrained or limited ex-periences than others have. Similar to other people, people with disabilities who have been raised in disadvantaged environments may also not have had access to an array of developmental opportunities and experiences. These individuals are likely to expe-rience additional challenges in identifying and pursuing a career.

3. Career development is strongly influenced by individual beliefs, such as self-concept and self-efficacy. These beliefs are shaped in part by culturally based beliefs about work and work roles, all of which influence a person's career goals. For example, a per-

son with a disability who has not had the opportunity to develop a positive vocational self-concept and who participates in a rehabilitation program that does not value work may experience significant barriers to identifying and achieving career goals.

4. Career development is influenced by societal beliefs. Such perceptions as prejudice, discrimination, and gender role stereotypes can play an important role in individual career development. People with disabilities may be subject to disability-related stereotypes that affect career development.

5. Environments influence career development. Such environmental influences include the labor market, employment practices, inaccessible buildings, and negative social attitudes, all of which have implications for job seekers with disabilities.

6. Career development is a lifelong process (Super, 1990), as evidenced by the ongoing career and job changes throughout an individual's lifetime. Over the long term, the need for accommodations and support due to a disability may fluctuate, thus affecting career development.

BARRIERS TO EFFECTIVE CAREER DEVELOPMENT

Since the 1990s, the emphasis on career choice and self-determination for individuals with disabilities has been growing, together with a focus on competitive and integrated work in the community. Despite this, full participation in employment among people with disabilities remains a challenge in our society, even though interest in working is as pervasive for people with disabilities as it is for any other group in America (Tschopp, Bishop, & Mulvihill, 2001). One reason for this phenomenon is the barriers to effective career development that one meets when challenged with a significant disability. These barriers encompass a number of external obstacles to career planning and development and include such circumstances as

- The unavailability of the types of vocational and career services and supports that are needed to assist in the career planning and development process
- Community rehabilitation programs that may not endorse or reflect the necessary values and commitment to competitive employment for all individuals
- Job development specialists and other staff who may not understand or who are not prepared to provide adequate career counseling and career preparation services
- Inadequate or outdated vocational assessment procedures and tools that may be used to discourage individuals from career planning, rather than assisting them to identify career-related goals
- Lack of knowledge among career planning and placement counselors and others regarding specific disabilities and their characteristics

- Time-limited services provision that may not offer adequate long-term supports necessary and sufficient to encourage career growth
- Lack of collaborative strategies designed to ensure a partnership between disability employment agencies and other community and government services

Employment specialists need to assess each individual's circumstances to ensure an understanding of any barriers that may affect the career development process. Effective career counseling and program implementation strategies should vary for each individual to ensure the optimum outcome for each person receiving job development services. For example, for some individuals, the presence of a disability may have little impact on their career development and life plans. Yet for others who may have the same type of disability, its presence may have a profound impact on their self-esteem, dreams, aspirations, and life experiences. A person's reaction to a disability is the result of the dynamic interplay of a variety of individual, social, and environmental factors, such as the person's abilities, interests, beliefs, gender, family, educational background, socioeconomic status, ethnicity, and culture and the interaction of these factors with the environment. Environmental restrictions and personal beliefs that relate to a specific disability, in combination, could change how an individual perceives and pursues various career options. In addition, the presence of a disability can reduce the type of life experiences a person has that help to shape his or her career exploration and career development (Enright, 1996).

FAMILY'S IMPACT ON THE CAREER DEVELOPMENT OF INDIVIDUALS WITH DISABILITIES

Career theorists acknowledge the family's influence on an individual's values and self-concept, variables that later affect career choice. If a child has a disability, family development and the subsequent career development of the child may be seriously affected. Such issues as family distress around disability issues can damage one's sense of self and the concept of the role of work. Families can also believe stereotypes about disabling conditions and inadvertently support misconceptions about the employability of their family member who has a disability (Tschopp et al., 2001).

On the other hand, families can play a very positive role in the career development of a family member's career development. During the transition from school to work, five major areas of parental influence can positively affect a young adult's career choices:

1. Providing job information
2. Motivating the job seeker's achievement and interests
3. Serving as role models

4.   Influencing self-concept

5.   Influencing the individual's developmental environment (Burkhead & Wilson, 1995)

Employment specialists need to be aware that some individuals with disabilities may experience developmental delays or uneven development in the specific skills and competencies that lead to effective career development and successful employment. Based on the circumstances of the disability, some individuals may never achieve certain skills, causing them to need ongoing supports in order to be successful in employment. Families, therefore, may need to cope with meeting these often significant support needs.

SUCCESSFUL CAREER DEVELOPMENT INTERVENTION

This section summarizes some important aspects of career development intervention, such as assessment, decision making, service planning, and follow-up. More detailed discussion of these aspects can be found in subsequent chapters.

Career development processes require that employment specialists learn as much as possible about the individual receiving services, career development theory, and the world of work. They assume that the individual conducting a career exploration will be and will remain actively involved in all phases of the process. Career development also assumes the use of ongoing, comprehensive, holistic assessment that applies multiple methods of evaluating the needs, skills, capabilities, limitations, resources, and patterns of interaction of the person with a disability and the environment. Assessment can take the form of formal instruments, such as intelligence and achievement tests, or informal methods, such as skills and competencies checklists, intensive interviews, behavioral observations, and questionnaires that lead to an understanding of the individual and his or her most significant strengths and interests. It can take the form of a self-assessment or an assessment conducted by a professional staff person. The combination of assessment methods should be chosen on the basis of individual needs, background, personal experiences, and personal characteristics, and it can include such mechanisms as values clarification and the development of an understanding of specific knowledge and preferred learning styles (Career Services, University of Waterloo, 2002). Chapter 8 presents a dynamic process for getting to know the job seeker that compliments and, in many cases, supersedes the need for a battery of formal assessments. It also produces a solid foundation for beginning a successful job and career development process.

Following a comprehensive assessment, the employment specialist's next approach is to assist the job seeker in developing a level of comfort with decision making, an essential process in successful career development and planning. Decisions should be informed, well thought out, and specific to the individual. The decisions made during this phase of the process and the results of a comprehensive assessment are the foundation for the development and implementation of individualized job-seeking strategies and plans. Knowledge about the job seeker is the basis for identifying goals and determining the learning and skill development experiences necessary for the individual with a disability to progress in the world of work. Skills that have been mastered and areas of underdevelopment are identified from the comprehensive assessment. Planning, like assessment, should be conducted early and should be comprehensive. All people significant to the individual should be included in the planning process, and plan implementation should ideally occur in the community in the most appropriate setting for the individual (Career Services, University of Waterloo, 2002).

Finally, the outcomes of the job and career search plan should be regularly monitored through follow-up to determine the appropriateness of the plan; to assess the success of the interventions in meeting the goals and objectives of the plan; to ensure accountability of the service providers, family members, and others included in the plan; and to identify and implement necessary modifications to enhance the plan's overall effectiveness.

CULTURAL SENSITIVITY IN CAREER DEVELOPMENT PROCESSES

The circumstances in which people live and the opportunities that are available to them are important influences on career development. In learning the major components of career development, it is sometimes assumed that people engaged in career exploration have adequate opportunity for choice, freedom to choose, and the background experiences that make it possible for them to make informed choices. Unfortunately, environmental constraints such as poverty, limited or inferior educational experiences, lack of exposure to vocational opportunities, stigma, and discrimination make these assumptions less valid for many individuals from ethnic and cultural minority groups. Employment specialists working with minority groups may need to understand not only the past experiences of their job seekers but also the immediacy of current needs (Szymanski, Trevino, & Fernandez, 1996).

Someone who is struggling to meet the basic needs of survival may find it difficult to concentrate on career planning. For this reason, professionals must consider the individual's background and current situation in order to implement the most effective planning and interventions. It should, however, be noted that one should not assume that an individual's ethnicity or cultural background has automatic implications for the type of interventions. All processes should be considered and examined on an individualized basis. Culturally sensitive interventions require an openness to continuous learning (Szymanski, Trevino, & Fernandez, 1996). Chapter 7 provides a more in-depth discussion on cultural diversity as it relates to job development and placement.

SUMMARY

This chapter outlines current career development theories and how these theories can be integrated into the job development process for individuals with disabilities. Employment is a primary determinant in the joy and fulfillment of someone's life. For most people, including people with disabilities, it is a function of who they are, and they should choose a career path accordingly. Although several career development theories have been cited in the literature, no one theory is designed specifically for people with disabilities, although any one or a combination of approaches can be instrumental in assisting people to find meaningful, quality employment, regardless of the nature of their disability. Employment specialists need to acquire an understanding of career development theory, career counseling, and the individual job seeker in order to help people with disabilities enter into chosen careers. It is important to include a person-centered, individualized process while maintaining a culturally sensitive approach to counseling in order to effectively implement career development theory and strategies into the job development process.

4

Employer Perceptions of Disability and Disability Employment Programs

*What business seeks, first and foremost, from an employment
service agency is a strong orientation to basic management principles.*

MARK DONOVAN, VICE CHAIR, MARRIOTT FOUNDATION FOR PEOPLE WITH DISABILITIES

The goal of employment service programs for people with disabilities is very clear: help job seekers obtain jobs and establish careers. The outcomes of these programs are also very easy to determine—either people get jobs or they don't. Thus, there should be little ambiguity in how these outcomes are evaluated. There should also be little ambiguity about the primary targets of employment service programs' activities. If the result of disability employment programs is jobs for people with disabilities, then it is reasonable to expect that this field would have developed very sophisticated and comprehensive interfaces with those entities that provide the jobs: employers.

Indeed, understanding employer perspectives about people with disabilities and the employment programs that assist them seems essential to any job development initiative. Yet, much more attention should be paid to employer perspectives in order to facilitate the development of effective relationships with employers and ultimately the achievement of employment outcomes. Ultimately, employment specialists should be pursuing these customers for repeat business. The purpose of this chapter is to bring the perspective of employers into a clearer focus so that we can examine how their views might inform the development of successful relationships between job development specialists and employers. This chapter summarizes relevant literature on employer perspectives of disability in the workplace and looks at what employers have said about programs that provide employment support to people with disabilities. The implications of these perspectives for job development and employment advocacy for people with disabilities are analyzed to establish an improved context for job development and business partnership initiatives.

WHAT EMPLOYERS THINK ABOUT PEOPLE WITH DISABILITIES

Employers' views on disability in the workplace have evolved along with general societal views. In many respects, employers now hold attitudes that are more enlightened and informed than in the past. However, there are many more remaining prejudices and misunderstandings. An examination of this evolution of employer perspectives follows.

Past Employer Views

Since the 1950s, employers have voiced wide-ranging and often conflicting views about disability and approaches to the concept of disability. In some cases, these views have merely reflected or were influenced by prevailing social issues and legislative policy related to disability. For example, the mid–20th-century views of disability as a medical condition to be fixed and mediated often translated into employer hiring initiatives that were motivated by reactions to charitable appeals. The "Hire the Handicapped" marketing campaigns of the 1960s were a reflection of what policy makers believed would motivate employers: corporate goodwill. Essentially, the message was saying that the status of people with disabilities as misfortunate citizens with problems merited employers' sympathy. This approach to marketing job seekers with disabilities to employers—however well intentioned—eventually became widely discredited as mostly creating negative images of people with disabilities as objects of charity rather than as people with individual competencies from which employers might benefit (Hearne, 1991; Luecking, 1997).

With prevailing societal views of disability and the way in which disability employment was marketed to employers, it is not surprising that employers might harbor prejudicial views of people with disabilities, as early studies often found (e.g., Fuqua, Rathburn, & Gade, 1984; Olshansky, Grob, & Malamud, 1958). Their views were really not much different from how society at large viewed disability. And indeed, there was no law until the Rehabilitation Act of 1973 (PL 93-112) that prohibited hiring discrimination based on disability, and even then it was only prohibited in federal employment. However, certain companies took a keen interest in disability employment. One of the most widely cited series of studies of employer perspectives on hiring people with disabilities was conducted under the auspices of a private sector company. Through studies conducted in 1973, 1981, and 1990, DuPont Corporation consistently found that managers positively viewed employees with disabilities, generally regarding them as easy to supervise and as producing as much as their co-workers without disabilities (E.I. du Pont de Nemours and Company, 1993). The results of these studies often found their way into employer recruitment materials to illustrate to other employers that there was good reason to consider hiring workers with disabilities. Still, stereotypes persisted. In fact, with the wide publication of the DuPont studies and the subsequent disability employment marketing campaigns, a new stereotype emerged: that of the super-achieving worker with disabilities who would go above and beyond to prove to an employer his or her worth as an employee (Hearne, 1991).

Fortunately, new attitudes emerged as society began to regard employment barriers for people with disabilities as external and environmentally created, as opposed to being based solely on a presumed problems with the person. Barriers to employment became an access and civil rights issue. This led to the passage of the Americans with Disabilities Act (ADA) of 1990 (PL 101-336). Among other discrimination prohibitions, the ADA prohibits employment discrimination against any applicant with a disability who, with reasonable accommodations, is otherwise qualified to do the job. The ADA has acted as a means of heightening employers' awareness of disability, and according to some studies, it has positively shaped the opinions of many employers (King, 1993; Thakker, 1997; Walters & Baker, 1995). Since the passage of the ADA, however, employment rates for people with disabilities have not improved (Louis Harris and Associates, 1998). Thus, it has become even more important to gauge employer perspectives to see what is preventing them from hiring more people with disabilities.

Emerging Employer Perspectives

Employers' views about disability have evolved along with society at large but still reflect many of the same conflicting views apparent in many early studies. The news is both good and bad. On the one hand, employers express generally positive attitudes toward workers with disabilities, and most exhibit very affirmative and humane views about disability (Hernandez, 2000; Unger, 2002a). These views, in many cases, reflect a relatively sophisticated understanding of disability, and often employers make a credible case for how company profitability requires the effective inclusion, accommodation, and management of previously marginalized workers, including those with disabilities (Luecking, 2003; Sinclair, 2002). However, corporate responsibility to the larger community is still often invoked when companies articulate a policy about workers with disabilities, rather than a belief in potential for productivity (Nietupski, Hamre-Nietupski, VanderHart, & Fishback, 1996; Unger, 2002a). In this respect, employer attitudes have not changed much from the 1960s, when charity was often a prime motivation for hiring workers with disabilities. This suggests that although some employers are much more enlightened about disabilities than in the past, many more are still holding outdated and even discriminatory views.

Significantly, employers still tend to have more negative attitudes toward workers with particular disabilities. For example, workers with physical disabilities tend to be viewed more positively than workers with intellectual or psychiatric disabilities (Diska & Rogers, 1996; Hernandez, 2000). This suggests an ongoing potential not only for misunderstanding but also for discrimination. The discrimination may be inadvertent, but it still represents a huge hurdle when recruiting employers to hire individuals from these groups. In addition, other invisible disabilities, particularly learning disabilities, are still widely misunderstood by employers because the needs for individual and specific accommodation may well be unknown at best or dismissed as unnecessary at worst (Gerber & Brown, 1997). Overall, in a review of 37 studies of employer attitudes toward disability, Hernandez (2000) concluded that employers' expressed willingness to hire applicants with disabilities still exceeds actual hiring, although this gap is narrowing.

Experience Helps   A very encouraging finding of the Hernandez review, and several other studies, is that employer views about disability tend to positively change with exposure. Simply stated, employers with prior contact with people with disabilities tend to hold more favorable attitudes toward workers with disabilities. Employers are more positive about workers with typically stigmatized disabilities, such as intellectual and psychiatric disabilities, when appropriate supports are provided (Cook & Razzano, 1994; Levy, Jessop, Rimmerman, Francis, & Levy, 1993). In fact, in many cases in which employers are given specific consultation from disability professionals, employers are willing to go well beyond the ADA requirements for reasonable accommodations by providing an array of supports to workers with significant disabilities (Unger, 2002b).

Many employers with experience hiring people with disabilities indicated that the presence or absence of disability was not a primary concern when making hiring decisions. One study found, for example, that 77% of the youth, regardless of the nature or severity of disability, who completed a standardized work-based internship program in high school were offered

A Mixed Bag: Employers' Views on Disability

- Affirmative and humane views are most often expressed.
- Prior contact usually results in positive perceptions.
- Many employers exceed the requirements for reasonable accommodation when competent support is available to help them do so.
- Diversity initiatives are often seen as contributing to the company's overall operation.

but

- Negative views and stereotypes are still held for particular categories of disability, especially psychiatric and intellectual disabilities.
- Invisible disabilities, such as learning disabilities, are often misunderstood.

ongoing employment by their host companies, even though the companies were under no obligation to retain the interns beyond the internship period (Luecking & Fabian, 2000). This strongly suggests that once these individuals are on the job and performing, their contribution to the companies' enterprise outweighs their disability in the eyes of their employers.

In fact, a history of research supports the idea that company hiring decisions are less influenced by the presence or absence of disability than by potential contributions by a job candidate to the company, especially when value is clearly being added to the employer's enterprise. Employers' more pressing concern is often simply matching a person to a specific company need. Under the right conditions and with available and competent assistance, employers are willing to develop new and augmentative approaches to meet human resource recruitment and retention needs, including hiring people who require extensive initial training and follow-up support (Wehman, 2001).

In fact, many companies with vacant positions, even though they may typically require workers with highly technical skills, can be persuaded to consider applicants with disabilities without the requisite skills. This is the case, however, primarily when these applicants offer something to an employer besides a straight worker-to-job match (Nietupski, Hamre-Nietupski, & DiLeo, 1997). For example, alternative and specific task assignment to a worker with a disability, sometimes called *job carving* by disability employment specialists, often makes it possible for other employees to accomplish more, thus contributing to increasing company outputs (Nietupski & Hamre-Nietupski, 2000). Assigning a person with a disability to deliver documents from one company department to another, thus allowing other workers to remain at their posts to more quickly complete more complicated tasks, is an example of such an arrangement.

Overall, there is reason for optimism. Despite some continuing misperceptions among employers, disability in and of itself does not trigger inherently negative employer responses. In addition, exposure to workers with disabilities usually yields improved employer views of disability. Key reasons, then, for persistently low rates of employment for individuals with disabilities are not due to inherent or pervasive unemployability or to ingrained negative employer attitudes. Rather, explanations for this circumstance may be found in how well prepared workplaces are to support the needs of individuals with disabilities. For this, employers need the expertise and support of employment service programs.

WHAT EMPLOYERS THINK
OF EMPLOYMENT SERVICE PROGRAMS

The challenge of enlisting more employers to hire applicants with disabilities is often exacerbated by employers' unawareness or naïveté about the availability of people with dis-

How Employers See Disability Employment Organizations

Those who have limited contact are

- Largely naïve about the availability of disability employment programs
- Confused by fragmented services and categorical programs
- Anxious about knowing how to support and accommodate workers with disabilities

Those who have contact but express frustration

- Resent simultaneous solicitations for job openings from numerous agencies
- Perceive job placement personnel as being naïve about or unfamiliar with their business practices
- Do not see placement personnel active in the business arena
- Are frustrated by general unreliability

Those who have contact and are satisfied

- See disability employment agencies as necessary and important intermediaries, linking them with workers and identifying supports and accommodations
- Receive help in addressing operational needs
- Believe agencies positively contribute to overall company operation

abilities as a supplemental labor pool (Unger, Wehman, Yasuda, Campbell, & Green, 2002). They simply do not know of programs that assist people with disabilities to find jobs. When they are aware of disability employment resources, employers are often confused by the fragmentation of disability-related information or worried about not having the experience and resources to adequately support the employment of people with disabilities (Butterworth & Pitt-Catsouphes, 1997). That is, even when employers express a willingness to hire people with disabilities, they are typically at a loss as to how to identify the resources to help them accomplish it.

In addition, employers are often frustrated by marketing efforts of disability employment programs. Employer focus groups consistently yielded three types of comments by employers: 1) they resent having numerous organizations soliciting for job openings simultaneously, 2) they perceive job placement personnel as being naïve about or unfamiliar with business practices, and 3) they do not see placement personnel active in the business arena (e.g., participating in trade groups, chambers of commerce and other forums important to employers) (Locklin, 1997; Luecking, 2000b). As a whole, employers are often confused by disability employment initiatives and how they relate to their enterprises. This suggests a fundamental shortcoming in marketing these resources to employers: Their awareness is low and the message is unclear or misdirected.

In many cases, employers have expressed frustration with the reliability of disability employment programs (Kregel & Unger, 1993). Yet, employers who have positive experiences with workers with disabilities often point to the importance of competent support of organizations that have disability expertise. Such organizations act as intermediary links between job seekers and employers and provide a number of supports to the work experience, including coaching the worker, training and preparing co-workers to interact with the individual with a disability, identifying effective individual accommodations, intervening to correct work behaviors and performance, and assisting the employer to identify task assignments. In effect, these are roles performed by almost any organization that provides employment support to people with disabilities. A series of essays written by employers consistently identified two factors in their success with workers with disabilities: the help of partners experienced in disability issues and the ability of these organizations to positively contribute to the companies' overall operation (Luecking, in press).

Disability employment specialists often miss this latter point, as illustrated in a focus group study that compared the responses and opinions of employers with those of employment specialists and job seekers with disabilities (Fabian, Luecking, & Tilson, 1995). Participants in three separate groups—employers who had successfully hired people with disabilities, disability employment specialists, and people with disabilities—were asked the same question: What factors contribute to successful employment of people with disabilities? Overwhelmingly, people with disabilities and disability employment specialists identified such factors as employers' understanding attitudes and having a flexible approach to accommodations. By contrast, employers pointed to high-quality service from employment specialists and competence in particular workers as contributing factors to successful employment. In other words, employers were satisfied when the needs of their enterprise were the ultimate focus. These contrasting views provide evidence that disability is not necessarily employers' primary concern when making hiring decisions but rather the support that they will receive from the disability employment agency.

The Bottom Line

Essentially, the extant literature on employer views of people with disabilities suggests that employers are generally willing to consider hiring people with disabilities but still hold confused and stereotypical beliefs about various aspects of disability. Many who might be interested still have trouble finding such applicants. Those who have had previously employed people with disabilities are typically satisfied with the experience, but as a general group employers may still be hesitant to hire people with disabilities, especially those with certain disability labels. These findings suggest the need for refocused employment advocacy, better honed marketing initiatives, and more employer-oriented processes in the delivery of employment services to people with disabilities. Advocacy and methodology, which have historically concentrated on aspects of disability, and associated incentives (e.g., tax credits) would be more effective when conducted in the context of the employers' enterprises and organizational processes. Such benefits are examined in the case studies in Chapter 6 and other succeeding chapters.

IMPLICATIONS OF EMPLOYER
PERSPECTIVES IN PARTNERSHIP BUILDING

It has often been said that employment of people with disabilities is mostly a matter of opportunity and support. The quantity and quality of opportunity, however, depend on how available, interested, and informed employers become. Furthermore, as studies on employer views of disability and disability employment programs illustrate, the target of the support should be as much the employer as the job seeker. Four factors that reflect this employer focus and that contribute to the formation of partnerships with employers are introduced in the following sections and expanded in Section II.

Marketing

Marketing to employers should be, by necessity, a continuous activity of professionals and organizations representing people with disabilities. Such marketing should feature joining business organizations, facilitating peer-to-peer contacts among businesses, and soliciting regular feedback and direction from businesses through such activities as participation in Business Advisory Councils and focus groups. The message of marketing should be about competent and quality service that is available to employers, and it should minimize appeals on the basis of disability and charity. Furthermore, marketing should touch on factors that motivate employer participation: individual company needs.

In any case, business needs should drive marketing, as an adaptation of an old marketing adage might say, "It is better to find out what the employer wants and needs and match it to what you have to offer than it is to try to get them to buy what you are selling." Disability programs' traditional experience of unsuccessful marketing to employers might well have been due to a misguided emphasis on trying to get employers to buy what they are selling. That is, the concept of disability employment is not what typically interests employers.

The "Hire the Handicapped" campaigns of previous eras have been widely discredited for their appeals that seemed more a request for charity than a reference to job seeker competence. Marketing has become more sophisticated but still leaves some with discomfort about how to most effectively represent the concept of disability employment in a respectful and accurate way. The challenge is exacerbated by the amorphous nature of the definition of *disability* itself. Marketing initiatives that involve the explicit reference to disability are tricky. However, experienced employers are not at all bashful talking about disability once they are familiar and comfortable with the concept. Here may be part of the solution to the challenge of promoting employment of people with disabilities without the implicit charitable appeals: Facilitate and promote employers talking to each other.

Peer-to-peer marketing, in which employers explain to other employers the benefits they have accrued by providing work experiences for people with disabilities, has the potential to demystify disability. Several evolving national and statewide initiatives are designed to do just that. They include such organized initiatives and activities as Business Leadership Networks and Business Advisory Councils, through which employers experienced in employing people with disabilities lead activities that inform other employers about the benefits of and the resources for disability employment. More about how to link with and organize these types of initiatives is presented in subsequent chapters.

Customer Service

Because much of the success of disability employment initiatives for employers has hinged on the benefits that accrue to their enterprise, the implication for the field of disability employment services is that there needs to be a strong focus on delivering quality service to employer customers. This seems obvious, but it is often underappreciated or ignored in this field. Section II addresses this area in detail.

Convenience

Given employers' oft-expressed concerns about confusing interactions with multiple entities representing people with disabilities, it behooves practitioners to look for opportunities to join forces and share resources with other practitioners and entities that are in the business to engage and partner with employers. Such collaborations potentially streamline contacts with employers. A related tack for practitioners involves identifying and cultivating champions for people with disabilities, within individual companies. This facilitates an individual's entry into a company and enables competent internal support once he or she is there. Case studies of such collaborations can be found in Chapter 6.

Organizational Focus

Given employers' views of disability and disability employment service programs, it is apparent that such programs often need to refocus operational approaches to make them more conducive to the establishment of employer relationships. Instead of having a primary focus on internal processes that might be influenced or required by funders and accreditation bodies, for example, these programs are likely to experience more success by looking externally to what the employer customer needs and wants. This will often require programs to significantly reshape the way they do business. From redeployment of staff to the development of more professional marketing materials to creation of a visible presence in the business community, disability employment programs will find that specific and bold steps are often needed to reorient their services to be more attractive to employers.

INCREASING PARTNERSHIP CAPACITY

The Individuals with Disabilities Education Act (IDEA) of 1990 (PL 101-476) and its amendments, the Rehabilitation Act of 1973 (PL 93-112) and its amendments, the Americans with Disabilities Act (ADA) of 1990 (PL 101-336), and the Workforce Investment Act (WIA) of 1998 (PL 105-220) each have either implicit or specific intentions to address employment outcomes for people with disabilities. At their core, these pieces of legislation represent a general national conviction that the presence of disability should not limit an individual's opportunity to enjoy a successful career. Unfortunately, this conviction has yet to be fully realized. One of the missing ingredients to improve employment outcomes is a better understanding of how to engage employers in the process. Research has given some clues about what employers think about disability and what they need from organizations that represent job seekers with disabilities.

Programs and professionals that facilitate work experiences for people with disabilities are in a position to offer employers far more than simply another source of labor. These programs and professionals can draw on their experience and expertise in accommodations, job analysis, and work skills training so that employers are able to identify how to not only hire more people with disabilities but also provide, adapt, and incorporate necessary supports in their workplaces. The capacity to provide these supports can often improve the company's overall operational and organizational processes. In turn, when job seekers and employment specialists become comfortable and adept at identifying ways that their assistance can improve the company, employer attitudes toward disability are rendered minimally relevant. Subsequent chapters include detailed discussions and presentation of case studies that illustrate how disability employment programs and employment specialists can

- Identify return on investment for companies that enter partnerships with disability employment service organizations
- Identify employer needs and market features of their services that complement these needs
- Help manage any changes in a company that might occur as a result of the implementation of workplace supports that workers with disabilities might need
- Identify workplace supports, interventions, and accommodations that also contribute to the improvement of companies' overall operational and organizational processes

- Interact comfortably and productively with employers and speak their language
- Identify well-structured contact and follow-up procedures that result in productive partnerships with employers
- Restructure organizational operations so that job development activity is more externally focused and "employer friendly"

SUMMARY

This chapter presents the evolution of employer perspectives on disability and disability employment service programs. With more enlightened societal views of disability and the passage of the ADA, employer perspectives on hiring people with disabilities have become more affirmative. However, there remain attitudinal disparities, especially about certain disabilities. Fortunately, employers who have experience with disabilities in the workplace develop more positive views, even when these workers have significant support needs.

There is a need to enhance the view employers have of disability employment programs, but those employers who have successfully hired and managed employees with disabilities credit the competent service and expertise of disability employment programs. These findings have important implications for how disability employment programs are marketed to employers, how staff are trained and supported, how service is provided to employers, and ultimately how disability employment programs are organized and managed. Subsequent chapters detail strategies for both individual employment specialists and organizations to become more effective at developing successful employer partnerships.

5

Developing Relationships for Effective Business Partnerships

It's not what you know, but who you know.

A WISE NETWORKER

This popular phrase is a common one in job placement, suggesting that it is often personal connections that result in job offers, regardless of the level of job the applicant is seeking. This phrase also relates to network theory, a model of business relationships that was introduced in the first chapter. Essentially, network theory states that business transactions, whether they involve hiring, buying, or contracting, often "depend on the nature of personal relations and the network of relations between and within firms" as the foundation for doing business (Granovetter, 1985, p. 502). Network theory does not contradict other job development theories described in Chapter 1, but it does account for the fact that the majority of jobs that people get, particularly good jobs that last, tend to be those secured through personal contacts, rather than those found through classified advertisements or employment agencies.

For business relationships, network theory suggests that the strength of the personal relationships that develop over time and the degree of trust and confidence they inspire motivate people to behave in mutually reinforcing ways. In other words, the more individuals trust each other and the longer that trust relationship is sustained, the more likely they are to do business with each other, whether the business context is hiring, purchasing, or contracting. This chapter describes how network theory relates to the job search process and to the fundamental assumptions that are the basic characteristics of building business partnerships.

NETWORK THEORY AND THE JOB SEARCH PROCESS

The network theory of job development was first described by Mark Granovetter in the first edition of *Getting a Job,* published in 1974. The book reported the results of a research study, in which Granovetter interviewed 280 men about how they had secured their current job. Almost 56% of the respondents used personal contact as the predominant job-finding method, as compared with 18% using direct application and 19% using formal job hunting methods such as responding to advertisements. As the research relied solely on white male respondents, later studies were conducted to ascertain whether these conclusions were generalizeable to the larger and more diverse world of job seekers. In fact, they were. Subsequent studies of diverse populations found that the proportion of those finding their jobs through personal contacts not quite as high as in Granovetter's sample of white males, but still significant. For example, a 1989 report of "disadvantaged youths" indicated that 51% of white youth and 42% of African American youth found their jobs through personal contacts (Granovetter, 1995). Later research expanded the sample base to include diverse groups and industries, as well as minorities, and typically found the same result: The majority of successful job offers came as a result of personal contacts of the applicant (Brown & Konrad, 2001). The consensus on the results regarding the best method for successful job searches is that finding jobs through personal contacts is a more efficient way to search, resulting in more job offers at better wages.

As a result of this body of research, job development professionals, including writers such as Richard Bolles who authored the *What Color Is Your Parachute?* book series, have been exhorting people to use personal contacts for decades in their job searches. The use of networking as the most effective job development strategy has also been found in research studies involving job seekers with disabilities (Fesko & Temelini, 1997; Hoff, Gandolfo, Gold, & Jordan, 2000).

However, what these writers sometimes neglect to emphasize and what is as important in understanding how networks function is that it is not simply the number of personal contacts that matter: Successful job leads depend on the expansiveness and diversity of the job seeker's personal contacts. In other words, the broader and more diverse the personal network, the more likely a positive result. As Harris, Lee, and Brown (1987) stated, "Using networks of informal relationships will only be an effective method of job search if those networks connect the job seeker with employment opportunities" (p. 184). It's not only the connection between the job seeker and the contact person but how well that contact person is connected to others that matter.

NETWORKING

The importance of expansive and diverse network links in the job search process was made clear in one of Granovetter's surprising findings from his 1974 research. That finding was that the more remote the connection between the contact and the job seeker, the more likely it was that the connection resulted in a job. He called this phenomenon the "strength of weak ties." Essentially, he found that weaker or more remote social ties resulted in more positive job connections because acquaintances were more likely to travel in different circles than the job seeker's own. For example, in the sample of men described earlier in the chapter, of the 56% who found a job through a personal contact, 80% of these reported that they had only infrequent or rare contact with the contact person. Later research supported this finding, with some reports suggesting that weak ties not only were better sources for job leads but also might even lead to better jobs (Brown & Konrad, 2001). As Gladwell (1999) stated, "The more people you know who aren't close to you, the stronger your position becomes" (p. 64).

The strength of weak ties—or the need to have connections beyond immediate friends and relatives—helps explain a barrier to networking encountered by people with disabilities. The methods by which networks are grown and expanded is through diverse experiences in all aspects of life: education, community, recreation, and work. Individuals with disabilities, particularly those with severe disabilities, may lack access to the diversity of activities and experiences that result in meeting people from different walks of life who can introduce or link them to jobs, a consequence that is made clear in the employment data on individuals with disabilities described in Chapter 1. Constricted access to diverse kinds of people has also limited job opportunities in the job market for adults who are part of racial minorities, again a consequence made clear in the fact that the unemployment rate of African Americans was 10% in 2003, compared with only 3.7% of white adults (U.S. Department of Labor, 2001). One of the presumed benefits of educational affirmative action policies promoted and enacted in the 1970s and 1980s, in fact, was to increase the exposure of minority youth not only to more diverse experiences but also to more diverse people. By getting out of their own neighborhoods, these youth would have the opportunity to make acquaintances "outside their own social world" and so get to "know someone who knows where all the good jobs are" (Gladwell, 1999, p. 62), by shortening the links in the chain that lead to good jobs. The same holds true for people with disabilities. In fact, a research study that we conducted illustrates this point.

The study involved examining follow-up data of a sample of more than 3,000 youth with disabilities who had participated in a school-to-work competitive employment internship program prior to school exit (Luecking & Fabian, 2000). Most of the youth participating in the transition program (85%) secured their jobs through the auspices of an employment specialist working with them prior to school exit. Although more than 85% of the youth in this study had competitive jobs prior to school exit, only 63% of them were still working 6 months later. Interesting, however, is that the percentage of youth still working who had located jobs through their own or other personal contacts grew proportionately through the follow-up data collection period. In other words, at 6 months 13% of youth still working found jobs through connections, 24% of those employed at 12 months did, and 36% of those employed at 18 months did, compared with 59% of those working who found jobs through service providers.

Even more important, youth who located jobs on their own had higher wages across all three of the follow-up intervals, compared with youth who got their jobs through employment specialists. One of the implications from these data is that the strength of personal connections and networks in terms of leading to better jobs at better wages holds as true for individuals with disabilities as it does for other groups. The data also support expanding the social connections of youth and adults with disabilities as a viable strategy, not only to assist them to find that first job but also to help them develop the networks that lead to subsequent and better jobs. Obviously, youth who secured their jobs through the efforts of job development specialists were also beginning the network building process that Granovetter (1974, 1995) and others (Hagner, 2003) found to be so important in fostering career growth. So, for effective networking results and for more effective partnerships, it is not just who the job seeker knows but also how many.

DEVELOPING NETWORKS

A major task for employment specialists, and a major benefit they provide to job seekers with disabilities, is to help develop and foster the types of connections that not only lead to the first job but also continue to be useful as individuals move through their work lives and careers. One of the major advantages of working with an employment specialist for the job seeker with a disability is the acquisition of connections the individual needs to link him or her to more opportunities. Empowering the individual in the job search and improving agency or institutional networks are two important considerations when assisting individuals with disabilities to develop and expand their networks.

Empowering the Individual in the Job Search

The Rehabilitation Act Amendments of 1992 (PL 102-569) mandated self-determination and choice as integral to the rehabilitation process. Self-determination and choice in the job-seeking process counteracts the older notion of job development, which was often described in terms of placing an individual in a job, as if he or she were a passive object of services rather than an active participant in the process. Although self-determination and choice are now routinely included in the way that agencies and professionals describe their philosophies and values, job seekers still feel placed in jobs by the agencies and individuals who work with them. This was made clear in a study that solicited perceptions of barriers to the job search process among job seekers with disabilities (Boyle, 1997).

Several benefits to job seekers taking an active or partnership role in the job search process are obvious. Studies have indicated that one benefit is that when job seekers are more active, employer reactions to hiring them are more positive (Godfrey, 1995). This makes sense, as positive contact with employers has been shown to reduce stereotypes and stigma related to hiring people with disabilities (Unger, 2002a). Another benefit is that taking an active role contributes to career self-efficacy and vocational self-confidence, the most important attributes for attaining a job and building a career (Fabian, 1999; Lent, Brown, & Hackett, 1994).

Empowering job seekers with disabilities in the job search process also contributes to network growth by expanding their contacts with potential employers (Lin & Dumin, 1986). Ensuring that job seekers with disabilities are included in all aspects of the job search—particularly in informal meetings with employers, information interviews, job interviews, and job fairs—diminishes employer stereotypes and builds network contacts. Information interviews may be a particularly useful resource to accomplish this, as the informal situation fosters open communication that leads to making important connections (Hagner, 2003). In addition, these situations provide opportunities to build the job seeker's self-efficacy in the job search process, while at the same time exposing him or her to potential opportunities. Even if the information interview does not lead to a job within that company, it is a normal and routine way for job seekers to make contacts that eventually lead to other jobs in other companies. The "strength of weak ties" finding strongly suggests that the more individuals a job seeker meets in a number of different contexts, the more likely it is that he or she will begin to acquire the types of remote contacts that lead to jobs.

Institutional Networks

The agencies and organizations in which employment specialists work also play an important role in terms of establishing institutional networks. Institutional networks may be as important as personal ones in expanding opportunities and encouraging employer investment, and some of the methods for developing viable and reputable agency networks with employers are described in the next section. At this point, it's important to note that an agency has networks among employers in the community that can benefit or harm the job development specialist's work. For example, an agency's adherence to standards, ensuring that a potential job seeker is suitable for a position, may negatively affect an immediate prospect for a job, but it is an investment in a future relationship with that employer. When supported employment agencies make untenable guarantees to secure a job by promising employers that job coaches will always be available to perform the work if the job seeker cannot, they may be getting a short-term gain at the expense of developing a long-term relationship. When an agency or an institution, such as a school, does not risk short-term gain for long-term relationship benefits, it is developing and strengthening its institutional networks so that it may eventually influence an employer's hiring practices and maximize opportunities for job seekers with disabilities (Rosenbaum, Kariya, Settersten, & Maier, 1990). The following sections explain the benefits of developing institutional connections and long-term relationships from the perspective of the employer.

NETWORK THEORY AND BUSINESS PARTNERSHIPS

Personal networks work to the advantage of the job seeker and are also beneficial to employers who face hiring decisions. One of the fundamental findings essential to understanding the benefits of relational information sharing about potential job seekers with employers is that information is not free (Stigler, 1962). In other words, in order to get information, people need to expend time, effort, and sometimes money. For employers, the cost of obtaining information necessary to make a hiring decision may be embodied in elaborate screening and testing methods. For the employee, the costs may be embodied in obtaining certifications and credentials to persuade potential employers of his or her productivity. As Granovetter (1979) stated, "It's neither accidental nor irrational for job seekers and employers to prefer to get information about prospective jobs or employees through personal contacts, rather than by more formal procedures" (p. 87). Obtaining information through personal sources is less costly than other means, and the information is frequently regarded as better quality. Thus, employers prefer to rely on personal networks or referrals to fill job vacancies rather than on more impersonal methods such as recruiting through advertisements or employment agencies.

The personal nature of the connection between job seeker and employer needs to be underscored because it helps explain the failure of rehabilitation and personnel agencies in representing job seekers about whom they do not have sufficient information to employers with whom they do not have a personal connection. The advantage of obtaining information from personal sources lies within the direct contact between the source, the employer who wants the information, and the resource who is providing it, the employment specialist. The longer the degree of separation of personal contact between the two, the less trust the source has in the information. This fact was clearly demonstrated in Granovetter's original research (1974), which indicated that the optimal distance between successful job searcher and employer was two chain links or fewer: The employer knows

Person A who recommends Person B for the position. The shorter the contacts needed to link job seeker to job, the more likely the employer is to regard the information about the job seeker as credible. In fact, links of four or more between job lead and job seeker *never* resulted in a job offer—the source was too distant to be regarded as reliable (1979).

The length of the link between job and job seeker in influencing credibility of information may be particularly critical for job development professionals, given the persisting stereotypes about people with disabilities. Job development specialists should assume that employers require more, not less, credible information about individuals with disabilities in order to counteract stereotypical attitudes that may include, for example, reduced productivity, heightened volatility, and additional employment-related costs (Unger, 2001). It is easy to see that specific employers would not regard employment agencies that represent hundreds of workers and have little personal knowledge of any individual job seeker as reliable sources of information about people with disabilities.

Employer Incentives for Partnerships

Employers have several incentives for relying on personal referrals to fill a position or to create a new one. First, personal referrals reduce the cost of searching to fill a job vacancy. It is much less expensive to obtain reliable information from a trusted source regarding an applicant's qualities than to engage in the processes required to evaluate a pool of applicants, such as résumé assessment, job testing, and credentials validation. Second, information obtained from known sources is more credible than information obtained either from an unknown job applicant or an unknown representative of the applicant, such as an employment service agency. Third, relying on referral information from a personal source reinforces the relationship for both parties so that future transactions are facilitated that are mutually agreeable.

The degree to which employers rely on personal contacts in making business decisions is critical in the job development process. Business transactions, such as job referrals, are embedded in personal relations or networks that generate trust and discourage doubt. In other words, employers trust information from those sources that, because of the desire to sustain positive relationships, provide honest and reliable information. In turn, the odds that they will continue to do business with that source are increased. It's no different than a consumer being more likely to purchase goods and services from businesses with which he or she has had a relationship or who were recommended by a trusted and credible source. In the sense that relationships between customer and business or business and business are based on trust, they are, to some degree, embedded in social relationships. That is, like all social relationships, business partnerships are based on and sustained by trust.

The social aspect of business relationships is an important one for employment specialists to understand. Other theories of how businesses operate tended to reduce the transactions—purchasing, hiring, and selling—to strictly economic, profit-motivated behavior. In this case, then, it would appear that the best strategy for assisting job seekers with disabilities to get job offers is to appeal to economic motivations of employers, such as tax incentives or a belief that "hiring the handicapped is good business." However, if network theorists such as Granovetter (1995) and others are correct, hiring decision transactions are embedded in social relations. This helps explain why a building contractor relies on the same subcontractors for job after job—not necessarily because they are least expensive or the best but because a long-term relationship has evolved between the entities, maintained by expectations of long-term beneficial outcomes. Engaging in a long-term partnership eventually pays off in terms of the parties learning to work together more effectively, and the eventual result is that such a partnership is more economical, whether the purpose is contracting, investing, or hiring.

The same rationale that is used to understand the transactions of individuals within businesses, such as employers making hiring decisions, can also characterize the relationships between organizations. Organizations rely on networks in their business transactions. In the job development arena, this reliance is most obvious when a company has an opening and it calls a particular employment service agency with whom it has an established relationship. Network theory provides a key to the fundamental values underlying business partnerships: trust, mutuality, and duration. These characteristics describe business relations that provide the types of results that employment specialists are seeking.

Trust   Trust is the basis for any relationship, whether personal or business. Trust represents the degree of confidence one imputes toward a person or an institution. It is the measure of credibility, based on integrity, that motivates any human relationship. In an economic sense, trust may be based on self-interest: If a real estate agent gets a reputation for over-selling properties or not divulging defects, his or her reputation will suffer as will the business. Trust is also motivated by the desire to sustain personal relationships, which are impossible without it. Sociologists and other theorists have used the dilemma created by people's behavior in a crowded movie theater to illustrate an important point about trust. When there is a fire in a crowded theater, even though all patrons know that orderly walking to the exits will result in less injury and save more lives, most people will not behave this way because they do not trust that others will behave similarly. In this situation, lack of trust leads to avoidable but desperate results: chaos, injury, and even death. Contrast this situation with one in which a home is on fire. Family members and friends in that situation never stampede for the door because they are confident that the behavior of others will reflect the mutual interests of all. From this dramatic comparison, it is easy to understand why organizations go to lengths to establish trust in their relationships with others. This maximizes their confidence that everyone will behave in a manner that will promote mutually beneficial outcomes.

Mutuality   Mutuality is similar to trust, in that institutions develop confidence or trust in each other based on the belief that each partner in a transaction operates in a mutually beneficial manner. It is mutually beneficial for people to exit a burning movie theater in an orderly fashion, but because one does not trust that others will behave that way, everyone panics and more are injured. In a business relationship, parties in the transaction—whether purchasing, contracting, or hiring—are interdependent. In order for both to succeed, they need to have mutually beneficial goals. In the case of hiring decisions, employers want a secure source of workers, and employment agencies—whether schools or rehabilitation services—want a good company to hire their applicants. Employment service agencies operating on the assumption that only economic principles guide hiring decisions might be tempted to inflate the productivity of an applicant. Employers, believing that employment service agencies are trying to sell them on hiring unqualified workers, may discourage such job seekers from seeking employment within their firms. Both parties are not seeing the mutual benefits that arise from a relationship established on credibility and fostered by a commitment to mutual benefit. Hiring transactions that occur within this context may succeed one or two times but do not lead to long-term partnerships.

Trust and Mutuality in School to Work Transition

A transition resource specialist working in a large secondary school was not having much success in finding competitive jobs for special education students in their year prior to exiting school. She managed to locate four medium to large businesses in the local school district and encouraged them to review the school's vocational training curriculum, to provide input about the types of job skills they determined to be critical, and to monitor their results. When these companies identified specific positions they anticipated, she only referred those candidates who had the requisite skills. In other words, she bypassed short-term gain for the long-term relationship. In 1 year, only one student got a job in one of these companies, but in the next year, eight students got jobs. These companies also provided numerous connections and referrals to other local businesses, many of whom now want to get involved with her school.

Duration   People tend to invest more in enduring relationships. For example, you might leave a larger tip in a local restaurant that you frequent often, as compared with one hundreds of miles from home. You are investing in the future in terms of ensuring good service. Similarly, businesses invest more in relationships in which past experience has paid off and future benefits are expected to continue. It is important to note that the duration of business relationships may well outlive the particular incumbent within the position. In this case, long-term relationships can be embedded within a position, rather than with the person who holds that position. For example, a company that always contracts for services through a particular purchasing agent will likely continue to do so if the relationship has been beneficial, even when there is a new employee in the purchasing role.

Trust and Duration in Job Development

Claudette was an employment specialist working with a variety of job seekers. A job seeker with whom she worked, Ned, was in his mid-30s and had schizophrenia and a history of substance abuse. Ned's employment history indicated more than 20 jobs, none held for more than 3 or 4 months. The one thing Ned was good at and loved to do was to work around cars. However, his history of work in garages and repair services was poor: He generally could not take the stress and was exposed to people who connected him back to drugs. Claudette was friendly with the assistant director of a large assisted living center for the elderly in her community. In fact, her aunt lived there. The center was a good contact and employment resource for Claudette, particularly for her job seekers who enjoyed being with elderly residents. Because the center owned and operated six or seven vans for transportation, she approached the assistant director to see how they provided regular upkeep and service for the vans and realized that hiring Ned to perform routine maintenance work would be a terrific savings for the center. The assistant director was aware of Ned's background, but based on the long-term relationship she had with Claudette, she agreed to try him out on the job. In this type of environment, Ned thrived. He was still working there after 1 year.

Each partner understands that the new occupant in the position has a stake in preserving the long-term relationship and will behave in accordance with these outcome expectations. The same is true when a hiring manager leaves a company but that company continues to call on a long-standing employment service agency partner. Of course, personal relationships within these roles may take some time to solidify, but again, it is more efficient and effective for businesses to continue investing in those partners with whom they have had long-term, stable, and mutually beneficial relationships.

IMPLICATIONS OF NETWORK THEORY FOR JOB DEVELOPMENT PROFESSIONALS

The implications of personal connections and their benefit to the job seeker or job development professional and the employer have been made apparent throughout the chapter. Some practical strategies arise from these discussions that are important to reiterate. Specifically, the following strategies need to be considered:

1. Expand the connections of your employment service agency outside of the realm of other social and human service agencies. Many agencies have strong ties and personal relationships within the human service or rehabilitation sector. While important, these are not the kinds of connections that lead to employment opportunities for job seekers. Strategies to expand agency connections include not only joining the chamber of commerce but also being creative in linking the agency to the community. This

can be done by participating in community volunteer activities; sponsoring sports and other teams; talking to political leaders about how your agency can benefit the business community; or providing free services such as diversity training, communication skills training, or advice and consultation on workplace accommodations to businesses in your areas of expertise.

2. Broker connections to good applicants. Remember that information costs money and that employers are as committed to reducing costs as you are. In order to reduce hiring costs, employers need to see the job development professional or organization as a credible, viable source of job applicants. They also need to understand that hiring referred applicants reduces costs associated with recruiting, screening, and evaluating applicants. If you cannot fill all of the employer's needs, then consider connecting them to other agencies who might fill particular positions. Offering this service to employers gains you and your agency important connections and builds the foundation for business partnerships. After all, as discussed at some length in Section II, this is really just good customer service, similar to when a desk clerk at a fully booked hotel arranges for a customer to receive lodging at a rival hotel.

3. Rehabilitate your agency's reputation in the community. Employment service agencies are often invisible in the business community in terms of their potential as a human resource solution. Or they may suffer from a poor image or from an image as an organization doing good rather than one that is good. Or, even worse, they may already have an untrustworthy reputation based on poor past relationships. Involving the agency in some of the activities already noted (e.g., sponsoring community activities, volunteer drives, and business roundtable groups) provides visibility and, if need be, helps to shift a bad reputation to a more positive perception of the value of partnering with the agency in developing beneficial relationships.

4. Behave in a credible fashion. Because trust is the foundation of any relationship, it is necessary to ensure that all professionals who represent the agency are reliable and honest sources of information regarding job seekers they represent and information they provide about the agency. The tendency to sometimes overpromise is a blight to the reputation of any potential business partner. To neglect this aspect necessitates returning to the third strategy: having to rehabilitate the reputation of your agency in the community.

5. Do not neglect long-term relationships because they have not resulted in job placements. The importance of relationships goes well beyond a specific employer offering a specific job. A relationship with one business can provide the connections to other businesses in the communities that do have jobs. Remember the strength of weak ties that may ultimately yield more and better job offers for job seekers within your agency.

6. Make job placement services, and therefore partnerships with business, central to your agency's operation, rather than either contracting the services out to other agencies or assigning the task to just one or two specialists. This is simply a good busi-

ness practice. Because business relationships are embedded in social ones, contracting job placement services to other agencies or individuals unaffiliated with the agency does not make sense. Remember that the fewer the links in the chain between job seeker and employer, the more likely it is that the individual will get a job offer. Developing and sustaining personal relationships with the business community are the keys to maximizing job offers in the world of work.

SUMMARY

This chapter presents the concept of network theory and related research on job acquisition that suggests the importance of personal networks in conducting a job search. Job search professionals have long relied on the maxim that getting a job depends on personal contacts. Those people who have broader experiences and broader social networks are able to find more and better job opportunities. Because people with disabilities are often handicapped by few job experiences and a small social circle, it is important for employment specialists to help expand employment opportunities for job seekers with disabilities by widening their own social and professional contacts and by helping job seekers expand theirs.

However, it is also necessary to understand the underlying rationale for this maxim, as well as to understand its economic and sociological context. Business partnerships are formed and sustained as a result of the trust engendered through social networks and the resultant relationships. Understanding the need to reach out to as many sources and contacts as possible, while stabilizing existing contacts and relationships, is an important area of job development expertise. Implications of network theory for job development professionals are presented in this chapter. Strategies and technologies to develop and manage such networks are covered extensively in Section II.

6

Partnerships at Work

ILLUSTRATIVE CASE STUDIES

Richard G. Luecking, J. Erin Riehle, and Mark Donovan

Inventing options for mutual gain is a negotiator's single greatest opportunity.
WILLIAM URY

When any set of partners establish a high level of mutual trust and when the partners all derive significant benefit, the possibilities are vast. Would Lewis have reached the Pacific without Clark, for example? Or would Hewlett have created monumental technology and business innovations without Packard? The concepts are similar for job development. Well-structured partnerships with a clear, common vision yield not only large numbers of employment opportunities but also jobs in many more places than would be evident at first glance.

This chapter provides examples of relationships between employers and disability employment services and professionals that illustrate the partnership principles described in previous chapters. Three major case studies are featured: One represents a partnership that was initiated by an employer looking to boost its human resources recruitment efforts, the second illustrates a specific approach taken by an organization that acts as an intermediary in linking hundreds of employers and job seekers with disabilities, and the third shows how an individual employment specialist developed a very successful relationship with an employer that resulted in a long-term partnership. Each has resulted in acquisition of jobs and careers by individuals with a range of disabilities. Each features the partnership building blocks of trust, mutuality, and duration. Each also has incorporated procedures and processes that are, at their core, extremely business friendly and that illustrate a strong focus on their external employer customers.

SEARCHING FOR A RELIABLE WORKFORCE: CINCINNATI CHILDREN'S HOSPITAL MEDICAL CENTER

Cincinnati Children's Hospital Medical Center (CCHMC) is a large multi-campus facility "dedicated to serving the health care needs of infants, children and adolescents and to providing research and teaching programs that ensure delivery of the highest quality pediatric care to our community, the nation, and the world" (2003). Like most hospitals, 70% of its staff members are professionals: doctors, nurses, therapists, and other personnel who are highly trained and educated. The other 30% are primarily support staff who receive the greater portion of their training on the job. At all levels, however, hospitals need people who are committed and well prepared. They also often take deliberate action to connect very directly with their communities, both as a healthcare provider and as an employer. Beginning in the mid-1990s, CCHMC began a significant diversity initiative to attract and retain the entire spectrum of the community's potential workforce. This initiative targeted people with disabilities. The reasons were threefold:

- CCHMC was experiencing a particular problem with attracting and keeping good entry-level support staff. It needed to upgrade and expand its recruitment approaches to include the large segment of job seekers who have disabilities, who want to work, and who are often represented by a variety of organizations that assist them in job preparation and job search.
- It needed to bolster the quality and intensity of its on-the-job education of new staff so that staff members were better prepared, performed better, and therefore stayed on the job longer. Eventually, disability employment organizations offered assistance to the hospital in designing ways of improving job training and support for people with disabilities.
- It adopted as a guiding principle the 1995 policy statement of the American College of Healthcare Executives, which states, "Healthcare organizations must lead their communities in increasing employment opportunities for qualified persons with disabilities and advocate on behalf of their employment to other organizations" (as cited in CCHMC, 2003).

Thus, the motives for the hospital to embark on a disability hiring initiative were both self-serving and responsive to a perceived community need. As CCHMC quickly learned, hospitals can be very good at providing medical services to people with disabilities who spend time under their care, but they are not always so good at recognizing the level of productivity that is possible for people with disabilities who have the right kinds of opportunity and support. Therefore, the hospital took small, incremental steps in developing what is now a well-designed, comprehensive partnership with disability employment service organizations that enabled it to eventually hire more than 100 people with disabilities in a wide range of jobs in a number of its departments.

Search for Assistance Begins

J. Erin Riehle was head of the hospital's emergency department in the mid-1990s. She was having difficulty filling some entry-level positions, such as stocking, and the hospital decided to support a disability employment initiative. She approached this initiative as a recruitment avenue. Not knowing exactly where to start, she first used the telephone book to locate such resources. After a few dead ends, she found a career and technical school that had some students with disabilities, the Great Oaks Institute of Technology and Career Development, and a state entity responsible for serving people with mental retardation and other developmental disabilities, the Hamilton County Board of Mental Retardation/ Developmental Disabilities (MR/DD). After many planning meetings, Ms. Riehle and her new partners initiated a training experience where youth and adults with disabilities were taught jobs that involved stocking supplies for the emergency room.

The arrangement worked so well that other departments wanted to try a similar approach. Soon, another area of opportunity was identified: The hospital needed reliable couriers to deliver laboratory and pathology specimens to laboratories and locations throughout the nine-building campus. Before long, 13 people were hired as laboratory couriers. The hospital, believing in the long-term potential of this hiring initiative, formalized the relationship with the Great Oaks Institution and the Hamilton County Board of MR/DD with a legal contract specifying the roles of all partners. Ms. Riehle was soon coaxed out of the emergency department to direct this new effort, now known as Project SEARCH.

Experience Leads to Adjustments

The initiative worked so well that the hospital decided to significantly expand it. It put out a call to a number of agencies that serve job seekers with disabilities, resulting eventually in the involvement of 6 different agencies that provided a total of 13 different job coaches at any given time. Unfortunately, this turned out to be a very unwieldy—and ultimately unworkable—arrangement. The hospital found itself dealing with multiple organizations whose staff had little direct knowledge of its needs. It had to train them *and* the employees with disabilities. It also had no control over who was hired to be the job coaches. If the job coaches were late or tardy, the hospital was at their mercy. If they did not perform up to the hospital's standards, CCHMC had little influence over improving their selection, training, or development. Overall, this was not a very employer-friendly arrangement.

So the model was changed. Through a contract with Hamilton County Board of MR/DD, the hospital now hires its own job coaches. It has developed its own follow-along program for the individuals with disabilities that it hires. In this way, the hospital can make sure that the performance of both the job coaches and the employees meets its standards. The job coaches become thoroughly acquainted with the hospital's needs and are better able to train and support the people with disabilities the hospital hires. And the hospital can more rapidly and conveniently address any performance or accommodation issues that may arise.

Significantly, the hospital has made Project SEARCH a single-point-of-entry system so that it can easily make contacts with schools and agencies representing people with disabilities. Project SEARCH coordinates referrals, the application process, and all hiring decisions, and it manages all of the on-the-job support, such as job coaching, adaptations, accommodations, final task definitions for specific jobs, and travel training. It also maintains employment status through on-site follow-along service and provides opportunity for career advancement. At any given time, Project SEARCH provides employment and educational opportunities for more than 75 individuals with disabilities. These individuals have a range of disabilities and accommodation needs. They are employed in a range of positions, with roughly 80% of these individuals working enough hours to qualify for benefit status.

Project SEARCH Targets Youth

Participants in Project SEARCH learn through demonstration, outreach, and education, combined with technical assistance, in several distinct programs. One of these programs is called the High School Transition Program, which began in 1997. This program, offered in partnership with Great Oaks Institute of Technology and Career Development, offers a 1-year transition program for students with disabilities who are in their last year of school. The program is geared toward students whose main goal is employment and who are interested in career exploration in a health care setting. It is a major vehicle for preparing and recruiting new hospital employees, although a number of the participants go on to work in other places.

During the school year, as many as 12 students spend the day at CCHMC, Provident Bank, or Clinton Memorial Hospital and rotate through three to four worksite experiences. These site rotations allow participants to build various skills, including communication, problem solving, and specific job duties, as they become ready for competitive work environments. During the second half of the school year, a process of individualized job de-velopment and placement occurs that is based on the students' experiences, strengths, and skills. Students are given support with accommodations, adaptations, and on-the-job coaching by on-site staff. As the school year ends, linkages are made to appropriate community services in order to ensure a successful transition to work, as well as retention and career advancement. Many stay on and become permanent employees of CCHMC.

What Makes It Work

In the past, the hospital's human resources department was approached by many different education and job placement professionals. It had no way of understanding who all of these people and organizations were and who they represented. These education and job placement professionals seemed to approach CCHMC as though they were seeking a favor from the hospital. Ms. Riehle stated that "such a model does not work for business. It is too complicated and confusing, too inconvenient, and too out of touch with our real human resource needs. Most often, applications from such sources ended up filed away and never considered." These professionals had not established a base of trust and mutuality.

The hospital strongly believes that it has been able to develop a viable alternative that is very effective in meeting its human resource needs and fulfilling the original intent of the disability hiring initiative. According to the hospital, the keys to making Project SEARCH work to its benefit are these:

- *A single point of entry:* Through Project SEARCH, the hospital posts jobs and makes them known to schools and organizations representing people with disabilities. These organizations then go through one place to get job information. The various hospital departments can then screen applicants.
- *Internal identification of job opportunities:* The position of Project SEARCH within the hospital allows it to constantly evaluate job opportunities and determine options, such as job restructuring, that meet the hospital's needs but that also offer unique opportunities for job seekers.
- *On-site and directly accountable staff:* Job coaches are employed by the hospital, not an outside disability employment organization, which enables the hospital to control the quality of the direct coaching and support that is necessary for many of its employees with disabilities to perform well.
- *Formal cooperative agreement with selected school and disability service partners:* The hospital retains a clear, formal contract with selected organizations who assign special educators and employment professionals who provide them with expertise in accommodations and training methodology when needed. They no longer have to use the phone book to find resources for expertise in disability and disability employment.

This program has received local and national awards and has been featured in mainstream magazines, such as *Family Circle*. It has also expanded beyond its own complex. It has linked efforts with other health care facilities, a prominent bank, and two retail stores to organize similar opportunities for people with disabilities in business peer-to-peer marketing of the initiative. What started as a way to meet a specific industry's need for a well-prepared, highly functioning workforce has evolved to equipping other companies in other industries to develop internal structures that will enable them to successfully recruit, hire, and manage employees with disabilities. The hospital's experience with an employer-driven approach clearly illustrates very effective ways to meet company human resource needs and increase the employment options for people with disabilities.

Partnership Lessons

The hospital had to cast about for the right partners, but it did eventually find and select disability service entities with which it could develop trusting relationships that were cemented with formal legal agreements. All partners receive significant tangible benefits. The hospital has received a host of workers, whose training, support, and supervision is totally under its control. The disability partners receive both an avenue for job preparation for individuals (the school transition program) and a direct link with many job opportunities for the job seekers they represent (Project SEARCH). For the Hamilton County Board of MR/DD, their investment in the contract with the hospital comes with a significant, and practically guaranteed, payoff: Public dollars invested result directly in jobs for people with disabilities. This long-standing partnership is likely to endure for many more years due to the formal partnership agreement and the fact that all parties are benefiting in significant and direct ways.

It is worth noting that this partnership is unique in two other important ways. First, the employer, CCHMC, initiated the partnership by finding trusted partners through the telephone book. It also had to revamp its hiring procedures when using so many agencies became unwieldy. This speaks 1) to a common need to increase the visibility of disability employment service agencies in the employer community and 2) to the typically disconnected way in which the myriad organizations who represent job seekers go about their attempts to connect with employers. This employer had to take things into its own hands to initiate what ultimately became a highly successful partnership. Had it not done so, applications from individuals represented by employment agencies would probably still be finding their way into a forgotten human resources file. The hiring initiative still requires a partnership with entities that have expertise in disability service to make it work. However, these entities have had to alter their usual way of doing things to fit their services to the needs of this employer, for example, by enabling the job coaches to be employed directly by the employer.

Second, not all employers are as large or have the resources, determination, and savvy to orchestrate such partnerships. It is rare that an employer would take on such a hiring program without outside stimulus. Thus, such partnerships are obviously not the only or necessarily the most desirable way to promote and arrange employment opportunities for people with disabilities. This is one unique and outstanding example that reinforces critical lessons that apply to employer partnership development.

Among the lessons from this partnership is that there is a clear *service* that disability organizations can provide and therefore market to businesses, as opposed to marketing the *concept* of disability employment. CCHMC is an employer that had a clear human resource need and obvious receptivity to trying different approaches to human resources recruitment. Disability employment organizations and professionals can also try new approaches to working with an employer by getting to know the specific human resources needs and the operational circumstances of the company in order to identify ways to offer assistance. Each employer has unique hiring needs. The employment specialists must not only identify these needs but also then match their services to these needs. Ultimately, expanded and innovative types of employer-friendly partnerships can emerge.

CREATING CONTINUOUS CONNECTIONS TO EMPLOYERS: MARRIOTT FOUNDATION FOR PEOPLE WITH DISABILITIES

The Marriott Foundation for People with Disabilities and its signature program, *Bridges . . . from school to work,* were established in 1989 to enhance employment opportunity for young people with disabilities. *Bridges* is an employer-driven program with two primary objectives: to help young people with disabilities identify and gain access to a future that includes productive and fulfilling employment and to help guide employers to a rich and largely untapped applicant pool. The program is a reflection of long-standing Marriott corporate experience with and commitment to attracting the broadest possible spectrum of individuals to its workforce. *Bridges* operates in seven communities: Atlanta, Chicago, Los Angeles, Montgomery County (Maryland), Philadelphia, San Francisco, and Washington, D.C. The program serves young adults (ages 18–22) preparing to leave high school by connecting them with local employers and supporting them in jobs developed with these employers. The program is funded by the Marriott Foundation's own resources, a variety of federal government grants, local school systems, local workforce investment programs, and targeted private-sector fundraising activities.

Since its inception, *Bridges* has helped more than 5,500 young adults achieve employment with more than 1,500 different employers. *Bridges* participants represent the range of students who receive special education services, including all disability categories and support needs. Reflective of a typical special education population, the preponderance

Table 6.1. *Bridges . . . from school to work* participant demographics

Demographic category	Percentage
Gender	
Male	53
Female	47
Primary disability	
Learning disabilities	57
Mental retardation	18
Emotional disabilities	15
Sensory disabilities	4
Mobility disabilities	2
Other disabilities	4
Race	
African American	50
Hispanic	23
Caucasian	20
Asian	5
Other	3

Source: Luecking (2000).
All percentages were rounded, resulting in more than 100% in one demographic category.

of the youth served by *Bridges* have learning and cognitive disabilities. Because almost all *Bridges* sites are located in urban centers, more than 80% of the youth are members of ethnic or racial minority groups. Table 6.1 illustrates the typical proportion of demographic characteristics of *Bridges* participants.

Maintaining an Employer-Driven Focus

The *Bridges* program has business origins, and it uses its business perspective as its local programs recruit businesses for participation. These businesses are drawn from each community in which the program operates and represent a wide range of industry clusters, including retail, service, finance, health, government, and manufacturing. Leveraging the Marriott name and presence in these communities, local programs recruit employers through several complementary and simultaneous activities:

- Business-to-business events, which promote *Bridges*, often hosted by Richard Marriott, Chairman of the Foundation. These events include introductory seminars on disability in the workplace, breakfast meetings, receptions, large-scale dinner events, and other functions to introduce the issue of disability in the workplace.
- Contacts through Marriott Business Councils, organizations designed to keep Marriott businesses in touch with each other in order to address issues of mutual concern.

These councils are natural vehicles to market *Bridges* within Marriott business operations, with some peripheral opportunity with Marriott business partners.

- Business Advisory Councils, established in each individual *Bridges* program. These bodies consist of local business people and other stake-holders, who provide guidance and recommendations to *Bridges* staff regarding local business issues, while engaging in peer-to-peer marketing of the program to the wider business community and other support activities.
- Active membership in business organizations. *Bridges* staff join and actively participate in chambers of commerce, boards of trade, and other local business organizations. These memberships provide a platform for the program in the business community, ultimately yielding increased credibility and a wider network of employer contacts.
- Job development efforts and contacts by *Bridges* staff using techniques that are typical of any intermediary representing job seekers, such as those outlined in Section II of this book

Table 6.2 shows the industry type of companies that have hired *Bridges* participants.

Keys to Effectiveness

Real progress on developing effective employer networks is made when it is clear to a business that what the program offers brings tangible benefit relative to their business imperatives. Thus, mutual benefit is the key to making *Bridges*, like any other relationship-building initiative, work. It is a priority that program staff supports *both* the employer *and* the employee as they embark on their new relationship. As necessary, *Bridges* staff assist

Table 6.2. Primary industry of employers participating in *Bridges*

Industry	Percentage
Retail	30.4
Food service/restaurant	19.1
Amusement/recreation	9.2
Health services	3.6
Educational services	3.7
Finance	4.3
Manufacturing	3.0
Lodging	3.3
Government	1.7
Public utilities	1.6
Communications	1.9
Other	18.2
Total	100

Source: Luecking (2000).

with new employee training, provide coaching for interpersonal and skills development, and help facilitate solutions when issues arise. Equally important, *Bridges* staff continually canvass the employers' operations to see how the youth they represent and the services they provide might affect it positively.

Several guidelines have been adopted by *Bridges* that clearly reflect the type of business orientation one would expect from a program so closely associated with the successful business practices of an industry leader:

- Under-promise and over-deliver to create longstanding and loyal partners.
- Never make a commitment that you are not confident you can keep—then do whatever it takes to keep the commitments you make.
- Know all parties, their circumstances, and their needs well before attempting to broker a potential relationship.
- Only broker a relationship that is a good fit for all involved.

These might well be adopted as principles for all employment specialists to live by. Trust develops from promises kept and from delivering more to the customer than what the customer expects (see also Chapter 12). Knowing what everyone might gain is important in the negotiation of a job referral. Thus, in the end all partners benefit.

GOING THE EXTRA MILE FOR EMPLOYER PARTNERS

Chantel, an employment specialist with TransCen, Inc., an employment agency with which the book authors are affiliated, was working with a young man who dreamed of being an artist. Michael had a long-standing interest in arts and crafts and was good at creating drawings and three-dimensional arrangements. He expressed an interest in working at an arts-and-crafts store near his home. The employment specialist learned of a job opening for a stock clerk at the store, which was having trouble finding good employees in a tight labor market. Knowing that Michael would have difficulty with a traditional oral interview, Chantel assisted the store manager to set up a series of common tasks so that Michael could perform them as part of a working interview. The store manager hired Michael after he observed that Michael could indeed perform the majority of the tasks, and Chantel showed the manager how she would help Michael learn the rest.

In effect, the employer was taught how to make an accommodation to his usual interview process. This experience ultimately led to changes in many of the hiring procedures of this and other stores in the franchise. At the request of the store manager, the employment specialist helped standardize the working interview as part of the store's recruitment and hiring system. In a region where English is the second language of many individuals, substituting sample task performance for oral interviews became a very effective way to screen applicants. Giving this additional assistance (i.e., helping the employer develop a process that he could use for a larger pool of applicants) was not really a requirement of Chantel's job, but this relatively simple act of going the extra mile for the employer partner resulted in a significant payoff for both parties.

Mutual Gain Leads to More Hiring Opportunities

This benefited the entire franchise in very obvious ways. First, it gained a trusted partner to whom it could turn when it needed positions to fill. Indeed, Chantel became the first person who was called whenever there was a vacant position in any of the franchise stores in the area. She could not always help them fill a position directly, but she often was able to find another agency that represented job seekers who had an interest in retail occupations. Second, the store acquired a process by which it could screen larger pools of applicants—not merely people with disabilities who may need such an accommodation but also applicants with limited English. Third, this employment specialist became a frequent source of consultation on other staff training matters. Her expertise became a boon to the employer.

Chantel, of course, gained a source of potential retail jobs for other interested job seekers. In fact, she occasionally was able to mine hidden job opportunities for job seekers who had fewer skills and less work experience than Michael. By working with the store manager to identify specific work tasks that might not be part of a standard job description, she found other jobs that contributed in some way to the store's overall operation. For example, one person was hired to only open boxes of new merchandise, freeing other clerks to more quickly stock the shelves. And finally, whenever Chantel needed a reference or a testimonial about her services, she could count on the store manager to provide it.

Making It Work

All of this occurred over the course of several months, but it resulted in significant payoff in terms of a relationship with an employer who became a repeat customer. In order to help Michael get the job in the first place and to identify ways in which her expertise could add value, Chantel drew on knowledge and skills common to people in the employment service field. Such expertise includes:

- Knowing the job seeker: She had to know Michael well, including his interests and needs for accommodation.
- Knowing the employer: She had to get to know the employer's operation and job tasks before she could offer any assistance or propose hiring options. She visited the store several times to talk to the manager and observe the stock clerk's job. Instead of ask-

ing the manager to consider hiring a person with a disability, she took the time to in-
quire about his needs and how employees accomplished the work in the store.

- Analyzing job tasks: She observed and analyzed how the jobs got done so that she
  could devise ways in which Michael could be interviewed.

- Using good communication skills: She displayed diplomacy and developed the rapport necessary to recommend alternatives to the store manager.

- Offering value-added service: After Michael was hired, she was willing to devote extra
  time to help the employer devise the alternative interviewing strategy that was eventually adopted for other applicants. Although some people may see this as outside of
  her job responsibilities, there is ample evidence that this kind of assistance is exactly
  what all good employment specialist can and should do. These characteristics of the
  employment specialist's approach to this employer illustrate some of the core aspects
  of what it takes to become a successful developer of partnerships. Chapter 7 examines
  in considerable detail the range of basic competencies that effective employment specialists possess.

Business-Friendly Processes

Michael's store manager ultimately found himself the beneficiary of the employment service of TransCen, Inc. He was assisted in hiring, as opposed to being the passive recipient
of a placement service. This is a subtle yet important distinction because from the employer's point of view, the encounter with the employment specialist was easy, helpful, and
clearly conducted to meet his business's hiring needs. An old marketing maxim states that
it is more effective to find out what the customers want and then match it to what you have
to offer, than it is to try to convince them to buy what you are selling. By helping the store
manager hire for a position hard to fill in a tight labor market, by helping the store to meet
a larger human resources need through a revised interviewing process, and by providing
value-added service, Michael's employment specialist used the skills she had to meet the
store's needs. She did not have to sell the idea of hiring a person with a disability.

SUMMARY

This chapter illustrates several highly effective partnerships between disability employment services and professionals and employers. All of the partnerships were characterized
by the development of mutual trust, mutual gain, and long-term relationships—the foundation for successful partnerships. All of the partnerships also featured processes that were

friendly to the employers' operations in that they were convenient, easy to implement, and reflected an appreciation for the needs of the employers' enterprises.

One partnership featured an actual legal and financial relationship. In this partnership, a large employer, CCHMC, initiated the relationships due to particular human resource needs. It eventually settled on a carefully designed internal recruitment, hiring, and training protocol to counter the frequent confusion and variable quality it had experienced when dealing with multiple disability employment organizations. Two of its partners built trust with the hospital when they delivered applicants and disability expertise, and eventually re-channeled employment service money.

Another partnership approach, developed by the Marriott Foundation for People with Disabilities, featured the broad implementation of a standardized process for linking young job seekers to area employers by using strong connections to the business community, including a range of industry clusters. The foundation's program, *Bridges . . . from school to work*, is based on a strong ethic of mutual return on investment, a concept central to any successful business partnership. Durable partnerships drive the success of this venture in each of the cities in which the program operates. As a result, employers of all sizes and from all industries have met human resource needs, and youth with a range of support needs and disability labels have achieved employment.

Finally, this chapter features the efforts of a single employment specialist who was able to help a particular employer adopt alternative processes for recruiting and evaluating new applicants that resulted in considerable mutual benefit. The principles of building partnerships apply to any relationship between employment services and employers, whether the relationship is initiated by employers, by service agencies, or by individual employment service professionals. Section II presents detailed strategies that lead to these kinds of results.

7

Fundamental Skills for Employment Specialists

A company is known for the people it keeps.

ANONYMOUS

Many professionals who provide employment services to people with disabilities have a variety of credentials and licenses. At the graduate level, some job development professionals may be certified rehabilitation counselors, licensed social workers, or licensed counselors. These credentials all require a master's degree. However, other professional associations, such as the International Association of Psychosocial Rehabilitation Services (IAPSRS), provide certificates to individuals who may not have graduate degrees but who have achieved a level of recognized practice in these particular fields. Still others, such as the Association for Persons in Supported Employment (APSE), have recommended guidelines that apply to anyone who provides employment support to individuals with disabilities, regardless of educational attainment.

However, there is no specific nationally recognized credential in the form of either certification or licensure for job development and placement professionals. In fact, these professionals come from a variety of backgrounds and disciplines, ranging from human service fields, such as rehabilitation or special education, to business fields, such as human resource development or marketing. Although there is no nationally recognized credential, there is growing consensus about the skills and competencies that are required for effective practice as a job development professional. The purpose of this chapter is to review the basic competencies required to be an effective practitioner. The chapter focuses on fundamental attributes and skills, and later chapters in this section address more specific skills requirements (e.g., marketing) that employment specialists need to know. In addition to basic attitudes and competencies, the chapter discusses ethics and multicultural competencies.

FOUNDATIONAL COMPETENCIES AND CHARACTERISTICS

Competencies refer to the basic or essential skills required to become a qualified professional. Competencies encompass specific knowledge and skills, as well as personal characteristics or attributes that are considered essential in performing a particular job. Competencies in the helping skills generally refer to three broad domain areas:

1. Attitudes and values. These refer to basic beliefs, values, and principles that undergird a profession. Attitudes or values might include ethical conduct, multicultural awareness, and endorsement of self-determination.
2. Skills. These are the building blocks of competencies. Skills incorporate the experiential level of competencies, being able to demonstrate mastery of a particular behavior. Skill areas include assisting with goal setting, assessing job seeker preferences, and communicating warmth and understanding.
3. Knowledge. Knowledge encompasses the context or background from which a particular discipline has evolved. Knowledge includes definitions and concepts, such as marketing or customer service, as well as principles or practices, such as career development or assessment.

Attitudes and Values

Attitudes and values shape who a person is as a professional and shape the nature of his or her services, interactions with job seekers and employers, and even the role in changing the system of services. Attitudes and values are particularly important for helping professionals, such as job development specialists, because they have a unique relationship with job seekers and the power to affect life changes. Before describing five of the fundamental attitudes that contribute to developing positive and effective relationships with job seekers and employers, it may be useful to present basic values that are characteristics of all helping relationships (Hodges, 1990, as cited in Weinstein, 2000), particularly relationships with individuals with disabilities.

- People want control over their lives. Although practitioners develop strategies and techniques for assisting individuals to get what they want, empowering others to do for themselves is a fundamental value in helping relationships.
- People cannot know what they can do until they have had every opportunity to try.
- A practitioner's job is not simply reducing discomfort or distress, it is actively working to increase an individual's skills and resources.
- Optimism and hope are sometimes the most important qualities practitioners bring to helping relationships.

Although many fundamental attitudes and values are critical in the helping professions, we have selected five that are the most important in developing the beliefs and values that inform effective job development practice. Attitudes and values cannot be learned in the same way the skills are acquired, but they can be understood and explored, providing the opportunity to challenge and, where necessary, to change them.

Communicate Respect for the Job Seeker   This attitude reflects what is the necessary and sufficient condition to foster change in any individual. Respect is communicated through effective communication skills but is based on the fundamental belief that all of the individuals you assist have the right to determine their own futures, to make their own choices, and to be integral partners in the job-seeking process. Communicating respect for the individual encompasses the values inherent in self-determination and personal choice and is reflected in enabling job seekers to take charge of their careers.

Believe in an Individual's Capacity to Change and Grow   Much of the literature on the effectiveness of counseling and psychotherapy concludes that it is the attitude and beliefs of the counselor that are important in fostering change, not the specific therapeutic orientation or theory that is used. Job development professionals can foster self-confidence or self-defeat in job seekers through the verbal and nonverbal messages they convey. In other words, you can contribute to an individual's confidence by communicating your own confidence in the job seeker's abilities, both explicitly (through encouragement) and implicitly (by offering opportunity). Ensuring that assessment techniques have a strengths-based foundation (as opposed to one that conveys limitations) is one way that job development professionals demonstrate their belief and faith in the job seekers they represent.

Be Aware of Individual and Cultural Differences   Although it is true that there is more difference within groups than between groups, it is critical for any helping professional to communicate respect for and understanding of human differences that have to do with culture, race, age, sex, disability, and ethnicity, among others. Developing listening skills and communicating respect are essential ingredients in fostering respect for diversity. More discussion on multicultural awareness and skills is included later in the chapter.

Demonstrate a Flexible Attitude and Willingness to Change   Excellent job developers are able to rapidly and accurately assess a situation and adapt themselves accordingly. Being able to think on your feet when challenged by an employer or a co-worker is, in part, a learned skill but more importantly, requires an open attitude toward others and a willingness to examine your beliefs and methods and make changes as necessary. Flexibility also means that job development professionals know when to shift approaches or strategies when one particular approach is not effective.

Maintain Self-Awareness   Self-awareness, or self-understanding, is the necessary prerequisite for being able to help others. Job development professionals who are not aware of their own attitudes, values, or beliefs run the risk of forcing their beliefs on consumers and job seekers, thus communicating disrespect. Self-awareness skills also require professionals to monitor their own reactions to stressful situations, to be aware of when their personal situations may be intruding on their job, and to watch carefully for the signs of personal frustration with the job, which can sabotage the best job development plans.

Fundamental Communication Skills

Unlike the values and beliefs described above, communication skills can be taught in human services programs and frequently are. Basic communication skills require a different type of listening and responding than what a person typically performs in everyday conversation. The following basic skills represent the building blocks that are required for job development professionals to form partnerships with job seekers and with employers.

Effective Listening   Effective listening skills that convey respect and understanding have been widely described in the helping literature (Corey & Corey, 1997). The ability to listen effectively is the critical skill in relationship building, whether with a job seeker or with an employer. Active listening eschews the types of behaviors that predominate in everyday conversations, such as giving advice, interrupting, telling, and talking too much. Essential components of listening skills include:

- *Active listening:* This means observing and responding to verbal and nonverbal messages. Paying attention to any obstacles to effective listening (e.g., personal biases that might filter the message) and being aware of the attitudes and beliefs conveyed by the speaker are essential in exploring and responding accurately. Active listening requires concentrating on the speaker, eliminating distractions (internal and external), and conveying interest and respect (through eye contact and body language).

- *Reflecting:* Active listening differs from typical conversations when the helping professional rephrases the verbal and nonverbal message as a means of signaling to the individual that he or she is being heard accurately. "You seem to be telling me that you want to look for work but are a little unsure about how to start the process" is an example of a *reflective listening* statement. "Don't worry, you'll get a job" is an example of a poor listening response.

- *Clarifying:* In active listening, the helping professional needs to highlight certain issues and bring them into sharper focus. This allows the job seeker to understand and prioritize his or her feelings and motivations regarding, for example, work or job seeking. "From what you've been telling me, you've made a number of different job contacts for the past year but are feeling frustrated that so far none has resulted in a job offer" is an example of a clarifying statement. "From what you've been saying, I can tell that you need to improve your ability to get a job" is a poor listening response.

- *Reframing:* Reframing is an important skill in helping people to defeat the types of negative attitudes and thoughts that may impede their ability to behave positively. Reframing examines a pattern of behavior and tries to reinterpret it positively. "You've told me you don't think you'll ever find a job because you've been looking unsuccessfully for a year. I wonder if we can look at your job hunting strategies and techniques to see if we can find better ways for you to achieve your goal." In reframing, the helping professional is presenting an alternative perspective to what has been labeled a problem.

- *Motivational listening:* Job hunters with disabilities have frequently encountered discouraging attitudes, negative messages, and outright discrimination in their job searches. Motivational listening is related to the reframing skill. It is a method of emphasizing and constantly focusing on positive thoughts, experiences, and behaviors in order to enhance another person's self-confidence and skills efficacy. An example of this is "It's hard to persist in the job search, but some of the activities you've done so far are really on target. Let's talk about how we can build on these to accomplish your goal."

Connecting Skills   Connecting skills reflect the ability to connect with people in a positive manner. In this regard, they are rooted in effective listening skills. They extend these basic skills by including what are called *interpersonal influence skills.* Interpersonal influence is a way of directing the focus or the content of a conversation or an interview in a manner that respects the participation of the other person but that provides structure and direction in order to achieve an objective. In this way, interpersonal influence skills help build rapport in a nonjudgmental manner in order to achieve mutually reinforcing outcomes. Connecting skills are also motivational because they focus on positive aspects of the interaction and of the message and influence its direction. Here is an example of a job development specialist speaking to an employer: "I understand your hesitation about hiring individuals with disabilities in your company, but I'd like to draw your attention to some of the positive features about our agency's services that may alter your feelings." Here is an example of a job development professional speaking to a job seeker: "I know you've had some problems with the rehabilitation services in the past, but I'd like to focus on how I can help improve things for you by understanding your vocational goals." Connection skills strengthen the capacity to make the types of positive contacts with others and facilitate positive connections between job seekers and employers.

Mediation and Negotiation Skills   These skills provide the basis for expanding partnership opportunities. They strengthen the relationship among people by emphasizing constructive feedback as a means of reaching an outcome that benefits everyone. Mediation and negotiation skills require helping professionals to be able to use effective listening and connection skills to work positively toward solving problems and reaching mutually satisfying outcomes. Negotiation skills separate the person from the problem so that problem solving occurs in a less personal, and therefore less threatening, environment. Focusing on the problem, not the person, avoids encounters that become power struggles and tends to result in people feeling defensive or resentful.

Here is an example of these skills in the context of working with an employer. After Joe, the supervisor, has indicated that he wants to terminate Nancy, the employee, you might say, "Joe, I understand that you have some real concerns about Nancy's being on time to work. However, some of the other aspects of her performance—such as her attitude and attention to tasks—are positive. It certainly is your option to fire Nancy, but I wonder if we might first try to brainstorm around her tardiness, so that you can continue to benefit from the positive employee aspects she offers the firm." Here is another example of negotiation skills when interacting with an employer who is hesitant to bring on a new employee. "I can see that business may not warrant hiring new employees right now. Perhaps I can help identify some operational efficiencies that would increase business or I can help have ready applicants when the hiring freeze is lifted."

Advocacy   All job seekers have to be self-advocates and self-promoters, and they must believe in their skills and the contribution they can make to a business entity. This is even more important for job seekers with disabilities because employers may be inclined to focus on their limitations rather than on their strengths. Advocacy skills are the natural extension of influencing and connecting skills. Employment specialists need to anticipate how social and employer attitudes may impede the job search (both explicitly and implicitly) in order to address them. Of course, in order to develop advocacy skills, you must know specific laws regarding employment discrimination, transportation, and access to services. This allows you to address these issues when necessary and to prepare job seekers to handle them during interviews. Advocacy skills may require practice or rehearsal, as they are often demanded when dealing with stakeholders or employers who are in a more powerful and therefore more intimidating position. To an employer who states that he or she is not interested in endangering customers by hiring "handicapped" people, you might say, "I'm impressed with your workplace and the kinds of things your business does. I also understand your commitment to customer satisfaction and think that you're wondering how hiring [Joe, who has a visible disability] will affect your customers and your business. It's easy to think in terms of negative reactions customers may have, but I think it's equally important to consider the positive aspects your business is displaying by its willingness to hire [Joe]. What specific problems or doubts do you have, and let's see if we can resolve them."

ETHICS AND THE EMPLOYMENT SPECIALIST

Certified and licensed professionals need to adhere to a code of ethics in order to retain their privileges to practice. Codes of ethics not only regulate the behavior of the practitioner but also provide reassurance to the job seekers they serve and the public regarding the practitioner's integrity and method of promoting job seekers' welfare.

Employment specialists who are licensed or certified must adhere to and uphold the specific code of ethics of their professional discipline, whether it is rehabilitation counseling, social work, or education. The majority of employment specialists, however, are not licensed professionals, but they are interested in delivering high-quality services to the job seekers with whom they work. Moreover, many employment specialists work in agencies and organizations that have established their own code of ethics or code of conduct. Other agencies and organizations adhere to codes of ethics that are consistent with accreditation bodies (e.g., the Commission on Accreditation of Rehabilitation Facilities) or professional organizations (e.g., the Association for Persons in Supported Employment).

Rather than knowing specific codes of ethics, employment specialists should have a general understanding of the basic principles behind most of these codes so that they can measure their behavior and conduct in accordance with these widely accepted principles.

Principle 1: Self-Determination and Autonomy   This principle states that helping professionals must behave in a manner that is consistent with conveying respect

José's Dilemma

José, a new job development professional, overhears some of his co-workers making fun of a consumer by telling a story about his experience on a job interview and what he did wrong. Although José does not engage in this behavior, neither does he try to put a stop to it.

- Was José acting in accordance with ethical conduct?
- What could he have done in this situation?

Mark's Confidentiality Dilemma

Julie has a psychiatric disorder and a history of substance abuse. As her job counselor, Mark is aware of her background, as well as the fact that she has been arrested for dealing drugs. A potential employer whom Mark meets at a social event seems open to hiring people with difficult backgrounds, perhaps because of a personal or family experience. Mark tells the potential employer about what he does and asks if he can have one of his job seekers set up an appointment to discuss working at the company.

- Was it okay that Mark did not actually reveal Julie's background and that the employer is left to draw her own conclusions?
- What would be the best thing to do in this situation?

and ensuring rights to individuals with disabilities. In this regard, practices include:

- Avoiding exploitive or dual relationships with job seekers
- Providing job seekers with complete and accurate information regarding the extent and nature of services
- Apprising job seekers of their rights and the risks of services
- Making service and intervention decisions apart from financial and other considerations
- Not condoning or engaging in any form of discrimination, stigmatizing practices, or biased practices
- Avoiding relationships or commitments that conflict with the interests of the job seeker being served

Principle 2: Confidentiality and Privacy

This principle states that job seekers have a right to privacy and an expectation of confidentiality regarding all information shared with the professional. In this regard, practices include:

- Holding in confidence information obtained in the course of service delivery
- Releasing information to others only with the specific informed consent of the job seeker
- Ensuring that job seekers have specific understanding of *informed consent*
- Safeguarding the maintenance, storage, and disposal of personal and confidential information
- Requesting only health- and mental health–related documentation that is relevant to the scope of practice
- Understanding and upholding state laws regarding privileged information and confidentiality

Principle 3: General Welfare of Job Seekers

This principle refers to behaving in a manner that promotes the well-being of job seekers. It includes:

- Promoting social justice for individuals with disabilities
- Addressing discrimination and acting as an advocate when required
- Advocating for changes in policy and legislation to improve the social conditions, justice, and well-being of job seekers
- Striving to eliminate architectural and attitudinal barriers to job seekers with disabilities
- Behaving in a culturally competent manner that reflects respect for diversity

MULTICULTURAL COMPETENCIES

The United States is rapidly becoming a true multicultural society. By the year 2020, for example, it is estimated that ethnic and racial minorities will make up the majority in California (State of California, 1998). The same trend is evident in other states as well. Since the 1980s, helping professionals have become increasingly aware of the biases, ignorance, or avoidance within their practices and have taken major steps to remedy them (Atkinson, Morten, & Sue, 1989).

It is as important for employment specialists to be aware of and committed to competent multicultural practices within their own work and within the agencies that they represent. Unfortunate evidence exists that individuals from different cultural and racial groups are less likely to have successful placement outcomes through rehabilitation service delivery systems (Wilson, Alston, Harley, & Mitchell, 2002). Whether this is the result of the attitudes of the helping professionals or the attitudes of employers, it is still a trend that needs to be reversed. Also, many of the same skills that are required for multicultural competence are those that are demanded of people who provide services to individuals with disabilities: being aware of stereotypes and biases, understanding the environmental and social context in which people with disabilities live, and having the skills to advocate and change things. In fact, people with certain types of disabilities—psychiatric conditions and some visible disabilities—experience similar stigma and discrimination as do members of ethnic and racial minorities in America. Finally, efforts to effectively create partnerships with businesses in the community and requirement to advocate within those partnerships for job seekers with disabilities are similar to those efforts required to expand opportunities for all people in America.

In many ways, multicultural competencies are similar to the other competencies described in this chapter in that these competencies are frequently described as consisting of three fundamental components:

- Awareness of personal biases and stereotypes that influence thoughts and behavior toward others
- Knowledge of how the environmental and social context of the world in which people live shapes their attitudes, beliefs, and behaviors

- Skills in being able to advocate for and empower individuals from different cultural backgrounds to expand their opportunities and to take new risks

Becoming a multiculturally competent professional means the capacity to understand and address the effects that discrimination, stigma, rejection, and isolation have had on the aspirations and goals of job seekers. Using the skills described in this chapter, together with an awareness of the need to be sensitive to the experiences of people with disabilities from different cultural and ethnic backgrounds, is a necessary and critical step in developing partnerships with job seekers and employers.

MEASURING JOB DEVELOPMENT CONFIDENCE

This chapter describes some of the basic attitudes and competencies that are the fundamental requirements for effective job development practice. There is another element, however, that is as important for effective practice and has more to do with the self-confidence and beliefs of the employment specialist than with his or her acquisition of skills. This element is the self-efficacy beliefs of the employment specialist and refers to the confidence he or she has in the capacity to acquire and perform the skills described in this section. Self-efficacy may be even more important than specific skill mastery in becoming a competent professional (Bandura, 1994), as believing in your own abilities is as important as having the skills to be a good job developer. With this in mind, we developed a Job Development Efficacy Scale (Fabian & Waugh, 2001) that measures three fundamental components of a job development professional's confidence regarding the job development and placement process:

- Believing: These items refer to the values regarding beliefs that job seekers with disabilities have the capacity to work and can find jobs consistent with their interest and goals
- Connecting: These items refer to the capacity to make contacts with employers, to use a variety of strategies, and to manage employer concerns
- Marketing: This item refers to the ability to effectively market agency services to employers, to respond to complaints, and to achieve consumer satisfaction with services

The 19-item scale is presented in Figure 7.1. Each item is marked to indicate whether it fits into category B (Believing), C (Connecting), or M (Marketing). You might want to use the scale as a tool to identify your beliefs, the confidence you have in your capacity to perform some of the essential functions of job development and placement, and the areas where you might want to focus on your own professional growth and development.

You can use the results of this scale to assess where you need to develop the confidence in your skills. For example, if you score low on items marked C (Connecting), you

Job Development Efficacy Scale

Item	Continuum of Agreement (from low to high)					Category
It is difficult to balance the competing demands of job seekers and employers in job development.	1	2	3	4	5	B
I am confident that employers are satisfied with my job placement services.	1	2	3	4	5	M
Even during times of high unemployment, I can secure jobs for job seekers.	1	2	3	4	5	B
I can usually find jobs that match the qualifications and interests of the job seekers I work with.	1	2	3	4	5	B
Even though I am nervous about contacting employers, I don't let that stop me.	1	2	3	4	5	M
I can usually find the right contact person within a company.	1	2	3	4	5	M
When the job market is tight, I can still find jobs for people with disabilities.	1	2	3	4	5	B
I can handle employer complaints about job seekers they have hired.	1	2	3	4	5	B
I do not rely on chance or luck in the job development process.	1	2	3	4	5	M
I am confident about how to describe my agency and the job seekers I represent in a positive fashion.	1	2	3	4	5	B
I am confident about dealing with employer stereotypes about the job seekers I represent.	1	2	3	4	5	C
I am comfortable meeting and talking with prospective employers.	1	2	3	4	5	M
It is easy for me to market my agency's services to prospective employers.	1	2	3	4	5	M
I do not let the fact that many of the job seekers I represent do not meet minimal job qualifications hinder my job developing activities.	1	2	3	4	5	B
I can use a variety of job placement strategies to develop and maintain job offers.	1	2	3	4	5	B
I am confident about explaining disability laws and accommodations to employers.	1	2	3	4	5	C
I am confident about addressing sensitive background or disability issues regarding the job seekers I represent.	1	2	3	4	5	C
I am confident about being able to assist job seekers with disabilities to secure employment, no matter how significant their disability.	1	2	3	4	5	C
I feel confident about discussing job seekers' needs for specific accommodations with employers.	1	2	3	4	5	C

Figure 7.1. Job Development Efficacy Scale.

might want to learn and rehearse new techniques for dealing with employer concerns regarding laws and accommodations. If you score low on items marked B (Believing), you might want to explore your values regarding job seekers with disabilities. If you score low on M (Marketing), review some of the skills related to communication and active listening, presented at the beginning of this chapter.

SUMMARY

This chapter sets the stage for the job development and placement process by identifying essential skills for employment specialists. It outlines basic competencies in skills that may be overlooked when working with job seekers with disabilities but that should compose the foundation of the job placement process. These include attitudes and values, communication skills, multicultural competence, ethics, and self-efficacy. All of these areas are the building blocks for developing the partnership skills that are required to sustain relationships with employers and with job seekers.

II

Job Development and Placement

A CUSTOMER-FOCUSED PARTNERSHIP

8

Knowing the Job Seeker Customer

Real education consists of drawing the best out of yourself.

MOHANDAS GANDHI

You might think of career development as having four primary aspects. The first one is self-awareness: How well do you know yourself? And how well do others know you? The second aspect is awareness of the world around you. More specifically, how much do you know of the opportunities and resources that exist in your community? Third, once you have identified your interests, skills, and goals, how many related hands-on experiences have you had? And finally, to what extent have you had opportunities to demonstrate your abilities in real work environments, especially through paid jobs? These four aspects play a repeated role in a person's career development throughout life. This chapter focuses primarily on that first critical aspect, self-knowledge. More specifically, the chapter discusses how employment specialists can get to know the job seekers and help them to become more self-aware. The real job search cannot begin until the job seeker and those who are supporting the search are armed with this knowledge.

TAKING AN INVENTORY OF ATTRIBUTES

Take a moment and reflect on your own personal experiences as a job seeker. Whether you have had numerous job searches in your career or are new to the process, one of the first things you have to do when looking for a job is take stock of yourself. Step back and think about all of the things you want people to know about you. These are the attributes that help you build a social network, and they are the characteristics that you capitalize on in your career.

What are your short-term job goals and your long-term life and career aspirations? What kind of skills and other attributes do you have to offer an employer and your community? What are the skills you particularly enjoy using and would like to use most of the time? What kind of an attitude do you convey to the people you meet? What are your preferred types of work environments? What things are most important to you about the job (e.g., helping others, earning a certain amount of money, flexibility, autonomy)? Do you have specific life challenges or obstacles to overcome in the process of obtaining a job? Perhaps without even thinking about it, you have conducted a mental inventory of your dreams, interests, temperament, values, and talents, as well as particular roadblocks you must confront when looking for the right job. Knowing yourself or taking stock of your attributes takes a great deal of energy, honesty, and courage. Some people are supremely gifted at objective self-reflection, while others have barely given a thought to who they are, in the context of finding life and career satisfaction (Boldt, 1999; Bolles, 2003). Many people, especially individuals with disabilities and other life challenges, may never have been given the opportunity or encouragement to take stock of who they are, their strengths, or what they would like to accomplish in their lives, much less in a career (Brown, 2000). Many individuals may have low expectations for themselves or adopt the low expectations that others project onto them. Some people may fear that because of their limitations, others will regard them as unfit or incapable, which leads them to overlook their strengths and potential contributions.

Employment specialists representing these job seekers have traditionally become acquainted with them through some type of vocational evaluation or client assessment. Historically, *vocational evaluation* has been considered a phase in which a variety of objective and subjective tests or situational assessments are administered to an individual in order to rate his or her vocational skill levels, behaviors, and potential. The extent and quality of vocational evaluation procedures and outcomes vary tremendously, depending on the competence of the evaluator, the tools used, the comfort level of the person being evaluated, and the degree to which the evaluation yields information that is useful to the individual and to those in his or her support network. There are numerous excellent resources on vocational and career evaluation (e.g., Sitlington, Neubert, Begun, Lombard, & Leconte, 1996).

However, some words of caution about vocational evaluations are in order. When examining the purpose of vocational evaluation, you can begin with the simple question "How do people get to know you?" One response might be that people get to know you by spending time with you or by seeing you in a variety of settings. It is unlikely that someone could really get to know you by seeing you for a short period of time in a setting that generates some anxiety for you so that the behaviors you demonstrate in that setting are atypical or are not necessarily characteristic. In fact, impressions based on a single encounter often prove inaccurate and are thus modified after later encounters with an individual.

People generally get to know one another through multiple meetings in a variety of settings at different times. This is precisely the way that employment specialists should become acquainted with job seekers they represent, particularly those whose disabilities and life challenges are significant. Research in social psychology regarding the ways in which individuals with disabilities are evaluated has demonstrated that when behavior is atypical (i.e., when an individual does not conform to pre-established standards), the inclination is to focus on his or her faults or deficits rather than on the environmental context that may be causing such a performance.

We subscribe to the notion that high-quality, individualized, and self-chosen employment begins with a thorough inventory of attributes—one that occurs over a period of time and helps the job seeker come to a greater understanding of him- or herself. It is one that highlights the individual's strengths and puts barriers in the context of possible accommodations, rather than merely deficits. It is also one that discusses possibilities for success, rather than merely limited options. Without self-knowledge, a job seeker is very likely to drift through his or her life and career in a rudderless fashion. Whether through formal or informal means, an inventory of the person's characteristics should yield information that can help an individual complete the first step in the job search process. This results in a positive personal profile (Tilson & Cuozzo, 2001).

WHAT IS A POSITIVE PERSONAL PROFILE?

Getting to know a job seeker requires that you hear the person's life story (Alea & Mullins, 1998). This requires substantial risk-taking and vulnerability on the part of job seekers; therefore, the person in a support role must be extremely sensitive and able to establish a rapport with each individual and in all instances, must maintain confidentiality and trust. Think of your role as a mentor to the job seeker, who is in essence a protégé. Valued mentors are those who know and understand their protégé (Zander & Zander, 2000; Zufelt, 2002). The purpose of developing a positive personal profile is to help job seekers identify as much positive information as they can about themselves. These data can be gathered over time through a series of one-to-one interviews with the job seeker and with others who know the person very well, especially family members and close friends; person-centered planning meetings; self-reporting checklists; observation checklists and logs; formal assessment tools (both paper-and-pencil and hands-on types); reports from specialists, such as therapists, teachers, and medical personnel; and actual products developed by the job seeker (or photographs, videos, and recordings of these products).

Features of the Positive Personal Profile

When becoming acquainted with a job seeker, guide the person (and others who know him or her) to identify his or her:

- Dreams and goals
- Talents
- Skills and knowledge
- Learning styles
- Interests
- Positive personality traits
- Temperament
- Values
- Environmental preferences
- Life and work experiences
- Education and training
- Support system
- Specific challenges
- Solutions and accommodations
- Possibilities and ideas

These are all characteristics, preferences, and details about each job seeker that the employment specialist has to learn.

Dreams and Goals   What does the person really want out of life? How does the person picture his or her life in the future? Where and with whom would he or she like to be living? What would he or she like to accomplish? What activities and work would be fulfilling? When it comes to dreams and goals, the sky's the limit; however, many people are reluctant to express these to anyone, lest their aspirations are criticized or they are accused of being unrealistic. Unfortunately, many people, especially individuals with disabilities and other life barriers, are discouraged from identifying and talking about their life dreams and goals, out of concern that they will be disappointed if they fail to achieve these goals. Yet dreams and goals are what propel each person to take action in his or her life (Boldt, 1999).

Dreaming Big

It has been our experience and observation that many people with disabilities never get the chance to dream big or to express those dreams without a lot of trepidation on the part of their families and paid service providers. And yet everyone knows how important it is to have those big goals. They fuel action and are intended to help people set short-term goals. Here are two examples from our own work with two job seekers. Both of these individuals with significant disabilities have similar dreams: to be movie stars. Though neither of them can read or write, they're both big hams and have had experiences in community theater. The big difference: one is working as a custodian—a job he hates. The other person is working for a professional theater company and loving life. One was given choices: clean the bathrooms at McDonald's or the bathrooms in an office building. The other was given different choices: perform an array of tasks at several local theater companies, fine arts museums, and theater departments of local colleges. Both of these career seekers have received support from employment service agencies. Both are receiving better than minimum wages. Both are working 30 hours per week and receiving benefits. But one dreads going to work and is in a program for problematic work behaviors; the other does not want to leave work at the end of the day. In the case of the custodian, the people who were supporting him were afraid of his life goal and at a loss as to what to do with it. Hence, they offered him no creative choices. In the second situation, people listened to the dream and helped this young woman set short-term goals. Whether she becomes a movie star is beside the point. She is working with creative people who share her passion.

Dreams and long-term goals enable people to think of the big picture of their lives. According to Nemko, Edward, and Edwards (1998), the "dream careers" of most people fall into six primary categories: 1) caring for others; 2) being a performer, including public speaking, singing, broadcasting; 3) leading or working for an organization that makes a difference; 4) owning a business; 5) generating ideas (e.g., planning, training or teaching, organizing, writing); or 6) working in any job that they are competent to perform, meets their needs, and has a minimum of negative factors for them. For every person out there seeking a dream job, opportunities are often found by being an assistant to someone else in that dream occupation.

Bear in mind, also, that many people want a well-balanced and complete life, which may mean they are willing to compromise somewhat on their career aspirations, as long as they are able to fulfill other life dreams and pursue their natural interests and talents. Every human being has dreams and goals, and it is a task of the employment specialist to help job seekers with disabilities to articulate their dreams and goals.

Talents   Everyone has certain abilities with which they seem to have been born; sometimes these are referred to as natural gifts. These talents might be in the arenas of athletics, music, art, creative writing, or other forms of expression. But they can also be represented by a warm smile and ability to get along with others, an aptitude for taking things apart and putting them back together again, a knack for noticing small details, curiosity, and the ability to express empathy. Every human being has some kind of natural talent.

Skills and Knowledge   These are abilities that are acquired through exposure, life experience, education, and training. They include abilities in the areas of academics (e.g., languages, mathematics, science); mechanics; daily living; creative arts; physical activity; communication (written, oral, and gestural); use of equipment, tools, devices, and computers; and analyzing and synthesizing data. Most career resources talk about work-related skills in terms of people, data, and things. If you ask someone, "What have you always had the knack for?" you are likely to find out about his or her skills and knowledge. Ask job seekers to think of times in their lives when they have been complimented. What skill were they mainly using? Every human being has some degree of skill and knowledge.

Learning Styles   Sometimes called *multiple intelligences, learning style* refers to the manner in which an individual naturally prefers receiving, processing, and expressing information. Psychologist and researcher Howard Gardner and others have identified the following learning styles: bodily kinesthetic, musical, visual-spatial, intrapersonal, interpersonal, verbal-linguistic, and mathematical-logical. In his book *Seven Kinds of Smart,* Thomas Armstrong (1993), a protégé of Gardner, referred to people with these learning styles or intelligences as being body smart, music smart, picture smart, self smart, people smart, word smart, and logic smart. The notion of learning style has significant implications for how people acquire and use skills, perform tasks, relate to others, and approach life. Not infrequently, the learning styles and intelligences of people with disabilities and other life barriers are overlooked or discounted. Every human being has a preferred learning style, or combination of styles and the capacity for developing those styles that are less preferred.

Interests   Interests are what grab and hold a person's attention, things that energize a person physically, mentally, emotionally, or spiritually. Interests are frequently expressed through hobbies, leisure pursuits, recreation, and avocations, as well as through occupations. You can tell when someone has a particular interest because you can observe the person engaging enthusiastically in that activity or intently focusing on an event or object. Interests are usually cultivated over time and require that a person first be exposed to that activity or object of interest. For example, a young child starts playing catch with her brother. Soon that activity intensifies. Every chance she gets, the girl plays ball. That early exposure leads to a lifetime passion for playing volleyball and other sports. A young boy watches his grandfather baking cakes and finds he enjoys doing the same. A boy who uses a wheelchair sees a show about space flight on television. He delves into science and

Investigating Possible Career Interests

A trap professionals sometimes fall into is to focus too narrowly on a job seeker's career interests. Certainly if someone you represent expresses very well-defined career interests, you should start there. But many job seekers with disabilities cannot identify their job interests. This means the employment specialist has to do some digging, along with the job seekers. How do they spend their leisure time? Do they have hobbies? What do they enjoy doing with family and friends? If they are movie goers, what are their favorite movies? In public places, what things or activities seem to grab their attention? Consider one young woman who has the label of severe autism. Her hobby was putting together one-thousand-piece jigsaw puzzles. She was declared unemployable by a vocational rehabilitation counselor. Someone else viewed her hobby as an asset, declared that she had incredible visual spatial ability, and helped her find a job with a high-tech firm assembling electronic security badges.

One more thing about interests. We have a motto: "Exposure precedes interest." If the only work experience Danté has had is folding sheets and he has never seen or tried something else and someone asks him his job interest area (or infers it), chances are, he will say, "folding sheets." This has important implications for the work of employment specialists: Determining the extent to which job seekers have been exposed to diverse experiences is necessary so that their interests are given a chance to emerge. This also has tremendous implications for choice making.

---

math, ultimately becoming an aerospace engineer. A woman with autism does not speak to anyone but is able to calm and treat injured animals. She volunteers 5 days per week at a wildlife rescue facility. A teenage boy from a disadvantaged family sees his first play and is interested in theater from then on. Exposure precedes interest. Often people with disabilities and other life barriers have a narrow set of interests or no expressed interests simply because they have never had a chance to get out in the world and see what exists. Many people have not explored the world of possibilities enough to have had an interest sparked. And in many cases, people have cultivated unhealthy or socially unacceptable interests because these are the areas to which they have been primarily exposed. People who have identified areas that interest them are usually highly motivated to pursue those interests. Interests fuel a person's actions. Also, people have no interest in or dislike certain things. In getting to know another person, it is important to identify those noninterests, as well as interests. Every human being has interests and preferences, likes and dislikes.

Positive Personality Traits   What are the things about a person's character that are genuinely recognized and appreciated by others? A beautiful smile? The ability to stay focused on a detailed task? Willingness to learn new things? Triumph over hardship? Frankness? A talent for listening to others? A sense of humor? Some believe that a sense of humor usually indicates the ability to keep things in perspective, even in the face of adversity—a leadership trait valued in many organizations (Metcalf, 1992). True, each person has certain personality traits that are less than ideal. Talking too much or becoming tired and grumpy in the afternoon are examples of normal human behavior, but they are certainly not traits that will win a person points in the working world. Part of getting to know someone is discovering the positive aspects of his or her personality. Every human being has positive personality traits.

Temperament   Temperament is closely related to personality. It might be thought of as a person's unique set of responses to different environments, people, and events. For example, some people are unflappable and seem to exude a sense of calm in even the most dire of circumstances. Others are easily flustered at the merest suggestion of a problem. Of course, there are people who fall into many spots on this continuum. Some express their feelings openly; others prefer to keep their feelings private. Some are always serious when focusing on a particular task; others seem to work best when they can express their sense of humor. Perhaps you are a person who has a perennial optimistic perspective on life, while your best friend tends toward a more cynical view. Temperament is more than simple mood; rather, it is an outlook, attitude, or philosophy about life. Often a person's temperament is an outward expression of his or her self-concept, and self-concept is considered to play a major role in career development. Can a person's temperament or self-concept change over time? Some argue that temperament is as fixed as the genetic code that composes a person, while others take the stand that often new life experiences (both positive and negative) can alter a person's self-concept. Consider temperament to be an energy type, energy level, and the manner in which each person uses his or her store of personal energy. Every human being has a predominant temperament.

Values   Values may be thought of as life philosophies or each person's unique perspective on what is important to attain in life. Often, the values a person holds motivates him or her to take particular actions. For example, someone may have a value that says having material wealth is of utmost importance. That person then may devote a significant amount of energy in this pursuit. He or she would likely expect a career that would be aligned with this value, dream of winning the lottery, or hope to otherwise become independently well-off. Compare this with the person who does not value material wealth but instead values simplicity and tranquility. Other values include having many friends; living a solitary life; wanting to apply acquired skills and knowledge; wanting to help others; making the world safer, cleaner, and healthier; gaining fame and recognition; making a quiet contribution; passing on skills and knowledge to others; being conventional; being nonconformist; and so forth. What people value in life may be reflected in what they do, say, and think. Values are closely related to personality and temperament.

In terms of careers, values may be reflected in such things as a person's desire for high status, a minimum annual income, an easy job, a casual (or formal) dress code, a specific geographic location or work at home, a short training time, recognition, an adrenaline rush (from competition or risk-taking activities), autonomy, work on the cutting edge, work indoors (or outdoors), an aesthetically pleasing workplace, opportunities for self-expression, and so forth. Every human being holds a set of values.

Environmental Preferences   Environmental preferences go hand-in-hand with temperament, values, and personality. For example, an unflappable person is more likely than her flustered friend to be well-suited to life activities, career areas, and jobs that are high-pressure in nature, that demand clear-headed thinking in emergencies, and that involve possibly dangerous situations, such as firefighting or child protective services. If a person thrives on being outside most of the time, an indoor job with no windows would probably not be a good work setting. If someone does his or her best work alone in a quiet setting, being employed in a factory would likely be a poor environmental match. Think about the implications for the person who craves routine, schedules, and predictable tasks of landing a job in a setting where the duties shift daily. Of course, people can have a combination of preferences, and one person can prefer a quiet workplace but a lively, family-filled home life, or vice versa. When people spend a good portion of their lives in settings that match their temperaments, they feel energized. The opposite is also true: If they find themselves spending too much time in environments that are contrary to their natural temperaments, they are likely to feel drained, stressed out, and beaten down. Every human being has environmental preferences.

Life and Work Experiences   The area of life and work experiences is one of the most overlooked in getting to know job seekers, particularly those individuals who may have had very limited or no previous job experiences. Employers want to know that a candidate has specific skills to accomplish specific company goals. How the individual job seeker acquired certain skills may be less important than the fact that he or she has them and can demonstrate them (DiLeo & Langton, 1993). A person can acquire skills in many ways, primarily through formal education and training, previous volunteer or paid jobs, and community service. However, skills can be acquired through informal training (e.g., a neighbor who teaches a teenager to repair a car engine, a teenager showing an older adult how to use the Internet) and self-training (e.g., an inmate who studies for the law school entrance examination, a young man with quadriplegia who teaches himself to cook using adaptive equipment).

Further skill acquisition occurs through hands-on experiences. Many skills are attained and developed through trial and error (e.g., negotiating an on-ramp on the freeway, writing grant proposals, giving a customer correct change). Some are fortunate to have learned many skills through on-the-job experiences (e.g., preparing budgets, selling products, detailing cars). Does this mean that those without job experience cannot acquire skills? No. This is where other life experiences come into play (e.g., entertaining young children, building model airplanes, sorting laundry, organizing parties). Often it is through chores, hobbies, and recreational activities that people acquire specific skills. When getting to know job seekers, try to ascertain what they—and people who know them well—have accomplished in their lives. What are they proud of? Have they received any special recognitions or awards? Even people considered to have the most significant disabilities have achieved specific milestones in their lives. The degree of complexity of those achievements varies from person to person; what matters most is that, for the individual, it represents a life accomplishment. And this bit of information may prove very valuable as you assist this person in finding a satisfying job. Every human being has life experiences that accumulate over time; that influence the person's acquisition of knowledge, skills, and personality; and that can be drawn upon during the job search.

Education and Training   Formal education and training is provided through organizations and institutions of learning and characterized by structured curricula and instruction (typically delivered by instructors who meet certain qualification criteria), performance measures, and specified outcome expectations. Instruction may be delivered in a variety of ways, including through classroom lectures, hands-on activities, and field experiences. Performance evaluation may be conducted using standardized tests, informal tests, computerized assessments, ratings based on observations of the student/trainee performing specific functions, checklists, ratings of projects, and so forth. Education and training organizations include public and private schools (preschool through high school), 2-year and 4-year colleges and universities, trade and technical schools, adult education programs, some prison programs, and some hospital programs; even some nonprofit organizations and private companies offer formal education and training courses. And of course, within elementary through secondary schools, a range of programs and services for academically gifted students and those with special education needs are available. At the postsecondary education level, there are also support services available to youth with disabilities and other life challenges. The degree to which people acquire skills and competencies through formal education and training—skills that are then recognized by employers as transferable to the workplace—varies tremendously from one person to another.

Although it is not within the scope of this book to address the many issues related to how education and training are delivered and made accessible to people with disabilities, it is extremely important to glean as much information as possible about the person's formal education and training and to incorporate this information into the positive personal profile. Bear in mind that holding a degree does not guarantee to an employer that a job seeker has the requisite skills to perform a particular job. By the same token, a job

Turning a Negative into a Positive

One of the authors worked with a job seeker who greatly annoyed his family and others because of his obsessive-compulsive behaviors. James had everyone stymied with his incessant need to pick things off the floor, lint off of people's clothes, and specks of dirt from surfaces. Naturally, they thought this pointed to work as a custodian. However, James really seemed to hate getting his hands dirty, so he refused to go to his jobs. A colleague tried a different approach. She asked herself what kind of jobs would require someone to gather items all day and not get his hands dirty. The solution was three part-time jobs. James now splits up his work week at a golf club driving range (gathering golf balls), returning clothes hangers to the storeroom of an upscale department store, and manning the frog-toss booth at an arcade on the boardwalk.

This is an example of taking a challenge and turning it into an asset. Always ask yourself if someone's negative attribute may, in fact, be a positive characteristic in the right setting. Stubbornness in one environment may prove to be persistence in another, obsession with picking up small pieces of paper may translate to attention to detail, a perpetually loud voice might be useful in a noisy setting, and so forth.

---

seeker may have dropped out of high school or may not have completed a degree program and may yet possess the skills sought after by an employer. Smart employers use a variety of ways to determine the true skill level of a job seeker. Knowing that a job seeker received her general equivalency diploma while incarcerated is valuable. Whenever possible, try to obtain school records and transcripts. They are particularly useful as a basis of discussion with the job seeker. For job seekers with disabilities who have received special education, it may be helpful to review their most recent individualized education programs and transition plans. Again, the purpose here is to use any and all methods to gather even tidbits of information that will help you round out the job seeker's positive personal profile. Most people in the United States and other developed countries have received some type and level of formal education and training.

Support System   A support system is the unique circle of support each person has around him or her. For some, this support system might be quite extensive, while for others, the circle may be very small or even nonexistent. A circle of support might include family members, significant others, friends, acquaintances, neighbors, co-workers, and classmates. You may even consider yourself to be in that circle. These are all people who are not paid to provide support. Then, there are supporters who may receive payment for being in the support circle, such as teachers, counselors, therapists, medical personnel, personal assistants, social workers, job coaches, human service organization personnel, and government agency representatives.

The Negative Résumé

Imagine that you are searching for a job, and you are necessarily concerned about making a favorable impression on prospective employers. Part of your job search involves assessment. You are given several pages listing questions such as the following:
Have you ever

- Been late for an appointment
- Forgotten an appointment all together
- Yelled at a co-worker
- Gotten a speeding ticket
- Called in sick when you really went shopping

Imagine that a report is made based on your responses to these questions that highlights each of your deficits and mistakes. Would you want that report released to prospective employers? This exaggerated scenario is intended to illustrate what often happens to people with disabilities: mistakes, weaknesses, limitations, and atypical behaviors are often highlighted by reports, while positive traits are unfortunately obscured.

For many people with disabilities and other significant life barriers, their support systems tend to be overly represented by paid supporters and underrepresented by volunteer supporters. This may primarily be due to society's tendency to shelter, protect, and intentionally or inadvertently isolate people with disabilities. The challenge to those who advocate for and support people with disabilities, then, is to help individuals build their social support networks. Every human being has a need for a support system of some kind, and every support system is unique.

Specific Challenges   The word *challenge* may be synonymous with the words *barrier, limitation, deficit, weakness, idiosyncrasy, pet peeve, shortcoming, roadblock, hindrance, problem, barricade, difficulty,* or *obstacle,* but it can also refer to risk and adventure. In fact, life may be thought of as a series of opportunities and challenges. Most people are born with certain challenges (e.g., a physical or cognitive disability, a medical condition, a propensity for behaviors that go against the norm, differences in physical appearance) or into challenging life circumstances (e.g., poverty; membership in an ostracized religious, ethnic group, or other demographic group). And certainly, everyone encounters numerous and diverse challenges throughout life. Some are better equipped or have adequate support systems to handle these challenges; others seem to collapse under the pressure of the challenges they face.

Sometimes, people face challenges because of opportunities they have never had, such as people who cannot read because they have never been taught how to read or individuals who cannot articulate the kinds of jobs they would like because they have had little exposure to the work world. And some people encounter a lifetime of challenges because of poor choices they have made (e.g., people with criminal records, those who stay in abusive relationships). People with disabilities face a unique situation: Often their disabilities are considered their primary challenges, when in fact, each person is affected by his or her disability in different ways. The disability itself is not the challenge. Rather, the challenge is the set of specific effects of the disability. For example, mental retardation is not a specific challenge, but not being able to read is. Having severe cerebral palsy is not a specific barrier; however, having unintelligible speech is a definite challenge. Not having access to public transportation might be the specific barrier for one blind person; another may have access to transportation but is not permitted by his family to use the bus, out of fear for his safety. The challenge of learning disabilities may be, for one person, the inability to write a coherent sentence. For another, it might be difficulty in picking up social cues and building friendships. A critical part of developing a positive personal profile is to identify those specific challenges that may get in the way of a person's pursuit of his or her life dreams and goals. Every human being faces specific life challenges.

Solutions and Accommodations   Once a person has identified the specific challenges in his or her life, that person can begin to think of creative solutions and accommodations. An *accommodation* may be thought of as any strategy that effectively alleviates, or lessens the impact of, a specific challenge. Here are some examples. Suppose you have been born into a family that lives in a high-crime, high-poverty neighborhood. One of your siblings dropped out of school, joined a gang, and was incarcerated for selling drugs. You developed a relationship with a mentor through Boys and Girls Clubs and went on to college and a successful career. Both you and your sibling faced challenges; yet you found an accommodation in the form of a mentor who had a positive influence. A common accommodation for a person who can read a book but cannot clearly see the signs on the highway is glasses for nearsightedness. A short person might need the accommodation of a step stool to reach a high shelf. Another example is Jack, a young blind man whose family would not let him ride the city bus for fear of his safety. A good accommodation for this challenge might be for a mobility specialist to take Jack's family with him on the bus to demonstrate the young man's skill at getting around.

Accommodations are creative solutions to specific challenges or barriers. They range from the common sense to the highly technological. They fall into three primary categories: 1) physical accommodations, such as equipment, devices, and modified spaces and buildings; 2) special services, such as those provided by interpreters, translators, personal assistants, job coaches, medical personnel, therapists, parole officers, and so forth; and 3) creative thinking and common-sense problem solving, by far, the most frequently needed and used category of accommodation. Every human being has a need for accommodations to address specific challenges.

Possibilities and Ideas   Most people have had the experience of doing something mundane and ordinary, like the laundry or walking down the street, when suddenly an idea pops into mind; they get a spark of insight into a solution for a problem or generate an appealing new activity or project. As you develop your own positive personal profile or assist someone else in developing one, you are likely to find yourself thinking about all kinds of ideas—such as job possibilities, things to explore, actions to take, and people to meet. Rather than waiting to brainstorm these ideas at a later time, you might want to record all thoughts and ideas, regardless of how random or unrealistic they might seem, at the time you think of them. There will be plenty of opportunity to sift through all of the ideas later (and to generate additional ones); however, these initial thoughts are often gems to be polished. Therefore, we have included the category of possibilities and ideas as a component of the positive personal profile. For every human being, there are an infinite number of possibilities and ideas for living a meaningful life and meeting life's challenges to be discovered through imagination, creativity, and determination.

An Important Note   For every one of these components of the positive personal profile, it is important to recognize and be sensitive to diverse cultural, familial, ethnic, and religious traditions of the individual job seekers. Factors such as personality, values, temperament, dreams and goals, and interests are likely to be influenced by these diverse traditions; and characteristics, behaviors and rituals valued by one culture or society may in fact be the antithesis of those valued by other cultural subpopulations.

STRATEGIES FOR DEVELOPING POSITIVE PERSONAL PROFILES

A variety of strategies are available for developing positive personal profiles. The four strategies presented in this section are 1) spending time with the job seekers and the people who know them, 2) developing résumés for job seekers, 3) identifying and addressing barriers, and 4) identifying possible accommodations. These are all ways of getting to know the job seeker and his or her strengths and goals.

Strategy 1: Spend Time with Job Seekers and People Who Know Them

Plan to spend as much time as possible with every job seeker in a variety of settings, including the local community, as well as your office. These meetings should be held in a combination of familiar and unfamiliar locations. Moreover, meeting times should be varied in order to determine whether behaviors are modified at different times of the day.

Formal assessment reports may contain excellent and useful information about an individual, so review any available files. However, when developing a positive personal profile, you must do everything possible to gather first-hand information about the job seeker. For every evaluation report, ask yourself, "What *don't* I know about this person?" Resolve to find answers to this question and remember to emphasize the person's positive traits.

Most of the information for the profile may be available from the job seeker him- or herself; however, some individuals may not have the speech or language abilities to communicate this information. It may seem quite hard to find out the positive attributes, skills, and experiences of a job seeker who may have significant cognitive disabilities and cannot articulate them or of an individual whose physical disabilities make it extraordinarily difficult for him or her to convey this information. In circumstances such as these, it is imperative that you contact others who know the job seeker well and interview them. This may include the person's family members, friends, neighbors, clergy, teachers, counselors, employers, co-workers, and others. You can interview them individually or even as a group. In either case, the job seeker must be included.

Important!

If the positive characteristics of a job seeker cannot be identified, then you should not represent that individual to an employer. Under this circumstance, it will be difficult to identify what the job seeker may have to offer a business. Should you encounter this situation, refer the job seeker to another employment specialist, or—better yet—form a team around the job seeker. Sometimes professionals can gain new perspectives on a job seeker when collaborating with colleagues.

This information gathering should have a positive, nonthreatening tone; after all, the purpose is to highlight every attribute that could potentially be matched to future opportunities. Even the negative aspects of the person's life can be addressed in a positive manner by putting them in terms of challenges, solutions, and accommodations. When determining what a job seeker can offer to an employer, everything possible must be done in order to identify that individual's strengths, talents, interests, and positive personality traits. When faced with the job seeker's limitations, the professional should ask, "What ideas can this person and I come up with for making accommodations that will help compensate for existing limitations?"

Strategy 2: Develop a Résumé

Among the career and job search books on the market, there are as many opinions on résumés as there are books. Some experts say résumés are a must when it comes to job seeking; others disagree. A résumé is one of the tools to be used; however, the format and precise use of a résumé will vary significantly from one job seeker to another. Some individuals might have a traditionally formatted résumé, others might use a portfolio that contains examples and documentation of past work and performance. The primary purpose of a résumé, in any case, is to highlight the types of information about the job seeker that will resonate with the needs, expectations, and desires of an employer. Rarely, if ever, will a résumé actually land someone a job offer; rather, it more often serves as a mechanism for introducing a candidate to a prospective employer. Most career experts agree: A résumé is only as effective as the person described in the résumé. Because so many resources on résumés and portfolio development (e.g., Mast, Sweeney, & West, 2002) are readily available, no examples are presented here. Suffice it to say, data for a job seeker's résumé can be derived from or based on the individual's unique positive personal profile. In essence, the profile is actually a functional résumé. Chapter 11 discusses how functional résumés and positive personal profiles can be used to achieve four different types of job matches.

Strategy 3: Accurately Identify and Address Barriers to Employment for Job Seekers with Disabilities

Just as important as obtaining a wide range of information about job seekers is the identification of barriers to employment they may face. People with disabilities are as susceptible to circumstantial obstacles as people without disabilities are. Barriers to employment may be classified into four major categories: voluntary, involuntary, psychological, and situational. A *voluntary obstacle* is exemplified by a job seeker who is unwilling to commute more than 5 miles to work. In this case, the individual is choosing not to fulfill a required condition of employment. By contrast, an *involuntary barrier* is something over which the individual has no control, such as the presence of a physical or mental disability or the absence of available public transportation. *Psychological barriers* occur when an individual assumes that a barrier exists when it, in fact, does not. Examples of this type of barrier are seen when women are unwilling to accept a position traditionally held by men or when a person who speaks with an accent refuses a sales position because he or she fears that customers may respond negatively. Finally, *situational barriers* are those that are inherent to a given situation and are independent of an individual's attitudes or beliefs. Consider the situational barrier for the job seeker with chronic asthma who applies for a position in a chemical factory.

It is imperative that professionals work with job seekers to identify existing and potential barriers. The professional should be guided by the following questions:

- What is the nature of the barrier?
- How could the barrier affect the applicant's job search?
- Is the barrier removable by the job seeker?
- Is the barrier removable with professional assistance?
- Does barrier removal require outside assistance?
- Is there a way to continue the job search despite the barrier?

Too often, employment specialists may be under considerable pressure to make a placement and fail to identify all barriers that will seriously affect a job seeker's ability to obtain and maintain satisfactory employment. The importance of identifying each of these barriers cannot be stressed enough.

Identifying Individual Barriers: A Short Case Study

A young man named Sam received the diagnosis of severe clinical depression at age 25. Sam's mental illness was exacerbated by the fact that he had experienced an injury to his spinal cord while in high school, an injury that left his legs paralyzed and therefore necessitated the use of a wheelchair. Prior to becoming physically disabled, Sam possessed impressive skills as a carpenter that he had developed while growing up and working alongside his father, who was a building contractor. Sam had excelled in his vocational classes and had even received honors for carpentry work done in a small housing development.

Despite his spinal cord injury, Sam was determined to continue carpentry work. Although he was restricted to ground-level tasks, he demonstrated that he was still very capable of utilizing most of his skills. At that time, Sam was living with his parents in a rural area, and his father drove him to work each day. Unfortunately, soon after Sam graduated from high school, his father died. Because his mother did not drive and Sam did not have a car, a transportation problem immediately arose. Further complicating the situation was the fact that there was no available public transportation where the family lived. One of Sam's friends offered to take him to work for several weeks, but the 50-mile trek ultimately proved to be too much for the friend and he was forced to stop driving Sam to work each day.

Sam subsequently became despondent and quit his job. His mother became concerned about his mental state and took him to see a psychologist. The psychologist suggested that Sam was showing definite signs of serious depression and recommended counseling. Sam's mother was opposed to counseling, saying that Sam should just get his act together. The situation deteriorated to the point where Sam refused to get out of bed in the morning. By the time a job placement professional met Sam, it was obvious that there were a number of significant barriers to employment. These barriers fell into four categories: voluntary, involuntary, psychological, and situational. The first step, therefore, was to work closely with Sam to clearly identify individual barriers and to devise an appropriate plan of action for addressing each.

Strategy 4: Identify Potential Accommodations

The hard work has only just begun as a job placement professional becomes acquainted with a job seeker's interests, skills, aspirations, personality, experiences, limitations, and barriers. An error frequently made by professionals is to believe that, despite the fact that a job seeker possesses some positive attributes that would benefit an employer, certain barriers (e.g., environmental or physical limitations) will ultimately preclude employment or severely limit employment options. It is a serious mistake for job placement professionals to determine a job seeker's employability without carefully considering ways in which a potential barrier may be alleviated or mitigated through some type of accommodation.

Accommodation is defined by the U.S. Equal Employment Opportunity Commission as any change in the work environment or in the way things are usually done that enables

What Does *Accommodation* Mean?

In simplest terms, *accommodations* are actions taken that alleviate, compensate for, or mitigate a barrier faced by a job seeker or an employee with a disability. Furthermore, appropriate and successful accommodations actually capitalize on and maximize an individual's positive attributes. Accommodations can be described as falling into three major categories:

1. Physical accommodations: Providing special equipment or modifying existing equipment or facilities, as needed
2. Services and resources: Examples include an interpreter for a job seeker who is deaf and schedule changes for a person who needs to attend therapy sessions or a substance abuse treatment.
3. Changes in how things are done: One example is reading an employment test to an applicant who is unable to read.

a qualified individual with a disability to have equal access to employment opportunities and to perform a job to the best of his or her ability (Pimental, Baker, & Tilson, 1991). Employment specialists must develop a much broader perspective regarding accommodation. Indeed, accommodations should be viewed as actions taken to address any identified barriers faced by job seekers.

The concept of accommodations and their provision is not limited to people with disabilities. In everyone's lives, accommodations are required to solve or respond to the many challenges that confront people each day. You strive for a simple, problem-solving approach to identifying barriers and providing appropriate accommodations for job seekers or employees with disabilities. What is the specific barrier? What can be done about it? How can accommodation be facilitated? What resources can be used? This process should be an integral part of becoming acquainted with job seekers. However, accommodations should be considered from the first meeting between the professional and the job seeker. Indeed, accommodations should be identified and provided before the job seeker starts his or her job.

An employment specialist's attention needs to remain on the individual, not on his or her disabilities. From the initial meetings with job seekers, the effective specialist works with individuals to identify and test potential accommodation strategies. This in turn invites creative problem solving that can substantially augment options and opportunities for individuals.

The appendix to this chapter includes a case study about Veronica. You should be able to ascertain the positive qualities and marketable talents that Veronica possesses. It is true that her disability poses potentially significant challenges. However, it is equally true that she has identified and effectively used accommodations that have helped her to utilize her talents. Imagine the potential accommodations and possibilities for Veronica that have not yet been explored. Her positive personal profile reveals a host of possibilities for her employment search, as well as the solutions to several challenges unique to her situation. Veronica's story and the other stories in the chapter appendix point to the importance of addressing job seekers' needs by drawing attention to specific solutions and accommodations to various potential barriers. Furthermore, they illustrate that options and possibilities are truly feasible when a positive orientation is utilized.

SUMMARY

Knowing the job seeker and the employer is critical for employment specialists and anyone else who may be assisting someone find meaningful work. Indeed, both job seekers and employers are identified as customers in the job placement process. Before employment services can be delivered to any customer, it is imperative that you learn as much as possible about each customer's desires, needs, and expectations. The ideal way to learn about customers or potential customers is to listen closely to them and establish rapport. Building rapport takes time, enthusiasm, consistency, and genuineness, and it necessarily presumes that each party has something to offer the others.

This chapter presents a critical concept and specific strategies for getting to know the job seeker customer through the development of a positive personal profile. This process, and its resultant document, provides a firm foundation for the job seeker's individualized job search plan and ultimate job match. It also better enables employment specialists to introduce job seekers to employers as known commodities who have specific positive traits that can be matched to the identified needs of employers. The next chapter discusses methods of getting to know what those employer needs are.

Appendix

CASE STUDIES

Following are brief descriptions of several individual job seekers with diverse characteristics and circumstances. Following the first case study is information that has been extracted and could be used as a starting point in developing the individual's positive personal profile. The remaining case studies may provide you with practice in extracting information to be incorporated into a positive personal profile.

Veronica

Veronica is a 25-year-old woman with a spectacular smile that lights up a room. She loves meeting new people. Veronica's family is extremely protective of her. They worry that she will be taken advantage of by others and do not feel that she is capable of holding down a real job. But this young woman is not about to be deterred. She has made it clear that she has aspirations: "I want my own job, maybe in show business, maybe working in a day care center. I want to get my own apartment. Maybe I'll get married." She has also expressed interest in working in a big office.

Although Veronica can only read at a first-grade level, she is amazingly adept at visual discrimination; that is, she can match words (including long ones) and distinguish between the slightest differences in colors. Recently, Veronica amazed some visitors who saw her working on a one-thousand-piece jigsaw puzzle of a Picasso painting. She had completed three-quarters of the picture! Regarding math skills, she can accurately count up to 15 objects and can read numbers up to 100. Understanding simple verbal instructions is difficult for her. Although she will nod and indicate that she understands oral directions, Veronica often gets them confused. When this happens, she becomes very upset with herself if she makes mistakes. Her education and training have all been in segregated programs for students with significant cognitive and other disabilities.

With lots of time on her hands, Veronica stays busy, nonetheless. She loves to go shopping any chance she can get and is very frugal with her weekly allowance. She prides herself on her appearance. Her sister has helped her learn how to apply make-up and select clothes. Veronica takes meticulous care of her clothes, washing and ironing them. She loves a wide variety of music and sings along whenever she hears a song she likes. People have commented on the beautiful quality of her voice, although it is difficult to understand her pronunciation of the lyrics. Even on her crutches, she has great rhythm.

Lately, she has been spending time volunteering at the physical therapy clinic where she receives services. Veronica helps out with such tasks as straightening up the waiting area, delivering mail, showing patients to various departments, helping staff clean equipment, and showing picture books to children. She has even demonstrated how to use certain exercise machines for visitors. She cheers on the patients who are struggling in their therapy sessions.

One of Veronica's paid work experiences while in school was at a fast food restaurant. Her favorite parts of that job were greeting the customers and making sure the condiment area was well-organized, supplied, neat, and clean. Customers complimented her on the way she performed this assignment. Another task was mopping the bathroom floor and cleaning the toilets, something Veronica frequently described as "nasty." Because of her refusal to do that task, she was let go from her job. The employment specialist from the school wrote, "Veronica lacks a positive attitude towards work."

Dreams and Goals

Wants to get a job, go into show business, work with children, have her own apartment
Dreams about getting married and having a family
Wants to work in a large office building

Talents

Can assemble a complex jigsaw puzzle
Has a great singing voice, loves to sing and dance
Is good at customer service

Skills and Knowledge

Can read numbers and count objects up to 100
Can match objects, printed words, pictures, and abstract symbols
Manages her allowance money skillfully
Can do laundry
Knows how to use variety of state-of-the-art exercise and physical therapy equipment

Learning Styles

Has several ways of learning, including musical-rhythmic, visual-spatial, bodily-kinesthetic, and interpersonal

Interests

Enjoys fashion, meeting people, jigsaw puzzles, art, music, dancing, shopping

Positive Personality Traits

Has a great smile
Is gregarious
Loves to meet new people
Has a fun sense of humor

Temperament

Likes to stay busy and to work closely with others

Values

Pays attention to her appearance, grooming, fashion

Values interaction with others, friendliness, and helpfulness

Believes in cleanliness, keeping busy

Environmental Preferences

Prefers being in settings where there is ample friendly interaction with others

Likes clean environments, indoors

Life and Work Experiences

Volunteered at the physical therapy clinic (tasks: straightening up the waiting area, delivering mail, showing patients to various departments, helping staff clean equipment, entertaining and watching children, demonstrating use of exercise machines, and encouraging patients)

Has gone to many locations around the city, using public transportation, with her friend

Education and Training

Graduated from a special education program

Met the goals on her individualized education program

Completed five different unpaid work experience placements, two in school and three in the community

Support System

Lives with very loving family (Note: see Specific Challenges)

Receives support from a sister, former teachers and therapists, and one friend with a disability

Specific Challenges

Her family is very afraid for her safety; therefore, they limit her opportunities.

Her family is not aware of her many skills and abilities.

She reads at the first-grade level and lacks essential literacy skills.

She has difficulty understanding and following verbal instructions. She pretends to understand when she does not, which leads her to make errors.

She becomes angry and upset when criticized or corrected.

She has limited exposure to career options related to her interests and skills.

An evaluation report from her fast food job stated that Veronica was not a good worker.

Solutions and Accommodations

Possible solutions to the fears of Veronica's family: Show Veronica's family what she is capable of doing. Assure them that Veronica will have the support she needs. Keep communications with the family open and frequent. Listen to and acknowledge their concerns as valid, while encouraging them to let Veronica take reasonable risks.

Possible solutions for Veronica's limited literacy: Capitalize on her other skills and strengths. Look for jobs that have tasks that do not rely on reading skills. If Veronica is interested, find a private reading tutor for her.

Possible solutions to Veronica's difficulties with verbal instructions: Model the tasks to be performed, and show pictures of the steps in the task. Have Veronica demonstrate the steps.

Possible solutions to Veronica's sensitivity about being corrected: Nonverbally correct her by continuing to model the task (or parts of the tasks) for her, then asking her to demonstrate. Congratulate her when she has demonstrated she is capable of performing the task correctly. Veronica might also benefit from a job club.

Possible solutions to limited exposure to career options: Travel with her around the community and observe job settings that are compatible with her interests, temperament, and so forth. Discuss her thoughts and reactions to these settings. Conduct job development and job search activities that are focused on Veronica's positive attributes and preferences.

Possible solutions for the poor evaluation: If possible, discuss the evaluation with the person who wrote it to ascertain the exact circumstances for which Veronica was rated poorly. Ask Veronica directly, "What did you like about your job at the restaurant? What did you not like about it?" Veronica would likely express her hatred of cleaning the bathroom and her preference for greeting customers and maintaining the condiments area. This would lead you to think of future tasks to avoid and those that would be acceptable to her.

Often, the reason a person does not do well on a particular job or training site is not because of his or her inability to perform a task but because of the person's disinterest or dislike of the tasks, the setting, the people, or other specific aspects of that job. It is critical to ascertain whether performance problems are due to lack of skill, desire, or even both and to respect a job seeker's right to find employment that is compatible, as far as possible, with his or her strengths and preferences.

Possibilities and Ideas

Explore jobs and tasks that employers need done that call for the types of skills Veronica has (e.g., making people feel welcome, paying attention to small details, using excellent small motor dexterity and visual-spatial skills, having a strong visual memory, having the stamina and ability to focus on a task for extended periods, being able to entertain small children and keep them occupied, having an appreciation and aptitude for fashion and grooming, keeping a workspace and supplies neatly organized).

Encourage Veronica to join a health club or other social club in order to meet people, make friends, and even date.

Take her parents on a few excursions around town, while exploring job possibilities.

Julius

Consider the case of Julius, a 50-year-old man with cerebral palsy. Since childhood, he has used a manual wheelchair that he guides with his feet. When first meeting him, one is struck by a number of things: the constant motion of his entire body due to extensive uncontrollable muscle spasms, his disheveled clothing that is frequently stained with food or liquid, the sounds he makes (his speech is virtually unintelligible), and the manner in which he struggles to eat. However, one is also struck by his twinkling blue eyes that respond instantly to anyone who takes a moment to interact with him and by his eagerness to display a worn three-ring binder with laminated pages of phrases and letters—his low-tech communication system. When a young visitor asked Julius if he minded getting older, his response was, "Heck, no! If I wasn't old, I'd be dead!" Wherever Julius goes, he gets people laughing along with him.

Julius' record and compact disc collection is impressive, composed primarily of opera and big band music. Writing poetry has been a hobby since he was a child, and it reflects deep thought and talent for verbal description. In fact, during the last few years, Julius has written several articles about his experiences as a citizen with a disability. These articles are well-constructed, informative, moving, and even humorous. He slowly creates these pieces on his computer at home, and he has even expressed an interest in approaching a publisher about some of his work. At home, Julius's level of independence is astonishing. He has somehow devised ways by which to care for himself, with only 4 hours of outside assistance per day. He bathes, gets into and out of bed, dresses, and even cooks frozen microwavable meals. Indeed, in all that he does, he has demonstrated his tenacity and determination.

Trace

Trace is a tall 57-year-old man who resembles one of those stately Civil War generals in old photographs. He looks quite distinguished, with his curly gray hair and a well-trimmed, full beard. Two years ago, Trace participated in a university study for people with IQs above 140. Through extensive testing, it was found that Trace has Asperger's syndrome, a form of autism. When describing his childhood, Trace revealed that he did not speak until age 6 and that he was frequently absent from grade school because of behavior. "Kids would beat me up after school, so I started doing things to get me suspended. Also teachers could not accept the fact that I did all the math in my head instead of writing out the problems." Recently, Trace learned from his mother that when he was 3 years old, he would put together jigsaw puzzles—in the dark.

Trace and his wife live in a rural area, approximately 30 miles from a mid-size town in a house Trace built 20 years ago from a kit he bought from the Whole Earth Catalogue. It looks like a flying saucer that has just landed in a field. Inside is filled with homemade electronic gadgetry, from stereo systems to musical instruments, to devices that will jam the radio stations of any passing vehicles that dare to play what he calls "intrusive, bass-thumping noise these kids call music." According to Trace, he has no problem with noise from engines and machinery, just loud contemporary music.

Trace has accomplished quite a few things in his life. He has a doctorate in physics and mathematics. He is certified to pilot several different kinds of small aircraft, is a licensed aircraft mechanic, and has taught many people how to fly. During the Vietnam War, Trace served 6 years in the Air Force, as a meteorologist and navigator for C-130 cargo planes. He received an honorable discharge because he was beginning to suffer migraine headaches and black-outs. After his employment specialist talked with him for a while, Trace revealed that he has always struggled to fit in socially with people. Although he has a number of close friends, he admits to being an outsider in most social circles. During his years in the military, he was often ridiculed for the clothes he chose to wear when not in uniform. His favored attire is a plaid shirt, striped tie, hand-stitched gray flannel vest, homemade trousers, red or orange socks, and impeccably-shined alligator-skin shoes. When outside his home, Trace likes to wear a top hat. He also claims that, in addition to his preferred clothing, many people do not seem to appreciate his favorite topics of conversation: his highly theoretical views on the universe. When he initiates conversation, Trace is extremely articulate, peppering his speech with words that require the use of a dictionary. He gives direct eye contact to his listener and appears quite animated. However, when he responds to a direct question, Trace's speech is often very halting and he stares at the floor.

Since his discharge from the military in 1975, Trace has been in and out of part-time jobs, in such diverse areas as bicycle repair, building maintenance, and other assorted odd jobs. Trace has also been a high school substitute teacher in math and science. He says teaching middle school kids was rough because he could not handle their behaviors. His wife would like for him to get a full-time job with benefits because she is an artist and needs health insurance.

Trace expresses a desire to work full time and is amenable to a variety of occupational areas "as long as I don't have to be around cigarette smoke and thumping music." When asked how much money he needs to earn, Trace says "I would hope to be remunerated at a minimum of $30,000 per annum."

Eric

Eric is a 19-year-old man who is very sociable and enjoys going to work. He has had experience bussing tables at the Campus Inn while attending a local community college course in word processing. For the past several years, he has also worked in a sheltered enclave in the dish room of a hospital, 10 hours per week, receiving less than minimum wage. Eric has a cognitive disability and epilepsy, and he has had several severe seizures on the job. He needs to take antiseizure medication three times each day. He also has a history of psychotic depression, which is currently controlled by medication that he takes twice per day. Eric is very talkative and detail-oriented, but he can also get moody. He is very sensitive at times and tends to take criticism personally. He has an excellent memory and sense of direction; as a result, he is able to make deliveries throughout the large multi-building hospital complex. His true interest in life is travel. At the group home where he lives, Eric keeps three file cabinets full of brochures and information about cities around the world: "I got 'em sorted. Hotels. Restaurants. Transportation. Yep, even got all the airports in the world. Yep. Got it all here." He also knows every airline in the world and the airports they fly into. He spends much time traveling with his family and enjoys flying to new cities. He is also a gambling aficionado, with a particular interest in slot machines, video blackjack, and video poker. He is very active with group home events and is not afraid to try new things. He enjoys sailing, camping, going to dances, movies, and eating out at new restaurants. Eric would like to leave his job with the hospital enclave and get his own job.

Rosita

Someone once referred to Rosita, a 23-year-old woman, as a whirlwind because of her tremendous enthusiasm for life, her expressiveness, and her dramatic flair. In fact, Rosita's fondest wish is to someday become a well-known actress. Since she was a child, she has expressed this career goal. Along the way, her family and teachers encouraged her to try out for school and community theater productions. Rosita has been in many plays and even acted in a movie created by a film student at the university. Many people express their surprise at how fashionably Rosita dresses. She prides herself on her appearance and learned about make-up and hairstyling at the part-time job she held as a shampoo girl. This was one of a number of work experiences Rosita had while still in high school, as part of her special education transition program. Her other work experiences have included delivering mail, collating training packets, photocopying documents, serving meals in the faculty lunch room, washing dishes in the cafeteria, and folding laundry in a large hotel. Of all those experiences, Rosita says her favorite ones were the administrative tasks and waiting on tables: "I loved talking to the teachers!" She is very vocal about the tasks she disliked: "The dish room in the cafeteria was awful! It was hot and made my hair frizz up. The laundry job, too. Yuck."

Rosita is highly motivated to develop her administrative skills. She is currently taking an adult education class in word processing. Although her speed on the keyboard is lower than average, her accuracy is outstanding. Her instructor thinks she should learn data entry. Although Rosita reads at around a fourth-grade level, her auditory memory is excellent. She can listen to a book on tape and repeat by memory much of what she has heard—verbatim and with the accents used by the speaker.

When asked what she would like to do as a career, Rosita always talks about being an actress; however, she is open to exploring other jobs in the performing arts field. Her teachers at school and her vocational rehabilitation counselor are concerned that Rosita's career goal is unrealistic and that she is setting herself up for disappointment. (Chapter 13 includes a case history of Rosita's job search and how her talents and interests were matched to the needs of a particular employer.)

Cindy

Cindy is a 21-year-old young woman with big brown eyes and a spectacular smile. She is in her last year of special education in a segregated school for students with severe and multiple disabilities. The majority of Cindy's classmates have severe mental retardation and physical disabilities. Cindy has cerebral palsy and a mild learning disability. Cindy uses a state-of-the-art motorized wheelchair with head-switch controls; the only part of her body that Cindy is able to move voluntarily is her head. Because she cannot communicate verbally, Cindy uses a computerized communication device.

Cindy has had no previous paid work experience, although she has frequently been willing to demonstrate and try out new adaptive equipment at the local rehabilitation hospital. On one occasion, she demonstrated experimental devices in front of 100 engineers and physicians from around the world. Her current school schedule includes speech, home economics, computers, and adaptive physical education.

Cindy enjoys spending time with friends and family. She can often be found outside lounging in the pool during the summertime. Cindy celebrated her 21st birthday by going out to a bar with friends. When asked about what she enjoyed most about her birthday celebration, Cindy responded enthusiastically, "The champagne!" She also loves going to the mall and running up her mother's credit card and going to the movies. Her favorite TV show is "Friends," and the color pink is prominent in her wardrobe. Cindy has strong literate skills. She is a very quick verbal learner with a tested reading level of seventh grade.

Shawn

At age 25, this gregarious young man just completed his undergraduate degree in computer programming at a state university. Since he was a little boy, Shawn has shown himself to be tenacious and adventurous. According to his mother, he had a passion for climbing trees, ladders, and jungle gyms. With considerable tutoring support from his mother and others, Shawn was able to progress through regular school programs even though he was born deaf and blind. At about the same time children his age were learning how to talk, Shawn was already able to understand and use sign language. His mother and a personal assistant would communicate by signing into Shawn's hands; he, in turn, would respond.

Shawn is fiercely independent and has taken an airplane by himself to visit a friend in another state. Shawn loves to meet people. His smile lights up a room.

With significant supports and accommodations—and much pressure on the local vocational rehabilitation office and the university's department of services for students with disabilities—Shawn has been able to get through the rigors of his undergraduate program. He has an adapted computer that reads and prints braille. A rehabilitation engineer has helped him experiment with a mechanical hand that actually signs into Shawn's hand whatever is on the computer screen. This has enabled Shawn to use e-mail. A number of experts have suggested that Shawn's tested IQ is likely to be extremely high; however, they have questioned the validity of any of the existing tests, due to his dual sensory disabilities. Shawn is clearly a person with big dreams and goals: "I want to get married and have a family. Living at the beach would be fun. Travel. And get a job, of course. Something that will use my computer degree." Vocational counselors have expressed their skepticism of Shawn's career aspirations. One report said that "Shawn's need for accommodations is so extensive that it is unlikely an employer would consider this reasonable. My recommendation is that he set her sights on an attainable goal, such as [a sheltered workshop]." Although Shawn's mother has been his staunch advocate over the years, she, too, is beginning to wonder what is in store for her son.

Gina

Gina is a tomboy whose father affectionately calls her "another one of my sons." She excels in many sports; in fact, she is a natural-born athlete. She also loves anything mechanical. She enjoys a reputation as the neighborhood whiz-kid when it comes to fixing things. The family first noticed this talent when Gina was 5. She took all of the handles off the drawers in the kitchen and drawers on the china closet and then switched them. When her folks took their car in for repairs, Gina insisted on watching the mechanics at work. When she was 8, her grandparents bought Gina a fully equipped tool box, which she still uses today at age 16. She has worked weekends and summers at her father's remodeling business, doing carpentry and painting. Customers rave about the quality of her work.

It took a long time, but Gina was finally diagnosed with attention-deficit/hyperactivity disorder at age 13. She attends regular classes for most of her school day, except for 1 hour with a reading specialist. Although Gina has excelled in sports and mechanics, she does not hesitate to tell people what she thinks about going to school: "I hate school more than anything! What a [expletive] waste of time." On school days, she has to be dragged out of bed in the morning, whereas she wakes easily during weekends, when she works in her father's shop. She gets mostly Cs and Ds on her report cards and has run away from home numerous times. When she gets a bad grade, Gina's response is usually to sneer and ask, "What do they know anyway?" Her parents are very concerned that she will drop out altogether. They have tried to convince her that doing well in school will enable her to go on to college, something no one in their family has achieved. They would even be happy if she were to go to a postsecondary trade school. Her mom has also suggested Gina might want to go into the military. Their biggest concern, however, is Gina's mental health. She has threatened to commit suicide on several occasions. Gina has seen a therapist who diagnosed her with clinical depression. Gina has since refused to go back to counseling or take her prescribed medication.

Jay

One thing strikes people right away when they first meet Jay: the serpent tattoo winding around his neck and face, up to his vivid green eyes. He dresses all in black. This short muscular man has served a total of 10 of his 35 years of life behind bars. His first stint in prison occurred just after he dropped out of high school at age 15 and stole a Jaguar from a dealership's lot. He subsequently gained some notoriety for being able to disarm complicated alarm systems on the nicest of vehicles.

According to Jay, he struggled through school from day one. "I just never could learn how to read. I could fake my way through some of my classes by looking at the pictures and diagrams, and I was good at math. But I guess I'm what you call illiterate. They tried to put me in special education in the seventh grade and I told 'em they could shove it. So they left me alone. Only other things I was good at was recess and art." In fact, during his last period of time in prison, Jay attracted some attention in art circles with what he calls his "junk sculpture," statues of people and animals he constructed of salvaged metal, wood, wire, and screws. His artwork was featured in a recent article in the newspaper about art that originates in unconventional places.

Now in a halfway house, Jay is determined to turn things around. "Maybe get my GED. Get me a decent job. Be nice to settle down and get a dog." Jay says he needs a full-time position with benefits because he has acquired chronic asthma and needs health insurance and prescription drug coverage. When asked about his family, Jay's mood shifts from optimistic to bitter: "They wrote me off a long time ago. Dunno. Maybe I wrote them off, too." He does have one friend whom he speaks of fondly. "Buddy of mine was a chaplain in the first joint I spent time in. His wife used to send cookies and his kids would paint pictures for me." Jay states that he is very concerned that his criminal record, dyslexia, and illiteracy will preclude his ever being able to earn a respectable living.

Greg

Greg is 17 years old and seems to have no idea of what he wants to do when he finishes high school. He has a history of mental illness and multiple hospitalizations due to episodes of severe depression and threats of suicide. This young man has held a part-time position at a cat shelter, feeding the animals and cleaning the cages. He seems to have a real interest in animal care, as evidenced by his menagerie of pets and his tendency to rescue injured wild animals and nurse them back to health. He has been known to say, "People are idiots. Animals have soul."

Greg takes a number of medications for depression, anxiety, and seizures. He is not very careful about taking them at the right times. On one occasion at the cat shelter, one of his co-workers spilled some cat food; Greg became livid, yelled obscenities, and threw the cat food dish across the room. When the cats became agitated, he knelt down and gently told them that he would make sure his co-worker did not harm them.

Greg prefers to work alone and has been known to be disrespectful toward supervisors when he felt they were spending too much time "looking over my shoulder and spying at me!" He seems to feel more comfortable in a low-stress, relaxed environment where he can be autonomous. When he works on a job he likes, his quality and accuracy are outstanding. Greg does not have a driver's license but uses public transportation and his bicycle to get anywhere he wants to go. He is an avid reader and can always be seen with a book in his back pocket. Greg frequents the local library and bookstores, where he sometimes spends hours. Greg's father bought him a membership at a local gym, and Greg likes to work out regularly. He scowls if anyone approaches him.

9

Knowing the Employer Customer

Nothing beats people showing me how they can meet my needs.

KATE STEWART, HUMAN RESOURCES DIRECTOR, ACT

After learning about some tools for getting to know the job seeker, it is important to look at the basis for developing the partnerships and relationships with potential employers of these job seekers. Employer customers are every bit as important to the employment specialist as the job seekers. How can an employment specialist truly meet the needs of employer customers without first getting to know them? Most people would not trust a real estate agent, a car salesman, a mortgage broker, or even a waiter who did not try to first get to know their preferences and their needs. The same principle applies to employment specialists who are hoping to capture employers' interest in employing someone the employment specialist represents. Why would an employer work with an employment specialist unless he or she was careful to understand the hiring needs, preferences, and operational activities of that employer? Without an orientation to understanding an employer's needs, the employment specialist is relegated to pursuing two options: 1) appealing to the employer's altruism, which does not work too well, or 2) hoping that just by chance the employer is desperate to hire someone, which also does not work too well.

A partnership orientation to job development and placement demands that professionals recognize employers as important customers of their service. To truly serve these customers, you have to know how you can meet their needs, which begins by getting to know them as thoroughly as possible. This chapter introduces ways of getting to know both the general employer community and specific employers in order to become valued providers of service to employer customers. General, straightforward, and fundamental strategies will be first introduced, followed by more intensive activities that have long-term but potentially significant job development payoff.

THE BUSINESS OF BUSINESS

There are almost no employers who are in the business of hiring people with disabilities. This is one reason that trying to sell employers on the notion of hiring people with disabilities is incongruent with business operation. How to get employers interested in hiring people represented by employment agencies when employers have no inherent interest in disability employment creates a fundamental conundrum for the field. On the one hand are job seekers whose circumstances of disability often create the need for employment specialists to help them find employment. On the other hand are the employers, who essentially have no economic or operational stake in whether or not a disability might present employment barriers. Addressing this situation requires first understanding of the nature of business and then applying effective strategies that match the services of employment agencies and specialists to the needs of a business.

For-profit businesses are in business to make money. Not-for-profit organizations are in business to address a specific societal or civic issue. Government agencies are in business to serve the public. In each of these cases, they employ people who will help them meet the missions of their operations. When a business utilizes the services of an employment agency or employment specialist, that business becomes a customer. Attracting and serving employer customers require first knowing their circumstances. Thus, the business of employment agencies and employment specialists must involve familiarity with the requirements of specific employers' operations, regardless of whether they are for-profit companies, not-for-profit organizations, or government agencies.

Depending on the experience of an employment specialist, the level of penetration into the employer's operation the specialist wants or needs to achieve, and the intensity with which the specialist has the luxury to pursue information on employers, there are several layers of possible strategies. At even the most basic level, these strategies have the potential to result in employment specialists first getting their foot in the door and then ultimately attracting employers to be customers of their service by hiring job seekers they represent. At the highest level, the strategies have the potential to create substantial, mutually beneficial, trusting, long-term partnerships.

GETTING ACQUAINTED

At the most fundamental level of job and partnership development are "get acquainted" strategies, that is, those that yield basic or cursory knowledge of businesses and employers in a community. This knowledge marks the first step in viewing businesses as potential customers. Through this knowledge, employment agencies and employment specialists can mount the marketing activities that help capture employer customers, introduced in Chapter 10. The following strategies are a few of the ways to get acquainted with employers in your community.

Strategy 1: Become Knowledgeable About the Business World and Join Business Organizations

It pays to be an ardent student of the employers in your community. Make it your mission to learn, in every way possible, about each of the various industries and companies that are prominent in your community. Business magazines, trade journals, and the business sections of local newspapers are excellent sources of information regarding opportunities, trends, and hiring projections. Read them and discuss them with your colleagues.

Talk with friends and relatives about where they work and what they do. Talk with people at community events and attend local business functions such as those at your local Chamber of Commerce. These activities may not lead to immediate or specific job leads, but you will develop an information base, and more important, an expanded network from which to identify job opportunities. Remember, it is from such networks that job leads arise. The more people you know, the more likely you will uncover such leads. Some additional ideas for expanding knowledge of the business community and at the same time expanding the network of employer contacts are:

- Join local Chambers of Commerce and other business and civic groups where business people associate. Become involved in various activities sponsored by these organizations.
- Ask colleagues, friends, and relatives for the names and telephone numbers of any people that they may know in the business world whom you may be able to contact for information about their particular industries.
- Ask employers with whom you already have a good working relationship to introduce you to colleagues in their company or industry. Ask for contact information for other companies that they do business with.
- Make a list of potential contacts in an array of industries and job types from people you know.

One employment specialist attended Chamber of Commerce meetings for months before an opportunity arose to use this network. At one meeting, she heard one of the members talk about a new contract his light manufacturing company received that would necessitate hiring dozens of new workers. In particular, the company needed individuals who were very precise in assembling small electronic components. One contact with the company led to another. Soon she helped one of her job seeker customers attain a job on one aspect of the company's expanded assembly line. This connection would never have been made without her knowledge of the local company's special hiring needs. What's more, she benefited from an expanded employer network that was created by her participation in the Chamber's events.

Strategy 2: Distinguish Between the Employer as an Individual and the Employer as Organization

The term *employer* can apply both to a company and to individuals within that company. This may seem like stating the obvious, but often employment specialists fail to see the importance of knowing both. Job development occurs at both levels: first becoming familiar with a community's employers as organizations (see Strategy 1 above) and then knowing the operation at the people level, the level at which interactions occur that lead to jobs.

Consider a single position within a given company, for example, a bakery supervisor. This individual has a business identity with a specific title and a defined role. However, a bakery supervisor in a store that is part of a larger grocery chain may have roles and responsibilities that are different from that of someone with the same title who works in a small, family-owned bakery shop. It is important for employment specialists to understand such differences in interacting with each individual.

One employment specialist helped a job seeker first find a job at a local, family-owned bakery by meeting and negotiating with the bakery supervisor, who was also one of the family members. The process was very informal, and the job placement happened relatively quickly once the employment specialist established a relationship with the supervisor and learned of the company's needs for a pasty chef assistant. However, the job seeker was dissatisfied with the job because it was too routine and uninteresting to him. He made the same pastries every day and was bored. He aspired to bigger and better things. He wanted more responsibility and more interesting job assignments, and he asked the employment specialist to help him locate another job.

The employment specialist contacted a large grocery chain to learn of the requirements of pastry chefs in the bakery departments of its stores. To get this information, she had to meet with several different individuals: the chain's human resource manager, the general manager of one of the stores, and then finally the bakery supervisor in the store. The process was different, the number of individuals with whom she met was different, and the bakery supervisor had different and larger responsibilities than what was the case at the family-owned bakery. But she had to work closely with each individual to facilitate the ultimate hiring of the job seeker with this company. He got the job because the employment specialist became acquainted with both the employer as an organization and individuals who perform employer roles.

Strategy 3: Learn How to Translate Your Services into Benefits for Employers

Customers like to be given choices. Thus, it is important to be prepared with a menu of options, not simply a list of potential job applicants. It is much easier to attract employer interest and reach an agreement with an employer when you are able to provide several options from which to choose. It is especially useful to be able to match the features of your service with how they might benefit employers. Table 9.1 shows how typical features of disability employment agencies convert to features to prospective employers.

One employment specialist was able to draw on his agency's features in meeting an employer's needs in a very resourceful way. When told by an employer that the company was not currently hiring anyone because it was revamping how it screened its applicants, the employment specialist offered to help design a recruitment strategy that would broaden where the employer might find qualified applicants. The employment specialist simply offered to make future job openings known to a host of other disability and workforce development organizations. The employer incorporated this offer into its new recruitment outreach procedure when the company was again ready to hire. This employment specialist became the company's first contact when recruitment was necessary because the agency promised to make other organizations aware of the company's hiring needs. He translated features of his organization—applicant screening and consultation—to benefits for the employer: reduced recruitment costs and responsiveness to a human resource need. More is said about translating features to benefits in Chapter 10.

Table 9.1. Translating services to benefits

Agency features	Benefits for employers
Employment specialist	Single point of contact
	Recruitment assistance
	Follow-up provided
Applicant screening	Prescreened applicants
	Reduction of recruitment costs
Training and consultation	Customized responses to human resources needs
	Education about managing a diverse workforce
Applicants	An expanded labor pool

Strategy 4: Learn the Decision-Making Process for Hiring

Every company has its own hiring processes and decision-making hierarchy. A logical question, then, concerns who has the authority to hire within a targeted company. Is there only one person who is responsible for hiring? How easy is it to gain access to the decision maker?

Several basic issues must be considered with regard to the hiring process:

- The company's current need to hire new employees
- How applicants are typically recruited
- The criteria by which the applicants will be screened and interviewed
- The final hiring decision process
- The time frame in which the hiring decision must be made

Depending on the size of the company, any number of people may be charged with resolving these issues. In fact, as new decisions are made, the process itself may change. It is misleading and overly simplistic to think in terms of one person being the only decision maker unless the particular company is very small and its owner makes all of the hiring decisions. Consider the following scenarios in which any number of contacts may have knowledge of or involvement in a company's hiring process.

- Through frequent visits to a local auto repair shop, you have gotten to know one of the mechanics. You've chatted with him and he's seen you with different job seekers. He is moving to another town. He is loyal to the shop and wants to make sure the shop finds a good replacement. He contacts you for ideas.
- A long-time friend is the personnel manager for a bank. Through the grapevine, he hears of a pending opening for a teller. Remembering his last contact with you at a Chamber of Commerce meeting, he gives you a call prior to advertising the position.
- You read in the paper that a local company is expanding its operations. You call a friend who works in the company, and she tells you who is in charge of hiring during the expansion.
- The brother of a friend has worked for a particular company for several years. Although his job has nothing to do with personnel or administration, he is a highly respected employee whose opinion is highly regarded by management. Whenever there is a job opening, management asks him for his recommendations.

Each of these scenarios depicts distinctly different ways in which hiring decisions are made, and each illustrates different people who might influence that hiring. The next step, finding out who makes the final hiring decisions, is best pursued by asking for some information from a person associated with the company with whom you already have developed at least a basic rapport:

- Is there one particular person who makes the final decisions regarding hiring?
- Does this person do the hiring for all departments?
- Are supervisors involved in these decisions?
- How does the company select candidates to be interviewed?
- How does the company recruit new applicants?
- How does the company decide what the minimum qualifications are for a position?

Through such contacts and through such processes for getting to know a company's hiring needs and processes, the need for cold calling is minimized. In fact, these are great ways to develop hot leads through developing basic relationships with company representatives.

Strategy 5: Do Your Homework on Particular Companies

There are many ways to research business needs and particular businesses. Read business publications—or better yet, subscribe to them. Weekly business magazines are common in many larger cities, for example. In any case, all local newspapers have a daily business section. Scouring it daily gives a perspective on the business of local companies. It covers the economic interests of the business community as a whole, as well as providing regular feature articles on local companies. One of our colleagues contacted a small furniture maker after the local paper ran a story on the company's plans to expand because of a new contract the company had landed. After several meetings with the human resources director, he facilitated the hiring of a job seeker he represented. The company needed precise assemblers, and the employment specialist knew of just such a person. He met the company's need because he had done his homework.

The Internet is also a valuable resource for learning about particular companies. It is easy to get companies' news and information from their websites. A wealth of information can be obtained from such reviews. For example, from the company reports, you can find out about the company's major products and services, how fast the company is expanding, what it projects its human resource needs to be, and other company developments.

Few things impress an employer more than when an employment specialist can talk knowledgeably about company activities. It demonstrates interest and competence. For the employment specialist, it often determines where, how, and when to try to get a foot in the door. Another colleague found a company whose web site made a continuous point of its emphasis on the quality of its products. When meeting with a hiring supervisor, she indicated her interest in the company's quality movement. There must be something in particular, she expressed, that the company does to upgrade the quality of its employees to ensure high-quality company outputs. From this question, the hiring supervisor began an animated description of the company's personnel training procedures. Given the interest of the employment specialist in this aspect of the company, a relationship evolved. Two job seekers she represented were eventually hired by the company.

Strategy 6: Seek Opportunities for Information Interviews

Information interviews are a popular technique for individual job seekers to hone their interviewing skills. It is especially espoused by outplacement firms that are hired by companies when they lay off workers. Outplacement counselors advise the laid-off workers to contact people and employers they know just to meet and practice interviewing. In the context of job development, it is also a great way to meet new employers and learn their needs without the pressure of trying to convince them to make a placement. Few employers will refuse a request for a meeting to share the company's business and human resource needs. One of the best ways for job developers to learn of employers' operational and human resource needs is to simply ask to meet with someone in the company. This would usually be someone in the human resources department but it could be anyone with knowledge of the company and the time to spend time talking about it. A few pointers for information interviews are:

- Make the request for a meeting easy to fulfill: "I'd like to find out more about your business so I can better understand the human resource needs in your industry. Can I meet briefly with you to ask a few questions?" or "I'm really interested in your industry. Is it possible for me to briefly visit and get more information?" or "Do you give tours? I'd like to join one if that is easy to arrange."

- Keep it short. Respect the employer's time. Fifteen to twenty minutes should be more than enough. Any more time can become an imposition and therefore threatens to sour the relationship on the first visit.

- Be prepared. Have your questions ready. There are only a few you really need: What is the main product or service of your company? What is your company most proud of? (Remember, it never hurts to get someone to talk about their shining moments!) How does the work get done? How many people do you employ? What kinds of preparation or training do the people you hire need? What are some of the biggest challenges in the industry, in your company? It is even better if you already know the answers to some of these questions because you have reviewed the company's web site and other materials beforehand. Then you can ask more knowledgeable questions such as "I learned that your company hired 15 new people last quarter. Is that hiring rate likely to continue?"

- Thank the employer for the time he or she took to meet with you. It also is wise to follow up with a brief, written, thank-you note. After all, you just added someone to your employer network and the residuals of a good impression could lead to future partnership activity.

The knowledge gained from these strategies put agencies and employment specialists in a position to develop and maintain broad employer relationships. They become aware of needs in a variety of industries and a variety of individual employers. More frequent and more effective marketing contacts are possible. And, of course, this ultimately means more job opportunities for the job seekers they represent.

BECOMING AN EXPERT ON EMPLOYERS IN YOUR COMMUNITY

In order to bolster knowledge of the employer community beyond that which comes with some of these fundamental activities, the most effective employment agencies and employment specialists are ready to become experts about local industries. That is, they are ready to take their operation to a higher level by upgrading how they learn about employers and upgrading what they do with this knowledge. Agencies and employment specialists who achieve a higher quality of information on employers begin to play "above the rim." That is, they are able to elevate their effectiveness to such a level that their goals become easier and easier to reach.

Two strategies in particular, if done well, provide extremely rich and useful information about employers. The first strategy is to have an organized group of employers who provide regular guidance and feedback to employment agencies on the employer perspective. Commonly called business advisory councils (BACs), these groups are ideally exclusively led by and composed of employers. The second strategy involves gathering selected employers together for facilitated discussions about particular issues that employers face as they meet their human resource needs. These discussion or focus groups require a little more expertise and skill to organize but they typically yield some of the best information and knowledge for launching or refining employer marketing activities. Both of these strategies position employment services to take full and best advantage of the circumstances that exist in their employer community so that they can develop truly dynamic employer partnerships.

Business Advisory Councils

Business advisory councils have been in use for a long time in the field of job development, with variable effectiveness. In fact, some funders of employment services for people with disabilities have required that organizations who receive their money must form a BAC so that business representatives can regularly and conveniently provide feedback on organizational practice and links to employment opportunities. On the surface, this seems like an eminently good idea. If these organizations are going to do the best job preparing people for work, then employer advice is of course helpful. In practice, however, such groups often became nothing more than rubber stamps for organization activity, or worse, groups organized solely to meet funding requirements. These are not the kind of BACs we are talking about.

BACs, in our experience, can be dynamic and continuous sources of both advice and jobs if they feature a combination of strong business leadership, a diverse mix of businesses and employers, a clear purpose, and a tangible direct benefit to their members. It also is important that they be supported by able employment professionals.

Five Steps to Establishing and Maintaining a Business Advisory Council

Step 1: Recruit team members. Start with a business person who is already known to the agency and who has benefited from the agency's services, especially through successfully hiring a job seeker represented by the agency. From there, other business people can be recruited, ideally by the members themselves. There is no optimal number of members, but the group should remain manageably small—no more than 15 or 20 members, no fewer than 6 or 8. The key is that the members can contribute a small amount of time each month or two to attend a short meeting. Also, recruitment of members should result in representation from the community's various industry sectors (e.g., finance, manufacturing, health care, hospitality) for a range of employer input and networks.

Step 2: Establish clear leadership. The leader of the group must be an employer who has a clear understanding of the agency's mission and is firmly rooted in the local business community. Ideally, this is someone who has connections to businesses and business organizations from which to recruit members and has credibility as a business professional.

Step 3: Establish a mission and member expectations. The group's work should have a clear purpose. It is not sufficient for the group to simply exist to provide advice and guidance to the agency, although that is important. A more dynamic purpose will keep the group together, such as to increase the number of satisfied companies that hire people represented by the agency. Similarly, the members should understand the parameters of their participation: attendance at meetings, contacts to other employers on behalf of the agency, occasional availability to agency staff who need advice or contact leads.

Step 4: Keep meetings focused and brief. Nothing loses the interest of a group of business people faster than unfocused and unprofessional meetings. A good leader will set a clear agenda that includes the purpose of the meeting, topics to be discussed, time limits for each segment of the meeting, and a desired outcome for each topic. Agency staff might support the meeting by taking minutes or reporting information when asked, but they should never run the meeting. Keep the meeting to no longer than 1 hour. Time is money to most of these people.

Step 5: Make it worth the members' while. Hold the meetings at a time of day least likely to interfere with the business day. And feed them! Early breakfast meetings are particularly recommended for this reason, although lunch meetings also work. The work of the group should also be continuously reinforced in agency publications. It usually does not hurt for businesses to get visibility for their work and to be associated with a winning program. However, one of the most important returns on the members' time investment is the opportunity to network with other business associates, sharing business and human resources concerns and solutions with each other.

Case in Point   Community Enterprises of Northampton, Massachusetts, has found that using a BAC is one of the best ways to not only learn about employer needs but also build long-term employer partnerships. Community Enterprises operates employment services in six locations in Massachusetts, Connecticut, and New York. It has established a BAC in each location, tapping local business leaders to become members. These councils include professional members from banks, telecommunications companies, colleges, local government employers, grocery stores, manufacturers, high-tech companies, and representative local businesses. In short, any entity that is an employer is a potential member.

At the time of this writing, Community Enterprises had a total of 82 business members participating in its six BACs. In addition to providing Community Enterprises with advice and council on its relationships with local employers, members agree to make a minimum of one employer contact each month to promote hiring of people with disabilities that live in that community. These contacts have lead to the development of more than 2,000 jobs since their first BAC was created in 1979.

The newest BAC of Community Enterprises, in Brentwood, New York, formed in 2000. Since its inception, it has recruited 18 members from 12 different companies and has achieved an impressive list of outcomes:

- Helped develop 85 jobs for job seekers represented by the agency
- Helped raise more than $20,000 for agency operating costs
- Developed and produced marketing brochures used by the agency to present to prospective employers
- Arranged exposure for the agency on cable television

Aside from the important role of helping Community Enterprises keep abreast of business issues in its communities, the BACs have essentially functioned as a peer-to-peer marketing arm for the organizations. One of the most effective ways to get across the idea of disability employment to employers is to have employers do the talking. According to Dick Venne, President and CEO of Community Enterprises, "Our most effective job development strategy continues to be our use of business advisory councils and the individual network each member has in meeting the ongoing employment needs of the individuals we serve. An added bonus has been that the BAC has also proven to be our most effective board recruitment vehicle" (Luecking & Tilson, 2002, p. 27).

Focus Groups

Focus groups have been a common and respected method for both social and marketing research (Greenbaum, 1993; Kreuger, 1994; Morgan, 1993). They have been adopted in both the private and public sectors to study values, attitudes, preferences, opinions, program materials, program effectiveness, and complex problems. Focus groups are an ideal way to get data-driven recommendations for program and organizational improvements and to develop marketing strategies based on more complete knowledge of a targeted group. Thus, they can also be one of the most useful ways to gain in-depth information and opinions from employers. Focus groups can help solicit:

- Interaction between employers around a particular issue
- Answers to "how" and "why" questions (e.g., How should employers be approached by employment agencies? Why is the job market changing?)
- Perceptions about gaps between employment professionals and employers
- Immediate feedback to questions or issues related to employment development
- Wide ranging and insightful employer opinions

Three primary uses of focus groups with employer participants are to learn about general human resource, or employer issues; pilot new materials, such as marketing brochures or services; and conduct formative program evaluation. In our work with employers and organizations around the country, we have conducted focus groups around each of these purposes. For example, focus groups have helped us to learn about general human resources or employer issues. We were able to:

- Get the opinion of a group of human resource professionals on how they prefer to be approached by employment agencies
- Find out opinions from experienced employers on what are essential ingredients to successful hiring people with disabilities
- Determine the most pressing human resource issues in a particular industry

We used focus groups to pilot new materials:

- Get opinions on a new brochure from an employment service program that targets employers
- Find ways to describe a particular service to employers (e.g., supported employment)
- Get reactions to a postplacement survey designed to gauge employer satisfaction with an employment service agency

We conducted formative program evaluation:

- Obtain feedback on how a particular program was meeting employer needs

- Determine ways to improve the contact with employers
- Test the potential effectiveness of proposed marketing messages of a program's materials

How Focus Groups Operate

Focus groups are not brainstorming sessions. Rather, they are carefully designed and conducted guided interactions among a specifically selected group of participants. Group interaction yields insights into an issue and produces valuable data that cannot be obtained any other way (Morgan, 1991). There are several common elements of a good focus group. They include:

1. A panel of 8–12 carefully selected participants
2. A comfortable environment
3. A skilled moderator who directs the flow of the discussion
4. A predetermined outline for the discussion, usually a list of sequential open-ended questions from which the moderator can elicit and guide discussion
5. A way of capturing and analyzing the discussion so that the most clear learning points can be extracted and used

Focus groups can last anywhere from 1 to 3 hours, but any longer than 1 hour leads to diminishing returns and stretches the courtesy of participants who usually have limited time to give.

The first step is to thoughtfully determine and then recruit employers who ideally would provide the kind of information you seek. It could be employers from a particular community, or a particular industry sector, or employers who have all interacted with a specific program. The composition of the group depends on what information you are after. For example, when we wanted to get input from employers about rehabilitation service features that characterized successful job placements of people with disabilities, we solicited employer nominations from agencies who had successfully placed individuals in companies that were then recruited. When we wanted to know how to market a particular program we were helping to launch, we invited employers who were generally looking to hire new employees but who had no previous experience hiring people with disabilities. We wanted to learn how they might respond as naïve users of disability employment services. Recruitment of employers in both of these cases involved a telephone call to them explaining who had suggested their participation and why. The telephone call was followed by a letter of invitation detailing the time and location of the meeting. Out of courtesy and respect for their time and participation, a small token for participation was usually offered, such as a gift certificate, small stipend, or service exchange, such as free human resource training.

The next step is to plan the questions for the session. Again, open-ended questions are important so as to elicit the most group interaction and the richest information. The questions that are asked of the participants will depend on what information is desired. For example, questions we have used to guide focus group discussions on general human resource issues include:

- What do you look for in applicants to your company?
- What are some of the biggest challenges in recruiting a good workforce?
- On a scale from 1 to 5, with 5 being the highest, how would you rate employee loyalty in your company? Why?
- What do you think about applicants who are represented or referred by an employment agency?
- What are the most important trends in your industry? How do they affect how you recruit, hire, train, and manage your workforce?

Again, these are just sample questions. Often it is useful to have a skilled facilitator work with the key users of the information to develop questions pertinent to the purpose of a particular focus group. Questions for piloting new materials might look like these:

- Please take a few moments to look over the materials. What one thing do you like the best? The least?
- If you could change one thing about the materials, what would it be?
- What would get you to participate in this program? Or under what conditions would you participate?
- What would you say to a friend to encourage him or her to participate in the program?
- Do you have any other advice for us to introduce this program?

In order to evaluate a program to plan for improvements, the questions might look like these:

- Tell us why you participated in the program? How did you participate?
- What did you like best about the program? The least?
- What should be changed?
- What should be continued or expanded?
- Do you have any other advice about the program?

From questions such as these, the discussion can yield active group participation and very useful information. But the responses are not helpful it they are not dually recorded. Thus, the next step is to establish a nonparticipant recorder. With the participants' permission, the session can be tape recorded for later transcription. If that is not feasible, a recorder (or two) is necessary to take down the main responses that occur during the session. Notable comments are especially important to record for later review.

Employers and Employment Support for People with Disabilities

In order to assist the state of Washington's Division of Vocational Rehabilitation to determine how employers would best like to be approached by agencies representing job seekers with disabilities, TransCen facilitated a focused discussion with representatives from nine companies and employers, all of whom had experience with hiring people with disabilities. These companies included a retail clothing chain, two temporary employee service companies, a university, a municipal government, an insurance company, a large national bank, and a telecommunications company. There were two main questions that structured the discussion:

1. What is your greatest human resources need?
2. What advice do you have for community rehabilitation programs when they contact you and partner with you?

A recorder transcribed the participants' responses, which are summarized here.

Greatest Human Resources Needs
All of the employers had needs unique to their company. For example, the bank needed people who were computer literate and had good customer service skills, while the university and the municipality each needed people for rigidly defined positions that were subject to well-established hiring processes. All of the employers, however, looked for people with many of the same characteristics: loyalty, good teamwork skills, and a good work attitude, that is, punctuality, attendance, and willingness for supervisory feedback. Of note, all of the non–civil service employers expressed a willingness to consider candidates who did not fit all of a position's requirements if they brought something of value to the job.

Advice for Community Rehabilitation Programs
It was a requirement of selection for this focus group for each of employers to have this experience. However, there were variations on the experience. Two companies had affirmative efforts underway to recruit employees with disabilities, and one company targeted people with disabilities as one of its markets for its products. Three participants maintained active membership in some type of disability-focused partnership. Thus, these were individuals who were, for the most part, extremely familiar with disability employment programs and who therefore could provide important personal perspective on their expectations of such programs. Here are their chief recommendations:

*   Be professional in both personal and written communication
*   Avoid too many points of contact
*   Use business terminology in describing services
*   Provide frequent follow-up after a placement
*   Adopt basic business etiquette
*   Find out what the business needs, rather than trying to simply sell disability
*   Offer direct assistance to meet those needs
*   Do not force a bad match between an applicant and the job

Typical comments revolved around the themes of professionalism and customer service: "I look for job developers who do what they say they are going to do, and follow-up." "Avoid messy applications and typing errors on résumés." "Explain how the service will benefit the business. This is more effective than trying to sell your program." "Always be attentive to the company's needs."

Sound familiar? These employers were clearly telling community rehabilitation practitioners to bolster typically effective job development approaches with a strong customer service orientation. From these responses, the Division of Vocational Rehabilitation and community rehabilitation agencies in Washington were able to begin crafting a more employer-focused marketing campaign. They were able to also institute professional development activities for rehabilitation personnel that featured such employer-focused orientations to marketing and job development.

Finally, the last step is to analyze the responses. The moderator and the recorders should begin to go through the proceeding immediately after the session while it is still fresh in everyone's mind. It is important to find the consistent thoughts or ideas and categorize the discussion into larger themes.

Private sector companies use focus groups extensively as they get to know their market and their customers. Similarly, focus groups are wonderful ways for employment professionals to get a good bead on the employer market and their employer customers. But planning and conducting focus groups requires careful preparation. Before conducting focus groups, it is useful to first participate in or observe them. If you want to delve into using focus groups as a way of getting to know employer customers, refer to Greenbaum (1994), Krueger (1993), and Morgan (1991, 1993), listed in the reference section.

SUMMARY

This chapter examines ways to get to know employer customers. After all, serving any customer well requires knowledge of the circumstances and desires of that customer. It is especially important to understand that the business of business is not to hire people with disabilities but to deliver products or services so that they make money (if they are for-profit companies) or to fulfill a specific social or civic purpose (if they are government or not-for-profit entities).

We introduce six general strategies that are easily implemented by individual employment specialists. These strategies help employment specialists both to learn about what employers need and want from prospective employees and to get a foot in the door with these employers.

Finally, we introduce two more comprehensive methods of getting to know employers and their views. BACs and focus groups both enable employment specialists and their agencies to tap into the views and circumstances of employers more deeply. Both require more than cursory expertise and effort. But they also promise to be rich sources of information and assistance as employment specialists and agencies strive to maintain a close and productive relationship with business partners. Getting to know the employer customer is the basis on which any kind of marketing activity is built. Chapter 10 details a host of marketing strategies that we have gleaned from our experience and from taking direct cues from our employer partners.

ting
pective
ver Customers

*...er needs and wants and then match it to what
...o get people to buy what you are selling.*

MARKETING MAXIM

Marketing involves two primary aspects: making sure that people know you exist and letting people know that your products and services are worthwhile. When a company has a commodity (i.e., products and/or services) to sell, it typically advertises its features, its cost, and its availability, as well as ways prospective customers can obtain it. Otherwise, the targeted customers have no idea that the commodity exists. Indeed, it may as well be nonexistent. Hence, if there is no market, there is no customer. Similarly, if a company does not communicate the value of its products, no one will buy them. No value, no customer.

In focus groups we have conducted with employers, we have sometimes asked the question "What are barriers to hiring workers with disabilities?" The typical answers, to our surprise, have not been issues of expense of accommodations, negative attitudes, or even discomfort. Most often, the barriers are related to not knowing how to find such applicants (Fabian, Luecking, & Tilson, 1995). This is an obvious indication that marketing disability employment services could use some improvement. The business community is largely unaware of such programs. There is also no doubt that the marketing message could use improvement. Marketing that is solely based on selling disability often inad-

147

vertently devalues job seekers and their competencies. This chapter provides strategies for marketing to improve the visibility of employment specialists and employment agencies in the business community and strategies to improve the marketing message to communicate value to prospective employer customers.

AVOIDING MARKETING MISTAKES

Too often the message sent to employers from employment agencies is about the human service missions of these agencies. Consider these marketing slogans and phrases sampled from actual agency marketing brochures that are currently in use to attract employers:

- "Helping people with disabilities enter the mainstream"
- "Maximizing the independence of people with disabilities"
- "Working to make a better life for people with disabilities"

As marketing messages, these phrases are not much more effective than the "Hire the Handicapped" slogans of past decades. They may communicate an effective message to individuals with disabilities who may want to use the services of the agency, but they miss the mark as messages to employers. They do not communicate anything of potential value to the employer.

The message about disability employment services should be delivered frequently, consistently, and in a way that communicates value. And the message should be derived and delivered based on what employers want and need, not on what you are trying to sell. Thus, phrases such as "innovative staffing resources," "meeting the human resource needs of employers since 1990," and "delivering human resource management services" resonate more with businesses than those that emphasize the service to people with disabilities. This is not to say that mention of disability should be avoided. It just should not be the primary basis on which the relationship is established. The message should feature the competency of the agency, the job seekers it represents, and the potential benefits employers can expect from the agency's service. A host of strategies deliver such messages and enable agencies to develop broad employer markets for their services.

PROACTIVE MARKETING

Chapter 9 introduces the importance of knowing the employer customer and offers strategies to gain that knowledge. Such activities are the first step in proactively inserting yourself into the world of employers and businesses. Once employment specialists and employment agencies begin to think in terms of how to convert the features of their service into benefits for the employer customer, marketing has begun to take shape. The following strategies are ways to build a proactive approach to marketing to employers.

Strategy 1: Conduct an Image Audit

Often, when disability employment agencies have any public image at all, that image reflects a pervasively human service orientation (DiLeo & Langton, 1993). That is not likely to appeal to employer needs. To see what kind of an image your organization might project, an image audit might be helpful. DiLeo and Langton suggested that employment specialists ask themselves and their colleagues a number of questions:

- Does the name of your service convey a business orientation? Names like Hope Center or acronyms like CARE convey an unmistakable image of charity and are not likely to give employers the impression that you have anything of value to offer their enterprise. Also, if the agency has a name that immediately identifies a particular disability, the image conveyed is not one that is business oriented. If either of these applies, consider at least changing the name of the employment service associated with the agency.
- Do job titles reflect a business orientation? "Employment specialist," "employer representative," or simply "associate" suggest a more professional, business-like image than do "job coach," "community facilitator," "rehabilitation specialist," or similar job titles.
- Are marketing materials and business cards professional and business-like? (See also Strategy 2.)
- Do the organization and its staff have a professional look? Dress, grooming, and behavior all leave important impressions.

If any of these items yields a "no" answer, then your organization is creating an image in the business community that is neutral at best. Quite likely, your organization may be portraying itself as one that is a poor match for business needs and is not likely to be taken seriously by business. An organizational name that sounds like a charity, shoddy marketing materials, poorly dressed and groomed staff—any one of these are likely to make employers do everything possible to avoid contact. All of the other marketing strategies in this section will be rendered minimally effective if a good first impression is not made. The old maxim applies: "You never get a second chance to make a good first impression." It might be time to renovate your agency's image: new name for the service, new job titles for the staff, new marketing materials (see also Strategy 3), and a new professional dress code.

Strategy 2: Be on the Lookout for Coffee Stains

Image is also often affected by any encounter a prospective customer has with a company. What do you think of a company whose sales clerks ignore you, a business whose service technician does not return telephone calls, or a restaurant that is late with your order? Business marketing experts call any customer encounter that that ends up leaving a distinctly bad impression a *negative moment of truth.* Tom Peters (1987), the well-known guru of business excellence, wrote that when a passenger boards a plane and pulls down a broken tray table covered with coffee stains, his or her immediate reaction is to question the quality of any aspect of the airline's operation, including the mechanical maintenance of the plane's engine. Peters thought that every service provider must identify their own existing and potential coffee stains, those factors that can negatively affect customers' opinions of an entire organization.

The same principle applies to employment agencies and their work with employer customers. There are many potential coffee stains to be avoided. Consider the following:

- After establishing contact with an employer, an employment specialist sends out brochure materials that are badly copied and misspells the contact's name in the cover letter.
- An employer calls the employment agency on a regular business day. The telephone rings and rings. Someone forgot to connect the answering machine.
- After visiting a construction site, an employment specialist goes to the corporate headquarters of a large company wearing muddy boots.
- An employment specialist shows up 30 minutes late for an appointment with a busy human resources director.

Any of these scenarios can result in creating a negative image for the employment service. Preventing coffee stains such as these helps build an image of quality that will help market the organization's services to employers.

Strategy 3: Develop and Use Professional Marketing Materials

Given the ease and relatively low cost of contemporary desktop publishing, employment agencies should have professional-looking materials to distribute to employers. Such materials are useful in introducing employers to your service and are often an important part of making a good initial impression. Some tips for creating marketing materials are:

- Use promotional material used by other businesses as models

- Avoid human services or employment service jargon such as "supported employment," "work adjustment training," "rehabilitation services," and so forth
- Use language and images that appeal to a business audience. Get reactions to draft materials from business advisors before finalizing the design and content

Poor or shoddy marketing materials are coffee stains. They make you look bad. Conversely, professional looking and sounding materials create an impression of quality and professionalism that will be attractive to any prospective employer customer.

Strategy 4: Study and Define the Market

Much of the activity described in Chapter 9 provides a means for studying the needs of employer customers. The next step is to define the market you want to target for your marketing efforts. Starting with particular market segments is often a fruitful base from which to grow the market. Do you want to pursue employers in a particular market segment, such as manufacturing, health care, or finance? Or would you like to work with employers in a particular geographical area, such as a quadrant of the city near public transportation or close to areas of commerce? Or do you plan to target only certain types of employer contacts, such as human resource managers or small business owners?

In any case, it is best to begin marketing from a small, well-defined base of activity. Trying to blanket the world with marketing activity will not have the penetrating effect that more targeted marketing will yield. One of our colleagues made it her plan to become well known by a group of human resources professionals. She first met with a friend who was a member of a local organization of human resources managers. She asked if she could audit a luncheon meeting. There she met several representative from local companies with whom she made follow-up informational visits at their companies. She also offered to make a presentation at a future meeting about the new placement program with which she was affiliated. Eventually, her contacts within this group grew to the point where she regularly received job announcements from more than two dozen companies. All of her contacts from this group became warm contacts. Not surprisingly, she had a very high success rate in helping job seekers obtain jobs.

Similarly, another colleague developed close relationships within several companies in the health care field by following a marketing plan that included making informational visits to every health care–related operation in her community: two local hospitals, several assisted living facilities, a physical therapy clinic, and many other health-related companies. By focusing on a defined market segment, you can expand your depth of knowledge and range of contacts, making all subsequent marketing more effective.

ACTIVE MARKETING STRATEGIES

Once you have established a unified look for your marketing efforts, crafted supporting professional materials, conscientiously taken steps to develop positive and competent images for the employer public, and defined and planned for a market segment, it is time to go out there and make the contacts that will result in employers gladly and frequently using your agency as a resource for meeting hiring needs. The following strategies have their origins in business marketing literature (e.g., Fox, 2000; Kotler, 2003; Levinson, 1993; Salzman, 2003) and from our own experience (Fabian, Luecking, & Tilson, 1994). All are adaptable for job development marketing and have been used in many different circumstances by our colleagues.

Strategy 5: Consider Your Business Card a Marketing Tool

The business card is a standard item for most business people. It is easily distributed and relatively inexpensive to produce. Most important, it provides your contact with basic information that they need about you: your name, your affiliation, your address and telephone numbers, and your e-mail address. Widely distributed, business cards can be one of the most readily available and easy to distribute marketing tools. Use them liberally!

Just as good conversation is characterized by interactive dialogue, an exchange of business cards is a gesture of communication. There are many occasions, both formal and informal, when business cards can be distributed to potential contacts. One technique is to write a brief note on your business card to remind the recipient of your initial interaction. This notation may subsequently jog the recipient's memory so that he or she remembers why he or she should contact you. Similarly, you may write a notation on a business card that you have received reminding you of when and why you should re-establish contact: "Met 6/23 at Chamber of Commerce breakfast. Has contacts for clerical positions."

Strategy 6: Develop an Elevator Speech

Can you explain your service concisely and compellingly enough to get your message across to a stranger in the time it takes to ride an elevator a few floors? If not, you need an elevator speech. This is a simply a way of being able to interest people in what you do during a brief, spontaneous encounter, such as during an elevator ride or at a Chamber of Commerce mixer. If you can catch the attention of a potential customer quickly, you have the chance to follow up with another contact. Here are a few examples:

- "We work with a variety of industries to refer them good job candidates. Our job seekers undergo a vigorous process to get them ready for job interviews. I've been at this for a number of years and love it when a good match is made!"

- "My organization, Preferred Placements, has worked closely with a number of our community's companies to improve their employee recruitment. If your company or anyone you know needs workers, I'd be glad to meet and explain our service."

Craft one that you feel comfortable with, explains your agency's service, and doesn't cause people's eyes to glaze over in disinterest. The fact that you represent job seekers with disabilities can be introduced or added to the encounter. If you get a response such as "it must be *so* rewarding," you have given the wrong impression. This is part of one good elevator speech we've heard: "Many of the people we represent require accommodations because of disabilities. What we are really good at is helping match their skills to an employer's needs and implementing accommodations that make them and their co-workers very productive." This communicates competence rather than human service charity.

Strategy 7: Use Past Partners as References

Nothing works better than the testimonial of a satisfied customer. People with whom you have had successful partnerships in the past will almost always be willing to provide references to your new contacts on your behalf. These references can be used in several ways. It can be as simple as identifying them or their company as a reference on agency materials (with their permission, of course). They could be given as a reference to call, or they can give a testimonial quote that can be used in marketing materials. They can also agree to contact a prospective employer on your behalf. In any case, references help deliver a marketing message that you have satisfied customers and they are willing to tell others about it.

Strategy 8: Turn Contacts into Prospects, Prospects into Customers

Given the importance of an ever-expanding network in the job search (see Chapter 5), it makes marketing sense to establish a large cadre of contacts. One goal should be to make as many people in the targeted market as possible aware of your service. Once people are aware of the service, an occasion may arise to turn them into prospects by having closer interaction, such as an initial appointment for a meeting. These interactions will eventually lead to these individuals becoming people who directly use your services: hiring a job seeker you represent.

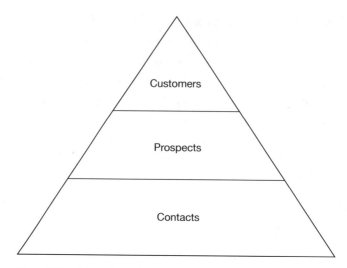

Figure 10.1. A larger base of contacts equals more job opportunities.

The universe of possible contacts is huge. Literally, it is anyone who comes to hear about you or your agency. Those contacts that become prospects are a smaller group, limited to the time and occasion you have to directly meet them. Prospects who become customers are a smaller group still because, of course, matching the needs of particular employer customers with individual job seekers will narrow the field. The operative perspective, however, is that the larger the base of contacts, the more opportunities you will have to find employers to use your service. This applies to any market segment you might want to target (see Strategy 4), and it applies to any broad marketing in which you engage. The more people you know, the more opportunity to cultivate a new customer. A schematic representation of this phenomenon is depicted in the pyramid chart in Figure 10.1.

Consider this scenario. An employment specialist meets a bank manager at a social function. They exchange business cards after discussing their respective lines of work. Thus a contact is made. The bank manager is someone on the list of people the employment specialist knows. A few days later, the employment specialist calls the bank manager to ask for an informational interview so that she can learn more about what the bank looks for in new tellers. The bank manager has become a prospect. If there are openings or human resources needs that the job developer can help meet, the bank manager will become a customer by hiring a job seeker represented by the employment specialist. In order to yield eventual customers, an employment specialist will always need a large group of contacts because the ratio of contacts to customers will always be largely in favor of contacts. Thus, a variation on the old adage is created: It's not just who you know but also how many people you know. The larger the base of contacts, the larger the top of the pyramid will be.

Strategy 9: Coordinate with Your Colleagues and Keep Track of Your Contacts

There are three reasons why coordinating with colleagues and keeping track of your contacts are important. First, as you roll out your marketing activities, it makes sense to divide the contacts into areas that are assigned to the organization's employment specialists in such a way that the targeted market is covered. Second, coordinating marketing contacts ensures that the same employer is not contacted by more than one employment specialist from the same agency, thus avoiding a coffee stain. Third, by establishing an internal system to regularly record and disseminate information on each employer contact and the status of each contact, all staff members have access to information on prospective employers that may be relevant for individual job seekers. This expands the number of contacts for all staff.

Strategy 10: Use Business Letters as Marketing Tools

Employment specialists can enhance their professional image and cultivate their contacts by adopting a habit of sending individual letters to employers. There are three tailor-made occasions for sending such letters:

1. As cover letters for marketing materials
2. To thank contacts for their time
3. To reiterate in writing an exchange that may have taken place verbally

Succinct business letters sent in conjunction with promotional materials to targeted employers is a good way to establish professional contacts. Business letters in combination with face-to-face meetings or telephone conversations can be extremely influential to prospective customers. Many successful employment specialists maintain a template that can be personalized for each occasion, saving time and making the activity relatively effortless. Three rules of thumb are 1) keep the letters to no more than two short paragraphs, 2) make sure they are grammatically correct and contain accurate spelling, and 3) end with clear next steps, such as "I look forward to calling you next week," "I will contact you if I have a candidate for future positions," or "Please contact me if I can be of any further assistance."

Strategy 11: Stay in Touch with Contacts

Even when good first impressions are made, people can easily forget about you as time passes and new priorities arise. Therefore, it is useful to maintain regular communication with contacts. Regular newsletters sent to employer customers are often used to keep an organization's name and service in front of prospective customers. Such newsletters can be either printed or sent electronically through e-mail Listservs. Another easy way to stay in touch is to develop a tickler file, which reminds you to call contacts after various intervals to find out whether their hiring needs have changed or to see if they have new circumstances for which they can use your services.

Strategy 12: Build Credit with your Business Partners

This simply refers to performing favors for employers that will create a lasting impression and a desire to reciprocate. For example, an employment specialist learns about an opening from an employer. The employment specialist does not know a candidate who could fill the job but puts the employer in touch with another organization that does. Not only is this good service, but it often creates a situation in which the employer feels that he or she owes the employment specialist. The likelihood increases that the employer will hire job seekers represented by the employment specialist. Examples of other credit-building activities include providing free training on interviewing accommodations, marketing presentations (see also Strategy 13), or even patronizing the company's business by trading there. One employment specialist, after making a marketing visit to the owner of a dry cleaning business in her neighborhood, decided to take her laundry there on a regular basis. She struck up a friendly customer relationship with the owner and when the store needed a new customer service associate, the owner hired a candidate represented by the employment specialist.

Strategy 13: Conduct Marketing Presentations

Often new contacts, prospects, and customers can be developed through invitations to seminars or similar events to which you invite targeted company representatives to learn about available services. This is especially useful in a tight labor market, when employers are having difficulty filling positions. They are inclined to come to seminars that promise to educate them about how to tap into new sources of employees. Such events are effective if they are brief (i.e., under 1 hour), informative, and professionally conducted.

Strategy 14: Ask for the Sale

All of the previous strategies are not very helpful if you do not know how to close the deal. This can be the bane of employment specialists unless they can become comfortable being direct with a prospective employer customer. Phrases such as these help, depending on the situation:

- [The job seeker] and I would welcome the opportunity to meet with you. Is there a convenient time?
- After reviewing our services, do you think you company would be interested in working with us?
- How does [the job seeker] compare with other applicants you have interviewed?
- I'd like to contact you next week. When would be a good time to call?
- How well did [the job seeker's] interview go? Is there anything I can help you with to evaluate her qualifications?
- When can I call you again?

Top-of-Mind Visibility

All of these strategies help maintain what business marketers refer to as *top-of-mind visibility* (Levinson, 1999), causing a targeted customer group to think first of a particular product or service. For example, what comes to mind when you think of fast food, luxury cars, appliances, or cameras? There are probably a few companies that come immediately to mind for each of these examples. These companies have made a concerted effort to make their products and services well-known to the public through consistent marketing. This is top-of-mind visibility.

A major goal of employment specialists and employment agencies should be to capitalize on the concept of top-of-mind visibility. You want employers to have your services come immediately to mind when they are thinking about hiring or when they have a particular human resource need. This is done by building strong relationships with employers, by providing excellent customer service (see Chapter 12), and by establishing a posture of high visibility in the local community.

SUMMARY

Assisting people with disabilities in obtaining employment necessarily requires thoughtful and dynamic marketing of the employment services of agencies and programs that represent job seekers with disabilities. In the past, such marketing has often been characterized by well-intentioned but ineffective appeals to the business community that have failed to recognize that, first and foremost, marketing is about finding out what employers need and want, not trying to get them to buy what we are selling. Thus, marketing that relies solely on selling employers on hiring people with disabilities is mostly misguided.

Business literature is replete with marketing concepts, ideas, and strategies. Unfortunately, marketing literature for the field of job development for people with disabilities is markedly scarce. However, it is easy—and productive—to incorporate and adapt business marketing strategies for this field. This chapter demonstrates several of the most time-honored and easily adapted strategies. All of these strategies have roots in conventional business marketing strategies, which are based on 1) getting the word out that a service exists and gaining top-of-mind visibility and 2) communicating that the service is worthwhile and that there is something of value to be obtained from contact with the agency or program.

11

Customer-Driven, Customized Job Matches

MESHING JOB SEEKER CHARACTERISTICS WITH EMPLOYER NEEDS

The deepest craving of humans is the need to be appreciated.

WILLIAM JAMES

Success is not the key to happiness. Happiness is the key to success. If you love what you are doing, you will be successful.

ALBERT SCHWEITZER

After becoming acquainted with both customers of the employment process, job seekers and employers, the true test of your effectiveness comes next: how do you bring these players together? Traditionally, this is called *job development and placement.* Typically, a job seeker with a disability or other life barrier comes to an intermediary and goes through an intake and evaluation process. From there, an employment specialist does most of the footwork in identifying job possibilities and makes the arrangements for the job seeker to meet employers. In many cases, the job seeker plays a very passive role in getting the job. Unfortunately, this model of job development does very little to empower the job seeker to take ownership of her or his career development. And all too often, when this approach is used, the job seeker feels no vested interest in the job obtained, which likely leads to dissatisfaction for both the new employee and the employer. When this happens, the employment specialist then is forced to spend substantial amounts of time and resources in fixing the problems. This chapter presents an alternative approach: customer-driven, customized job matching. Using this approach, the employment specialist helps to broker the relationship between a job seeker and potential employer, ensuring that both parties are essentially in the driver's seat.

DEVELOPING AND IMPLEMENTING A CUSTOMIZED JOB SEARCH PLAN

Because each job seeker has unique life circumstances and goals, it makes sense that the approach to helping each individual should be customized. If you intended to take an overseas vacation, you would probably develop a customized plan of action. People develop customized plans of action for weddings, choosing a college, buying a house, and any number of other life events that call for some forethought and organization. Surprisingly, many career books note that all too often people give little thought or planning to their career development—they plunge into job opportunities in a haphazard manner, with little regard for the goodness of fit between the job they obtain and their attributes, life dreams, and goals. A customized job search plan promotes a goodness of fit. Consider it a job procuring campaign that is tailored to the individual's positive personal profile. Although each campaign or plan will be unique, it will likely fall into the following three primary categories.

- An autonomous and independent approach, with or without consultation from an intermediary
- A semi-independent approach, with intermediary coaching from the sidelines
- A team wrap-around approach, with considerable assistance from an intermediary

The Autonomous Job Search Plan

Not all of the job seekers who seek job search assistance will need to have extensive, direct interventions. Once you assist them in developing their positive personal profiles, all you may have to do is suggest resources through which they can explore job leads and make employer contacts. Although you would make yourself available for consultation as needed, this job seeker would do the footwork of preparing a résumé, making contacts in the community, conducting research on employers, conducting informational interviews, completing employment applications, interviewing, negotiating terms of employment, and so forth.

The Semi-Independent Job Search Plan

In other situations, after you have helped a job seeker develop a positive personal profile, you and the job seeker may determine that there will be a need for considerable direct support from you during some or all of the job searching and obtaining process. How, when, and what supports are provided will all depend on the individual's circumstances. And in all cases, the job seeker should be shouldering the primary workload of his or her job search. After all, any job the job seeker obtains will belong to him or her, not you.

The Team Wrap-Around Job Search Plan

Once you have helped a job seeker develop his or her positive personal profile, it may become apparent that he or she will need extensive supports throughout the entire process of searching for a job, getting it, and keeping it. Here is where a team can come together to build a *team wrap-around plan.* The goal is not for one employment specialist to assume the entire responsibility of providing employment support but to pull together a network of supporters, including other professionals and significant people in the job seeker's life.

JOB MATCH TYPES

Just as each job seeker's job search plan and need for support will vary from person to person, the types of job matches achieved will be unique. There are four primary categories of job match:

1. Match to well-defined job description
2. Match to modified job description
3. Customized job match through an employment proposal
4. Entrepreneurships

Each of these job match types is described in the following sections, using the job seeker case studies from the appendix to Chapter 8 to illustrate the concepts.

Match to Well-Defined Job Description

Many job seekers with a disability or other life barriers can obtain and be successful in positions that are clear and well-defined in a given job description, as announced or posted by an employer. In this case, the job seeker's profile is an excellent match with the specific job characteristics and expectations defined by the employer. In this situation, you are likely to achieve a match to a well-defined job description.

Jay   Recall Jay, the 35-year-old former inmate with artistic and mechanical talents (see p. 127). An employment specialist first spent time talking with him and observing him build one of his sculptures. The specialist also arranged for him to take a battery of formal career assessments and occupational interest surveys. He also completed an informal learning style checklist. In addition, the employment specialist asked him questions about the skills he used in conducting his criminal activity (disarming high-tech alarm systems and stealing expensive cars). All of this information was incorporated into Jay's positive personal profile.

Jay's life and career dreams and goals are "to get a decent job that pays the bills and gives me health benefits, doing something where I can use my artistic abilities and eye–hand coordination. Where I can be around people some of the time but get to work independently. I don't want to have to be on all the time for customers." He also said he'd like to earn his graduate equivalency diploma, get a motorcycle, and eventually bike around the entire United States.

Besides his natural artistic talents, the employment specialist was able to pinpoint Jay's uncanny ability to think on his feet and his fine motor dexterity, combined with his keen eye for detail. His skills and knowledge are extensive: electronics, metal work, and use of small tools, to name a few. His two dominant learning styles are visual-spatial and intrapersonal. Most of Jay's interest areas came as no surprise: art, cars, tattoos, and body piercing; however, a few other interests emerged: classic blues music, Zen meditation, listening to historical novels on audiotape, pets, and teaching art to others. Reading his criminal record would have given a one-dimensional impression of Jay's personality. In getting to know him and talking with others about him, the employment specialist was able to identify many positive personality traits: Jay is friendly and has an engaging demeanor. He is a hard-worker, and he is modest and self-effacing with a dry sense of humor and infectious laugh. He is also empathic and very forthcoming about his shortcomings.

Jay's temperament might be characterized as easy-going and laid back. He is soft spoken. It takes a great deal to get him riled up. His values fall under the "live and let live" category. The things he values most are creating objects of beauty that are fully appreciated and enjoyed by others. He says he would welcome an opportunity to teach teenagers some of the skills he has. Ideally, Jay wants to work in a casual setting where he can dress the way he wants to and "not catch grief" for his tattoos and body piercings.

After much discussion, Jay and the employment specialist agreed that he would be well-served by a work environment that is informal and relaxed, with people who are open-minded and who appreciate Jay for his good qualities. He also agreed that the ideal boss would be someone who communicates clearly what she or he wants and then lets Jay have autonomy in getting the job done. Jay's life and work experiences form a rather jumbled picture: he has had many part-time jobs, both in and out of jail, and can point to an extensive portfolio of photographs of his artwork, along with clippings from art show reviews of his work.

Jay's support system is rather weak. He has few friends that he stays in touch with and no significant other, and he is estranged from his parents and siblings. As support, he has a strong sense of self-reliance and a parole officer who encourages him and has put him in touch with the local One-Stop Career Center. In addition, the employment specialist suggested he keep in contact with some of the people who have purchased his artwork.

There were a number of specific challenges that Jay faced in his life that were likely to affect his job search and ultimately his employment success: his illiteracy due to his dyslexia; no high school diploma; his criminal record; a spotty employment history; no formal postsecondary skill training, certification, or trade license; his choice of dress and general appearance; and his asthma. With him, the employment specialist addressed each of these issues and brainstormed possible solutions or accommodations:

1. Illiteracy and lack of high school diploma: Jay could enroll in the adult education night school program and work towards his general equivalency diploma, with assistance from a reading specialist through student services for individuals with disabilities. He could find a volunteer tutor. He could also communicate to others how his reading deficit does not hinder his ability to perform the essential functions of the types of work he is interested in and capable of doing.

2. Criminal record: He had several options open to him:
    *   Write on the job application, "I will discuss this further during the interview."
    *   Enter the code number of the crime.
    *   Write, "See attached." Attach a sealed envelope containing disposition papers, with the following written on the envelope: "To the attention of human resources only."

    This latter strategy would demonstrate to employers that as an applicant with a criminal record, Jay is able to approach a difficult subject professionally. The employment specialist also encouraged Jay to develop a network of friends and acquaintances who could get to know him for his talents and positive attributes and develop a rapport over time so that he could talk candidly and openly about his past. His parole officer also recommended that he attend a support group for ex-offenders, where employers are frequently guest speakers and mentors.

3. Spotty employment history and no formal postsecondary training: Jay developed a functional résumé, one that would highlight his skills and downplay the chronology of his past jobs. He also polished up his art portfolio. Regarding his educational level, Jay joked that he would tell employers he had a "degree from the school of hard knocks." He agreed that it was best to seek out jobs that would not require a diploma and that he would inform prospective employers that he was enrolled in night school. Once again, the employment specialist discussed the value of his establishing a network of contacts who could get to know his talents and advocate for him.

4. Choice of dress and appearance: Because Jay had made it clear that he was not willing to alter his style of dress, remove the multiple rings in his face, or hide his tattoos, he agreed with the employment specialist that this meant he would have to seek out employers who were willing to accept his appearance. Jay seemed well aware of the challenge this might pose to his job search.

5. Health concerns: Jay's asthma apparently worsened during his last stint in prison. Medical staff were able to find a prescription inhaler that was effective. The only problem was that this medication is extremely expensive and Jay lacks health insurance. The employment specialist was able to get him declared "a charity case" at a local hospital, and they have kept him in supply of his medication. The hope was that ultimately Jay would find a full-time position with health benefits. The worse-case scenario would be that he might be eligible for social services or disability-related medical benefits.

While the employment specialist was helping Jay develop his positive personal profile, he also recorded possibilities and ideas that came to him during various discussions. For example, some of his ideas were to:

- Contact the local art league to see if they need a teacher
- Sell his sculptures at local open markets and via the Internet
- Talk to companies that create and install alarm systems for luxury cars
- Set up an informal exhibit and get press coverage
- Volunteer to be a guest presenter in high school art classes
- Design tattoos and body jewelry
- Design and sell jewelry

This list grew substantially as Jay and the employment specialist progressed through the profile, and Jay actually followed up on some of the activities. The next step was to jointly develop an individualized job search plan for Jay. Being a gregarious and confident person, Jay felt optimistic that he could represent himself to employers without the employment specialist's direct involvement. Behind the scenes, the employment specialist helped him to develop his résumé and make his portfolio look more professional. He was referred to a local support and networking group composed of ex-offenders. At one of those meetings, Jay met a stockbroker who had volunteered as a mentor.

One thing led to another, and the stockbroker introduced Jay to his friends at a local yacht club, many of whom purchased Jay's artwork. One of his art patrons got to know Jay and told him the club was going to be hiring a company that installs electronic alarm systems on luxury boats. Knowing Jay's background, he felt that Jay would have an insider's perspective in the trade. He arranged for Jay to interview with the security company. Jay was hired on the condition that Jay's friend at the club would have him bonded. Jay subsequently worked for the security company for 1 year, 30 hours per week with medical benefits. During that time, he became fascinated with boats, learned how to work on engines, and started his own business. Between income from his job as a ship's machinist and sales of his artwork, Jay makes a comfortable living and is able to purchase his own health insurance. He has purchased a motorcycle but says with a laugh, "I'm too busy working to go on vacation. Maybe some day."

This is a detailed example of one job seeker who was able to find a job match with a set job description in spite of having a disability and a number of significant life barriers, including a criminal record. It also shows the extensive initial consultation that was provided by the employment specialist, although Jay was able to represent himself to employers independently.

Match to Modified Job Description

In another case, you and the job seeker may determine that an employer's job description does not match the job seeker's profile perfectly; however, the job seeker definitely has some of the skills and qualifications desired by the employer. You may agree that this is the time to work toward a match to a modified job description.

Eric   As with Jay, an employment specialist worked with Eric, his family, and others who knew him well to develop a positive personal profile that would provide a departure point for his job search. Eric has a lot of positive attributes and is very interested in the travel industry (see p. 124). In fact, his fondest desire is to work for a travel agency. He has a very supportive family and lives semi-independently in a group home. He met the employment specialist he works with in a dish room of a local hospital; his co-workers are people with disabilities. Eric worked there for a number of years and was eager to find another job. He faced a number of specific challenges, such as health and mental health issues and poor stamina (he can only work for 3 hours at a time and then has to take a nap; when overly tired or stressed, he is prone to having severe seizures); he has significant mood swings and tends to take even the slightest criticism personally; and instead of having a high school diploma, he has a certificate of attendance from a special education program.

In collaborating with Eric and his support network, the employment specialist agreed that his job search plan should incorporate numerous opportunities for him to make contacts throughout the local travel and tourism industry, including travel agencies, transportation companies, resort hotels, and the local amusement park. Part of Eric's job search plan involved keeping a log of all of his contacts, something Eric came to enjoy a great deal because he already kept extensive files on the international tourism trade as a hobby. It was imperative that his needs for accommodation be addressed up front. The most important issues were his health and stamina. Everyone agreed that Eric seemed to disengage after 3 hours of focusing on any task, whether a physical task such as washing dishes in the hospital or a mental task such as being engrossed in his favorite leisure activities. This appeared to indicate a possible need for adjusting his medications. However, after extensive medical evaluation and attention, it was finally decided that Eric's current medication was the most effective and that he would need to find work that would allow him 3-hour shifts. Regarding his well-known mood swings, the employment specialist discovered they were much less likely to occur when he was engaged in his preferred leisure activities. His most frequent emotional outbursts were reported on his hospital job. The typical punishment for this behavior was to send him home and dock his pay, which was not much of a deterrent. His family finally allowed him to quit his job in order to devote more hours to his job search.

Eric wanted business cards of his own, so the employment specialist helped him design his. He gave himself the title "Travel Consultant." The employment specialist also devised a combination résumé and press release for Eric, which highlighted his unique hobby and the transferable skills he demonstrated in the pursuit of this hobby. Anyone who found the article interesting was asked to disseminate it and to let their contacts know that Eric was looking for a part-time job as an assistant somewhere in the travel and tourism industry. This unconventional approach was quite intentional: The employment specialist knew that in spite of his skills and positive attributes, it was unlikely that Eric would be able to sell himself using the traditional job search route. Why shouldn't he try to sell himself in a nontraditional manner? This approach paid off. While participating in a Chamber of Commerce special event, one of the employment specialist's colleagues became acquainted with a mid-level manager of a large resort hotel. She told the manager about Eric and gave him his press release. Several days later, she received a call asking if she thought Eric could handle the concierge desk at the hotel, responding to guest requests for local sightseeing spots and restaurants. The hotel was seeking two part-time workers. Upon visiting the hotel and discussing the position, it was decided that Eric would be best suited to the least busy shift, in the morning. In learning more about the job, it was also decided that Eric might have difficulty handling more than one customer at one time or answering the phone while with a customer. When she discovered that the hotel had a tough time keeping brochures, maps, and other printed material on hand and organized, the employment specialist suggested this would be a good task for Eric to do as an assistant to the concierge. She assisted them in developing a modified job description. The human resources contact for the hotel met Eric and had him demonstrate how he would do the job. Then she made him an offer. He is now working 15 hours per week, with a salary of $7.00 per hour, and he loves his job.

This was an example of a job match to a modified position description. The company was willing to make changes in their job description, and considerable support from the employment specialist was provided to both Eric and his employer.

Cindy   Another example of a job match to a modified position description occurred for Cindy. Cindy wanted to work for a large company, wear nice clothes to a fancy office building, use a computer, and "work with fun people" (see p. 125). In spite of many detractors who claimed that her physical disabilities were just too serious for her to achieve such lofty goals, Cindy and her mother persevered in their quest. Again, the first major task was to help Cindy develop her positive personal profile. This took some time because Cindy's physical, verbal, and medical challenges were extensive and required a concerted team effort to identify effective accommodations. The team was undaunted in drawing out Cindy's many positive attributes and decided that with certain adaptive computer equipment, Cindy was capable of doing data entry and using a high-tech communication device that could speak for her.

With technological accommodations, Cindy could do very accurate data entry, although it would be at a slow pace. At the same time, it was highly unlikely that Cindy would be able to fit right into a job description or opening, as advertised by an employer. So the employment specialist started by using her (and Cindy's family's) personal and professional networks to identify big companies (with nice offices) that might have a slew of records to be entered into the computer, where accuracy, not time and deadlines, were of major importance.

Demonstrating once again that networking is an essential factor in any job search, the employment specialist met a friend of a friend who knew somebody at a large multi-national research and consulting firm. It turned out this company had just won a federal contract to re-analyze raw data that had been collected several years before. They were looking for data entry clerks and statisticians. Upon review of the data entry clerk job description, it appeared that Cindy had the skills to perform half of the tasks listed. The employment specialist came back to the team, and together it was decided it was worth presenting Cindy as a candidate and suggesting some modifications to the job description.

Upon meeting Cindy, the company representatives were clearly mesmerized by her smile, her ability to use her adaptive equipment, and her eagerness to demonstrate her skills. After the meeting, the employment specialist outlined her ideas for modifying the job description. They agreed to hire Cindy for 30 hours per week, with an hourly salary slightly below the salary given to the other data entry clerks (because she had less responsibility). However, at the end of the probationary period, she was given a raise, due to her productivity and overall contribution to her workplace.

It is important to note that a substantial level of time, energy, and creativity was required to make this job match a reality. However, the return on investment of effort was significant for Cindy and her employer with this match to a modified job description.

Customized Job Match through Employment Proposal

Let's say you have helped someone develop a positive personal profile and in the process you have both agreed that it might be extremely difficult, or just not desirable, for this job seeker to obtain a job with a predetermined, set description or to apply for a job opening using the traditional channels and methods. This does not mean the job seeker is unemployable, only that previous experience, skill development, need for accommodation—or any number of other factors—present the need to look for a job with a particular niche in a company. This is likely to be a situation in which a customized job match through an employment proposal is in order.

Veronica   Revisit Veronica's positive personal profile (see p. 118). Here is a young woman who, in spite of significant barriers caused by her disability and life situation, has a burning desire to make something of herself. Consider her gift for making people feel welcome and appreciated. She has remarkable visual discrimination skills and the ability to focus on small visual details for extensive periods of time. She is a very hard worker, when given tasks that she can do and enjoys. The goal involved searching out work environments that were friendly and that had many tasks that would capitalize on Veronica's visual detail orientation.

Not exactly sure where to begin, the employment specialist began researching local companies, as described in Chapter 9. The employment specialist made an informational site visit to a new company, Forecast, Inc., and came away from his tour with a wealth of ideas and possibilities.

Forecast is a rising star among high-technology corporations. Established in 1995, the corporation has around 1,500 employees. The company's primary objective is to act as a server for the delivery of any kind of software application a customer might need. For instance, a customer (another company) may want all of its employees to use specific database software that is continually upgraded. Rather than the customer having to invest in its own network and software installation—and go to the expense of trouble-shooting and upgrading—Forecast provides up-to-date software, feeding it to the customer from a Forecast satellite office housing a state-of-the-art mainframe computer and digital relay. Forecast runs a highly secure operation to ensure that hackers cannot invade the customer's system. Forecast's employees ascertain the customer needs, identify appropriate software, train the customer on software usage, and provide upgraded software as it comes on the market. The customer pays Forecast a monthly service fee.

Forecast's customers also include public school systems, mid-size local banks, nonprofit organizations, and small businesses. They include engineering and architecture firms; law offices; web designers; and other companies working in the industries of arts and entertainment, media, software design, medical facilities, agriculture, and manufacturing and retail.

The employment specialist visited the company's high-security computer facility, where he observed staff monitoring multicolored security codes on gigantic video screens. Several employees mentioned that tracking the lighted blips and configurations could get very tedious. One said, "Believe me, they start to look alike after a while. This is a burnout job."

Another task observed was the manufacturing of electronic identification badges. This is a multistep process that includes photography, scanning, programming of digital codes, and production of microchips that are then all assembled in ordinary-looking badges. In discussing the process with one of the managers, our colleague discovered that there are numerous lower-level tasks requiring excellent manual dexterity. The engineers were constantly griping about the busy work that seems to take up substantial portions of their day, especially the sorting of components and maintaining ample supplies.

Developing a Task List   Following this site visit, the employment specialist put together a list of the specific tasks that needed to be performed on the site, particularly those tasks that were cumbersome for current staff or for which the company seemed short-handed. Some of the tasks included the following:

- Monitor the codes on the tracer board
- Inform security manager of discrepancies in the lighted signals
- Stock and replenish component parts for security badges
- Assemble badges in preparation for programming by engineers
- Maintain clean assembly area

Identifying a Potential Candidate   Although there were no posted job openings for this branch of Forecast, it was clear that there were some challenges within the operation that the employment specialist might be able to assist them in solving. During discussions the employment specialist had with colleagues, someone immediately thought of Veronica as a great candidate. Her skills matched beautifully the tasks on the task list.

Preparing the Proposal   The employment specialist decided to combine a proposal with a thank-you letter to her point of contact at Forecast (Figure 11.1).

Outcome of the Proposal   As stated in the letter, the employment specialist followed up the letter with a telephone call. It turns out her proposal letter had caught the attention of a few people at Forecast. Intrigued, they asked her to come in with Veronica. As a result, Veronica was offered a 25-hour-per-week position as a security assistant (a position and title Forecast created for her), making $15 per hour. In negotiating for the position to be probationary, the employment specialist, the employer, and Veronica agreed to a performance review and salary renegotiation scheduled for 1 month later.

Rosita   Rosita's positive personal profile outlines numerous strengths and characteristics that would be desirable to employers. The challenge is that her stated goal is to become an actress, and most employment specialists would be stymied at how to help her realize this dream, because the *Occupational Outlook Handbook* cites the grim realities: Most working actors, if they are fortunate enough to find acting jobs, are perpetually looking for work and make poverty-level wages. Also, there is the concern that Rosita's Down syndrome would limit her options for roles in a business that puts much stock in physical perfection.

In exploring professional theater companies in Rosita's community, the employment specialist learned that most of them are nonprofit organizations that operate on very tight budgets. Most of the paid staff fulfill several roles and have theater, business management, or finance degrees. Much of the work is carried out by temporary employees, seasonal workers, college interns, and volunteers. Given that Rosita has demonstrated strong

March 20, 2005

Mr. Steven Botchie
Manager of Human Resources
Security Division
Forecast, Inc.
7533 Carroll Avenue
Trenton, New Jersey 08609

Dear Steve:

Greeting and recap

It was a pleasure meeting you last Monday. I greatly appreciate the time you took giving me such a thorough tour of your headquarters, not to mention your arranging for me to visit the security division. That is truly an amazing operation. Thank you also for the opportunity to give you and your colleagues information about our company, TransCen, and the services we offer companies such as yours.

What you observed:

Potential benefits of your services

During my visit with Kate Forbes and her colleagues, it seemed that there were two major discussion items: 1) a concern over the shortage of engineers to manufacture the security badges and 2) errors due to fatigue on the part of the personnel monitoring the tracer board. Once the processes were explained to me, I realized that many of the basic tasks might be undertaken by assistants to the engineers and the security staff, which would greatly free up your engineers to focus on the highly technical aspects of their jobs and provide more frequent breaks for the security staff. TransCen could be a resource for you in addressing these needs.

Match applicant skills to specific tasks:

Request a meeting

I currently represent a job candidate named Veronica Dee Mayfield whom I'd like you to meet. Although Ms. Mayfield has had limited work experience, I can vouch for her dynamic personality and her tremendous desire to work for a company such as Forecast. I believe Ms. Mayfield is well-qualified to perform the following:

- Monitor the codes on the tracer board as a relief worker
- Inform security manager of discrepancies in the lighted signals
- Stock and replenish component parts for security badges
- Assemble badges in preparation for programming by engineers
- Maintain a clean assembly area

Further benefits

In the event you hire Ms. Mayfield, as with all of the job candidates we represent, Forecast would receive any necessary supports from TransCen in accommodating this qualified applicant—at no cost to your organization.

Next steps and closing

Steve, I look forward to discussing this proposal with you and arranging for you to meet Ms. Mayfield. I will call you next week. In the meantime, please do not hesitate to call me at 300-555-3535. My email address is Pamela.Jones@tci.com.

Once again, thank you.

Sincerely,

Pamela Jones
Recruitment Specialist

enclosure: Résumé for Veronica Dee Mayfield
cc: Veronica Dee Mayfield

Figure 11.1.   A sample thank-you letter.

administrative support skills, has a winning personality, and is determined to work in a theater-related environment, the employment specialist opted to use the customized job match through an employment proposal approach.

Based on Rosita's positive personal profile, the employment specialist helped her develop a functional résumé. She then identified all of the theater companies in her town and made a plan to visit each of them, for information gathering. After visiting six different theater companies with Rosita, the employment specialist learned that they have in common some challenges (e.g., tight budgets, overworked and low-paid staff). One of the largest theaters has several unique challenges. First of all, it has a huge costume shop, with costumes from every historic period, every size, and every type of show. To generate additional revenue, the theater rents out costumes to other theaters in town and across the country, as well as to individuals for costume parties and special events. All of the costumes are cataloged. Tracking the rental transactions has become an overwhelming chore, and the staff at the theater are instituting a new computer system, which will entail entering voluminous amounts of data. They are currently paying a temporary employment agency to handle this and a number of other administrative tasks, such as assembling press kits, photocopying contracts, and inserting handbills into programs. The one full-time office manager is working 60 hours per week. The employment specialist took careful note of these and other needs she observed and created a task list.

It was determined that Rosita was highly qualified to perform the array of assignments on the task list, so the employment specialist next estimated the amount of time these tasks might take up during a week's time—anywhere from 20 to 50 hours per week. After doing a bit of sleuthing to find out typical hourly wages for temp workers and office assistants and using minimum wage as a base salary, the employment specialist proposed to the theater that they hire Rosita for 25 hours per week at a starting salary of $7.50 per hour to perform critical tasks that are now costing the theater $15 per hour for up to 50 hours per week. A 1-month trial employment period was proposed, after which time the theater would be under no obligation to continue Rosita's employment. However, should the theater feel that Rosita's contributions to the work team were of sufficient value to keep her on as an employee, it was agreed that the employment specialist would help Rosita renegotiate her hours and salary. Furthermore, the employment specialist explained that she would be available to offer whatever supports were needed to both Rosita and the theater staff.

The theater was surprised by the employment proposal; it had never received one before, and it was currently in a hiring freeze. Nonetheless, the staff were impressed with the planning that went into the proposal and the extent to which the employment specialist was willing to learn about their operations, expectations, needs, and constraints. To top it off, doing the math showed them that this was also a significant potential budget saver.

The employment proposal was accepted, Rosita was hired for a month, and she was subsequently offered an ongoing position with the understanding that her hours might fluctuate slightly due to seasonal conditions. She has become part of the theater family, gets to see all of the shows for free, is getting some experience in the costume design department, and is in a free acting class. As far as she is concerned, "I'm living my dream!"

Advantages of an Employment Proposal

First and foremost this approach does two things: It capitalizes on the specific talents of a job seeker, and it meets specific and clear needs of the target employer. There is no vagueness in the job description or major upheaval in the company due to provision of accommodation for the worker. Certainly there are drawbacks, chief among them the substantial time it take to research the company, to develop and present the proposal, and to do the follow-up. However, job development using the more traditional methods still requires extensive amounts of time and energy. The advantages of creating an employment proposal far outweigh the disadvantages. On top of that, employers really get to see you at your best: as a bona fide business problem-solver who "can find the need and fill it" (Nemko, Edwards, & Edwards, 1998, p. 290).

This approach is forthright, timely, and proactive. Although it may not work every time, the act itself of preparing and making the proposal really impresses employers. If they do not feel in a position to accept the proposal, submitting a proposal still establishes your credibility as a viable business partner. In some cases, an initial approach may pay off later and when openings come up, the companies may contact you for applicants. The steps to developing an employer proposal, along with some other sample task lists, are summarized in Tables 11.1 and 11.2.

Table 11.1.   Steps for developing an employment proposal

Visit company sites

Observe the environment and several jobs within the site

Identify all major tasks for each job

Order the tasks from most complex to least complex

Identify essential tasks from each job that could be reassigned to capitalize on the skills of the job seeker you represent, while maximizing the employer's resources

Combine tasks across different jobs

Determine reasonable time and wage to conduct these tasks

Prepare and submit a concise and professional proposal

- Up front: Request employment for a specific candidate
- Highlight skills of the candidate
- Explain your role as an accommodation specialist
- Outline the benefits to the company
- Explain how you will follow up

Follow up

Table 11.2.   Sample task lists

Business	Position	Area or department	Tasks
Book store	Office assistant	Human resources	Collating new hire information packets Entering name, address, or salary changes Distributing paychecks Responding to résumés submitted for openings Filing or shredding personnel information
		Marketing department	Sending out review copies of new books Sorting and tabulating results of research projects Collating press kits Faxing press releases
		Accounting department	Logging and photocopying accounts received Mailing billing statements Shredding budget information
		Office management	Taking inventory of office supplies Restocking printers and photocopiers Sorting and delivering incoming mail, faxes, and packages Picking up or delivering artwork or other routine errands Cleaning conference rooms and kitchen areas Metering outgoing mail
		Shipping and receiving	Processing invoices and requests for product information Taking inventory of backstock Filing invoices Maintaining the database of vendors and contracts

Retail clothing store	Sales assistant	Stockroom	Processing merchandise
			  Sizing
			  Attaching security devices
			  Stripping packaging and shipping materials off of clothing
			  Hanging clothes
			  Pricing stock
			  Sizing and organizing backstock
			Collecting hangers from store floor and sorting
			Organizing and cleaning the stockroom
			Returning unpurchased hold items to the sales floor or stockroom
			Steaming clothing

		Sales floor	Straightening and sizing racks and tables Marking down clearance items Assisting customers Cleaning and stocking cashwrap Cleaning mirrors, displays, and windows Vacuuming and edging the sales floor and fitting rooms Restocking

Specialty bakery and café	Kitchen assistant	Kitchen	Food preparation
			  Washing lettuce
			  Smashing avocados
			  Doing basic set-up for sandwiches
			  Slicing tomatoes
			  Mixing cream cheese spreads and other simple recipes
			  Destemming pepperoncinis
			Making salads
			Setting up or stocking the salad bar
			Dishwashing
			Putting cookies, bagels, and breads on trays for baking
			Sweeping and mopping
			Restocking soda coolers
			Rotating stock and produce in walk-in refrigerators

Entrepreneurships

Some people are born to be entrepreneurs. They have unique skills and talents that enable them to create and provide services and products for which there is a market. In other words, there are people out there who are definitely interested in purchasing the types of products and services the entrepreneur has to offer. Entrepreneurs are often thought of as self-made individuals, people who have started their own businesses and have created great wealth for themselves. This is certainly possible. However, in most cases, there are entrepreneurs who have been very successful at earning a modest, but satisfying, living by using their unique attributes. You may find yourself representing a job seeker whose positive personal profile indicates that he or she would be a good candidate for this type of job match. Keep in mind that starting and maintaining a small business, even a sole proprietorship (in which the entrepreneur has no other employees but him- or herself) takes a great deal of hard work and perseverance. Most people are not experts in small business start-ups, but there are numerous resources out there (e.g., Griffin & Hammis, 2003). Some other good resources include Richard Bolles' *What Color is Your Parachute?* series and Laurence Boldt's *Zen and the Art of Making a Living* (1999). Many other books are available to individuals considering starting their own businesses.

Julius   Julius is a 50-year-old man of many talents, interests, and dreams but no paid work experiences (see p. 122). He has significant challenges posed by his disability and isolation in a small town. When the employment specialist got to know Julius and helped him develop his positive personal profile, many ideas were generated that seemed to suggest an entrepreneurial approach: self-publishing his books of poetry; teaming up with an artist to develop a line of inspirational greeting cards; designing book marks; consulting with hotels, restaurants, and theaters on how to make their businesses more comfortable for people with severe physical disabilities; doing Internet research; writing human interest articles on daily life for people with disabilities; and motivational speaking, to name a few. Julius is currently writing a book about his life, which he thinks would make a good screenplay. He has created a network of people who are championing his work and putting him in contact with publishers and other entrepreneurs. Although he has not earned much more than $1,000 from his ventures at this point, he feels hopeful. "It's a lot better than sitting in a day care center for adults. And not too bad for a senior citizen," he jokes through his communication device.

Trace   Like Julius, Trace has considerable skill, knowledge, and many positive attributes (see p. 122). Unlike Julius, he has had many work experiences and life experiences that could be applied to a work setting. Trace's first employment goal when the employment specialist met him was to find a full-time job that paid health benefits, in the areas of teaching (physics and math), aircraft mechanics, meteorology, or any other occupation that would let him use his skills in electronics. He made an exhaustive search of companies and organizations in these fields, all within a 50-mile radius of his home in a very rural region. In the process, he met many people and was able to expand his professional network. He also had a chance to see first hand a wide variety of work environments and was then able to evaluate those settings in terms of their match to his temperament and personality.

Unfortunately, after 6 months of exploration, putting in applications, and even going through a number of interviews, Trace was unable to find a position. The employment specialist's next step was to try the employment proposal route. This was a valuable exercise because in the process of gathering employer data, developing task lists, and reviewing Trace's skills, goals, and needs for accommodation, Trace came to the conclusion that "If I had my druthers, I'd just as soon spend most of my time at home. Don't mind driving but people just don't go the speed limit and it's stressful. Maybe I could just drive some of the time." Because Trace has proven himself to be an excellent physics and math teacher (for those students who are serious about the subjects), the employment specialist suggested he open up a tutoring business that caters primarily to high school students eager to pass advance courses to get into top colleges and professionals going back to college. The employment specialist and Trace investigated several nationally recognized private tutoring companies and determined that Trace could charge (and receive) a very hefty hourly rate. With very little trouble, he would stand to earn his target salary of $30,000 per year. Because his wife was no longer working due to health problems, she could be his business manager and marketer. They could then afford to buy their own health insurance or investigate joining in a consortium with other self-employed people. Running this type of a business would afford Trace the privacy he enjoys, time to pursue his many hobbies (including flying), and an opportunity to use and be appreciated for his skills without having to deal on a daily basis with people who think his idiosyncrasies are a major deficit.

JOB MATCHING FOR CAREER GROWTH AND JOB SATISFACTION

Consider how unique the approaches were for each of the job seekers in these case studies. Some of them were able to find and secure good job matches through traditional search methods; others needed unconventional approaches. Several of them, with just the slightest coaching from the sidelines, were capable of navigating the process quite independently, while others needed significant direct assistance each step of the way. What all of them have in common is the desire to apply their talents and to earn a living doing so. And all of them started the process by developing comprehensive positive personal profiles. From there, individualized job search plans were launched: outlining tasks, deadlines, expectations, and responsibilities of the job seekers, as well as those of the people assisting them. The employment specialists remained wide open to possibilities and opportunities and continually generated new ideas. Once the job seeker secured a position, employment specialists made sure that the new employees (and their supervisors and co-workers) were able to navigate the initial stages of salary negotiations, orientation, and training.

Ultimately, a good job match should result in mutual satisfaction for the job seeker and the employer. Job and career satisfaction are subjective; the employee and the employer will determine whether they are satisfied with the employment arrangement. However, there are things that employment specialists can do to increase the likelihood of customers' satisfaction:

1. Facilitate and guide a strong job match. Often dissatisfaction arises because the employment outcome was not a good fit from the start. Taking the time to find a good fit is likely to pay off later.
2. Know the indicators of satisfaction and be able to read them (see Chapter 12).
3. Be prepared to offer the right kinds of support, at the right times, to the right people.

Indicators of career satisfaction include such things as:

- Expressed satisfaction with career and quality of life (see Table 11.3)
- Achievement of career goals
- Ample opportunity to use strengths and skills
- Continued self-improvement through education and work
- Success in obtaining and holding jobs
- Economic self-sufficiency

These factors will give all players in the employment equation evidence that an employee is finding satisfaction in his or her work. Employment agencies that operate "place and run" outfits will not be very successful. It is important to be concerned with the long-term career development and advancement of the people with disabilities and other life barriers whom you serve. As you continue the dialogue with these customers, ask them the types of questions in Table 11.3.

Help your job seeker customers to build mentor networks for ongoing support and guidance and to seek out people at work and in the community who can help them with various aspects of their lives (i.e., job, career, community, social/interpersonal relationships, and recreation). After all, quality of life is usually defined as a balance of all of these aspects of a person's life. And just as the opportunity to work can influence one's happiness in other life arenas, satisfaction in those other life domains can significantly influence the level of satisfaction one feels toward a job and ultimately a career.

Sample Customer Service Questionnaire for Job Seekers

1. How would you rate our services overall?

   1 - Excellent   2 - Good   3 - Not very good   4 - Poor

   Suggestions/Comments:

2. How would you rate your job developer's willingness to listen to and respond to your interests and needs?

   1 - Excellent   2 - Good   3 - Not very good   4 - Poor

   Suggestions/Comments:

3. How would you rate your job developer's willingness to take care of any special concerns you had?

   1 - Excellent   2 - Good   3 - Not very good   4 - Poor

   Suggestions/Comments

4. What part of our services was most important to you?

5. What part of our services was least important to you?

6. What changes should we make to improve our services?

7. Would you recommend our services to other job seekers?

                    Yes   No

   Why or why not?

8. Would you use our services again?

                    Yes   No

   Why or why not?

9. Other comments:

Thank you for taking the time to share your thoughts with us.

Figure 11.2. Sample customer service questionnaire for job seekers.

Table 11.3.   More clues to career advancement

Have you added value to the workplace (in comparison with peers)?

Do suppliers and customers like what you do?

Do you have long-term career goals and specific strategies to achieve them?

Have you received any promotions (e.g., higher level tasks, a raise, more benefits, more hours, bonuses, recognition)?

Are you actively upgrading your skills and learning new skills on the job?

Have you offered up suggestions for improving the way the company does business and have those suggestions been taken up?

Do co-workers and bosses seek you out for your expertise?

Are you getting to try new tasks?

Do most co-workers like you?

Do you have any co-workers who have become friends outside of work?

Do you volunteer to take on new tasks and projects?

Do people outside of your work area or department know you and your skills?

Do you ask for feedback? Do you change your behavior because of feedback?

Have you created a community network in case you need to look for a new job?

Do you have portable skills (i.e., skills that will transfer from one setting to another)?

Do you receive above average to excellent performance appraisals?

SUMMARY

The focus of this chapter has been on the job search process and strategies for achieving job matches that genuinely meet the needs and expectations of both job seeker and employer. We present a number of methods and ideas for customizing the job search plan. This customized approach is based on each job seeker's unique positive personal profile and the unique requirements of the individual workplaces. Matches can be achieved in several ways: 1) match to well-defined job description, 2) match to modified job description, 3) customized job through employment proposal, or 4) entrepreneurship. Case studies illustrate these concepts in action.

12

Quality Service and Customer Satisfaction in Job Development and Business Partnerships

Delivery of outstanding customer service is the most effective marketing tool.

JAY LEVINSON

Since the days of my dad's root beer stand, a guiding principle of Marriott has been total commitment to customer service. Our reputation in the hospitality industry and our business success would not have been possible without it.

RICHARD E. MARRIOTT

Successful business enterprises know that keeping the customer is just as important as attracting the customer. Ensuring customer satisfaction is central to marketing success in any field. Building a solid base of satisfied, repeat customers leads to an enduring market share for any business. The success of such business giants as Marriott illustrates this point. The same principle is true in job development. After all, it is a service business—service to the job seeker and to the employers.

Business partners of employment specialists and disability employment services are attracted by high-quality and effective marketing, and they remain partners only as long as they are on the receiving end of good, solid service. Negative perceptions and lost customers are the consequences of inferior services and products. If an employer partner feels neglected, mistreated, or manipulated, he or she is likely not only to cease the relationship but also to tell others. Conversely, if customers are pleased with an agency and its services, they will be inclined to boast to others about these services. This chapter presents basic customer service techniques for employer customers that yield enduring employer relationships. They are adapted from the business world (e.g., Connellan & Zemke, 1993; Gitomer, 1998; Zemke & Anderson, 2002) and from our and our colleagues' experiences (Fabian et al., 1994). This chapter also presents ways to measure and improve customer and service satisfaction.

SERVICE AND SATISFACTION

Think of the last time that you were a customer. What were your expectations? What stands out in your mind about the customer service you received? Do you recall the service being: a) fantastic, b) quite acceptable, c) fair, d) poor, or e) downright horrible? From a customer's perspective, you can identify what pleased or displeased you. You can readily pinpoint the precise action (or inaction) that caused your pleasure or displeasure. Whether customer service is viewed as being fantastic, downright horrible, or somewhere in between is influenced by the individual customer's perspective. Customer service is thus difficult to define because it is a subjective concept. Also, there are obviously degrees of satisfaction.

Although it is a subjective phenomenon, satisfaction can be measured by formal customer surveys, informal discussions, and correspondence rating pleasure or displeasure with services provided. Most important, however, satisfaction can be measured by the degree to which customers disseminate positive information about services. In general, people are satisfied when the products or services they receive benefit them—or are perceived to benefit them—in some distinct way, however large or small. And they are willing to share that experience.

Customer service involves the full range of activities that begins with the provider's attitude and progresses through development, marketing, delivery, follow-up, and evaluation of the service. Implementation and maintenance of high-quality services thus occurs through one continuous feedback loop, as illustrated in Figure 12.1.

Tom Peters (1982), the world-renowned co-author (with R. Waterman) of the business classic *In Search of Excellence* and author of a number of best-selling management books, thought that even customers who receive unsatisfactory outcomes may become satisfied customers if they feel that they have been treated with courtesy, respect, and a genuine attitude of helpfulness. Peters (1993) expanded on this notion, saying that it is not simply a question of satisfying the customer. Although that may be adequate to help a business to stay relatively productive, it will not propel that business to prosperity. Businesses must "delight, thrill, and dazzle" customers. The message to employment specialists is that basic competence is required, but outstanding performance is what customers appreciate, remember, and ultimately publicize.

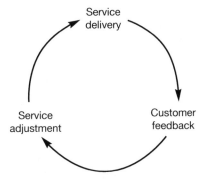

Figure 12.1. Feedback loop of implementation and maintenance of service quality.

As shown in Figure 12.2, Connellan and Zemke (1993) represented customer service excellence and retention with a customer service grid that illustrates the likely results of good and bad customer service processes (how it is delivered) and outcomes (what is delivered). Even if customers are fairly satisfied with the process of a service encounter and the outcome meets their expectations, the risk for retaining customers still exists because someone else can come along and dazzle them with a wonderful process and add value to the encounter so that the customers get more than expected. The key, then, is not only to convince employer customers that your services meet their unique needs but also to give customers the impression—based on observable, tangible results—that your services are the best services presently available. Persuading an employer to commit to using your service by hiring a job seeker you represent may seem like the goal, but it is really just a beginning. Delivering promised services in a timely, convenient, effective, and value-added way so that the employer remains satisfied is in fact the ultimate goal.

		Customer Retention		
Outcome	(1) Value added	At risk	Loyal	Advocate
	(2) Expectations met	Searching	At risk	Loyal
	(3) Expectations not met	Gone	Searching	At risk
		(C) Dissatisfied	(B) Satisfied	(A) Dazzled
		Process		

Figure 12.2. Likely results of customer service processes and outcomes. (*Source:* Connellan & Zemke, 1993.)

STRATEGIES TO FACILITATE
CUSTOMER SERVICE AND SATISFACTION

A host of techniques are available that generate customer satisfaction and loyalty among employer customers of employment services for people with disabilities. They are highlighted here, along with examples of how they have been implemented in job development practice. Many of them create basic, solid foundations for long-standing partnerships with employers. Others may result in employer customers being "delighted, thrilled, and dazzled." All of them offer immediate opportunities to improve and expand job development initiatives.

Strategy 1: Adopt a Customer Service Mentality

It is easy to tell when certain companies wholly embrace customer service and satisfaction. The way staff answer the phone, the helpfulness exhibited by everyone associated with the organization, the delivery of just what you wanted are all clear examples of how customer service permeates the company's culture. Such companies have adopted a customer service mentality by making it a part of their entire structure to honor and serve their customers. They customize their service so that each customer feels special and appreciated. In most cases, the result is a successful, thriving business.

Embracing such a mentality is likewise critical to operating a successful, thriving employment service. A sincere desire to please the employer customer should drive the activities of the employment specialist and the employment service organization. Such a mentality is necessarily grounded in 1) a strong belief in the job seeker ("I represent a good service with a good product"), 2) an attitude that anything is possible ("Whatever I can do to help!), and 3) a commitment to customers' needs ("Let me know what you need"). In high-performing organizations, strategies to achieve customer satisfaction are widely adopted in an employment service organization and permeate all staff training. Customer service delivered by staff is rewarded and customer satisfaction is celebrated. This way, customer service is always on the minds of everyone associated with the employment agency.

Adopting a customer service mentality also requires developing the ability to see you and your service through the lens of the employer customer. Simply ask yourself, "If I were an employer, how would what I am doing look?" Employment specialists and employment service agencies that continually perform such self-examination create a mentality in which customers' needs and perspectives drive their work and the following strategies are implemented as a matter of course.

Strategy 2: Customize Your Services

More and more organizations, representing an array of job seekers and job seeker categories, are competing for employer attention. With increased competition and greater service choice for employer customers, employment specialists and employment service agencies must be able to respond uniquely to each employer's human resources needs in order to set themselves apart from the competition. Employment specialists must therefore provide flexible service, as well as shift and modify services to meet the needs of the employer customer.

Tips for customizing service to employers include:

- Be ready to adjust appointment or work times to meet the employer's circumstances, especially if such times are after ordinary work hours for your agency
- Provide the follow-up that the employer wants, for as long as the employer wants it, not just what funding regulations call for
- Follow whatever screening and hiring procedures the employer wants. Some employers want applicants from an employment agency to follow standard company procedures, and others want them specially adapted.
- Define and deliver your service in ways that make the most sense for individual employers. Terminology such as *transitional employment, supported employment, job coaching,* and *work adjustment* are foreign and irrelevant to most employers. Use terminology and characterize your assistance in terms that communicate that the employer is a customer, rather than another human service agency.
- If the employer wants and needs something that you cannot deliver, link the employer with another service that can. For example, if an employer has a job opening that you cannot fill with a job seeker you represent, offer to contact other agencies to see if they might fill be able to fill it. This is akin to building credit with employers (see also Chapter 10), but in this context, it is a way of giving a customer what he or she wants.

Strategy 3: Respond Quickly

The quickest way to give a positive customer service impression is to be ready to immediately offer assistance when a customer needs it or asks for it. Conversely, there is nothing more annoying to a customer than to have to wait for a service or product long after it is expected. It is equally as annoying to have to wait for a response when things go wrong with a product or service and you cannot find someone to help you promptly. Thus, a quick response time can mean the difference between making or losing a sale and keeping or losing a customer.

Often, human service organizations are notorious for slow responses, not the kind of slow response that comes from careful study and concern with quality but the kind that comes from complacency or a "business as usual" mentality. However, employment specialists and employment service agencies can perform many activities to make rapid response time a defining feature of their employment services in the eyes of employer customers. Consider these examples:

- Return telephone calls and e-mail messages before the end of the business day or within 24 hours, at the latest. When you call someone right back, he or she usually expresses real surprise and appreciation, each of which is a great impression-builder. It makes people feel that they are important to you.
- Respond quickly to correspondence, by the next business day if possible.
- Confirm appointments 1 day ahead of time. This communicates that you respect the customer's time and also provides an opportunity to quickly prepare for any additional requests the employer might make in advance of a meeting. For example, the employer might ask if you can come at a different time or for additional time. Having made the call allows you to respond accordingly and quickly.
- Respond immediately in cases of emergencies or pressing situations. Such responses communicate a concern for the circumstances of the employer customer and may in fact make the difference between keeping and losing that customer. Our colleagues have been in more than one situation when some event at a worksite prompted an employer to call for help with a situation related to an employee we support. Fast responses have saved many relationships with employer customers, especially when coupled with additional service (see also Strategy 4).

Strategy 4: Identify Silk Ties

In any business, mistakes will inevitably occur. Even the finest companies have experienced foul-ups resulting in customer dissatisfaction. Some examples include late room service at a hotel, the wrong merchandise delivered, late delivery of ordered merchandise, an inexperienced sales clerk giving wrong information—the list is endless. The key to mitigating the situation is to turn a mistake into an opportunity.

Most customers tend to have a higher tolerance for mistakes if there is a timely and genuine response that communicates that the situation will be addressed. Attending to the problem immediately and encouraging feedback from dissatisfied customers are essential customer service activities. In fact, often the customer frequently knows exactly what the solution might be to fix the problem, but even in situations where this is not the case, identifying how the problem can at least be addressed and then coupling that action with a service that adds value to the encounter breeds strong customer loyalty. This added value is often important because even fixing the immediate problem is not always sufficient to make the customer happy. Innovative companies will therefore deliver extra customer service, what Tom Peters (1987) called "silk tie incentives" (p. 110).

In a frequently told encounter that Peters originally reported, a businessman was in need of a new suit. At the advice of his wife, a devotee of Nordstrom department store, he went to Nordstrom to buy the suit. After picking out a suit he liked, he requested that necessary alterations be made before he left on a business trip that afternoon. Returning later in the day, he learned that the alterations were not completed as promised. Annoyed, he left for his trip. The next day at his hotel, the front desk worker called him to pick up a package. By overnight delivery, Nordstrom had shipped a box that contained not only his new suit but also two matching, complimentary silk ties that he had not ordered. The stories he heard about Nordstrom's legendary customer service were confirmed. Where do you think he bought his next suit?

What is instructive about this story is that there was both a quick response to correct a customer service problem and something extra to make up for the mistake—in effect letting the businessman know that the company cared about his business. The silk tie, then, is an analogy for anything that adds value to a problematic customer service encounter and that fosters customer satisfaction. In employment service programs, there are a number of potential silk tie moments and potential silk ties to address that moment:

- A job seeker fails to show up for a scheduled interview. You ensure that apologies are provided and arrange for complimentary lunch for the hiring manager at a local restaurant.
- A job candidate has a bad day during his first week on the job. You show up the next day with a dozen donuts for co-workers.
- A printing company hired one of the job seekers you represent, and she took longer than you expected to learn the job. You arrange to have your agency's brochures printed at that company.
- A job candidate that you accompany to an interview accidentally breaks a lamp in the reception area. You offer to replace the lamp and have it delivered.

The list of occasions where one must correct an inadvertent customer service error or problem is endless. The list of potential silk ties is also endless. Innovative and effective employment specialists will have them ready. The reward is likely to be intensely loyal customers at best and at the least, people you do not have to hide from when you see them again.

Strategy 5: Solicit Complaints

Human nature being what it is, most of us do everything we can to avoid negative experiences, including complaints from others. However, complaining customers are often valuable assets to employment specialists. The premise is simple: A customer complains because he or she honestly believes that you can do something to take care of a problem.

Handling a complaint causes three things to happen: 1) you learn that a customer is unhappy, which is better than having an unhappy customer you do not know about, 2) you can do something about it to appease that customer, and 3) you can prevent it from happening again.

A well-handled complaint often breeds more customer loyalty than existed before the complaint (Peters, 1987). It is far better to have an angry customer turn into a happy one than to have an angry customer just go away. Dissatisfied customers are also likely to tell lots of other people about the encounter, so it should be a regular order of business to ask customers to tell you what they do not like. Opinion cards in a hotel room asking for feedback on the service are really a way for the hotel to get customers to tell them what is wrong with the service so that the problem can be corrected for that customer and all future customers. It is a way to solicit complaints. Several ways to encourage employer customer feedback and complaints include:

- Establishing a clear organization policy whereby you are open to receiving feedback from any customer, regardless of the customer or the circumstances
- Providing a number of ways by which customers can give feedback (e.g., telephone, e-mails, interviews, surveys). See the next section on measuring customer satisfaction.
- Encouraging customers to complain immediately when they are displeased or concerned
- Listening! Do not argue or be defensive. Ask for or offer solutions to fix the problem. Nobody ever wins an argument with customers. Even if you know the customer is wrong, make him or her feel that he or she is right. Sometimes a complaining customer just wants to be heard.
- Making sure that under no circumstances are employers' concerns or complaints ignored or minimized. Doing so is delivering a message that you do not care about them as customers. You might as well forget them because they will not likely do business with you again and they are likely to tell others not to do business with you.

Strategy 6: Convert Basic Competence into Outstanding Performance

Average service is likely to keep people interested only as long as it takes to find someone else who can deliver outstanding service, as illustrated in the customer service matrix in the previous section. Mere competence may suffice, but as funds grow tight and job seekers exercise more individual choice of service providers, professionals and agencies that demonstrate excellence will be the winners. Think of outstanding job development performance in terms of four levels of Peters' (1987) total product concept:

- *Level I: The generic product.* The generic product is a perhaps useful but very basic service. Many employment agencies deliver the generic product to employer customers. They help them hire job seekers the agencies represent.

- *Level II: Expected service.* Expected service occurs when employment specialists or agencies operate ethically and match job candidates with appropriate job tasks. This is better than merely placing someone with an employer, but it is still a minimal, or merely expected, level of service.
- *Level III: Augmented service.* With augmented service, the employment specialist is not only matching the job seeker to job tasks but also providing extra assistance from time to time, such as checking in to see if help is needed with teaching the employee new job tasks even though the case is inactive.
- *Level IV: Potential service.* Many employment specialists are able to deliver services that are well beyond expectations so that the employer comes to rely on the specialist to help in other areas, such as participating in interviewing candidates not represented by the specialist or helping design general interviewing protocol.

Outstanding performance rarely goes unrecognized by employer customers. In fact, it is those outstanding performers who are able to develop the kinds of partnerships that both thrive and endure. One of our colleagues helped a store manager devise an interviewing procedure for stock clerk applicants who did not speak English well. This was definitely not required, but her competence delivered a service that resulted in the store manager, and others in the chain, hiring many of her job seekers over the years. (See Chapter 6 for an expansion of this example.)

Strategy 7: Treat Colleagues as Customers

Teamwork makes the best organizations function. It therefore makes sense that teamwork is fostered in the same way customers are courted—by providing mutual assistance, adding value to the team, responding to the needs of team members, and so forth. Conversely, colleagues are unlikely to treat customers especially well if they are not also treated well. Coming late to meetings, refusing to help because you are too busy, and not responding to colleagues' e-mails are just a few examples of failure to model and reinforce the same kind of service to internal customers (i.e., colleagues) that is necessary to deliver to external customers (i.e., job seekers and employers) for ultimate job development success. In fact some business writers advocate that the customer comes second: Until staff are treated well, they will not treat external customers well (Rosenbluth & Peters, 1992).

Examples of customer service to colleagues include:

- Covering for a colleague at a job site who has an emergency to attend to at another job site
- Sending a thank-you note to a colleague who covers for you or treating him or her to a lunch

- Responding to telephone and e-mail messages from colleagues in the same business day
- Passing on to colleagues job leads from employers you have met
- Giving a colleague a ride when transportation is not available to him or her
- Dropping everything to help a colleague who must address an emergency at a job site

The list is really endless. All that is really required is to be thoughtful and helpful.

Strategy 8: Celebrate Customer Service Successes

It is useful to organize agency activities so that customer service successes are celebrated and reinforced. Again, this is modeling internally what is desired for external customer service. Three easy ways to do this include 1) having a regular staff meeting agenda item for sharing examples of excellent customer service delivered by colleagues, 2) publicly displaying examples of outstanding customer service (e.g., we have a "Wall of Fame" where we display framed letters from satisfied customers), and 3) making regular notations in staff personnel files when compliments on service provided by individual staff members are received.

Strategy 9: Listen to Your Customers (and Keep Listening!)

An old sales adage says that one should spend 20% of the time talking to the customer and 80% of the time listening to the customer. By tuning into what employers say about their needs, high-performing employment specialists can deliver the service that employers want and need. One of our colleagues heard an employer say that he did not have any job openings, but he really wished he could get one of his departments to finish its reports faster. The employment specialist could have thanked the employer for his time and left. Instead, he asked if he could observe the department for a short time. The observation led to a suggestion by the employment specialist that reports would be processed more quickly if one person was assigned to copy and distribute the drafts for review. Eventually, this process was adopted and a job seeker represented by the employment specialist was hired for just that task. Processing time for reports was cut in half.

Another colleague was told by an employer that one of the individuals she hired was not getting the job done fast enough. She wanted to know how she could better prompt him for faster performance. The employment specialist could have gone to the worksite and provided more training and coaching to the employee. Instead, she heard correctly that the *employer* wanted to learn how to prompt the employee. Therefore, the employment specialist spent time teaching the employer how to deliver the prompts. Performance improved as a result. The employment specialist listened first, then acted.

Strategy 10: Underpromise and Overdeliver!

The true hallmark of outstanding customer services is when the customer receives more than what was promised. Consider the car dealership that not only makes the repair on your car but completes the repairs before they were promised *and* washes and waxes your car. You get more than promised or expected. Of course, you are likely to maintain a customer relationship with that car dealership. The same principle applies to relationships with employers. It should go without saying that you deliver what you promise. If you do not, you have lost the confidence and trust of the employer. But to deliver more than promised is to cement the relationship for the long term. Here are some examples:

- A person with slow keyboarding speed due to a mobility disability was assisted to enter data faster by using macros on her computer. Her employment specialist arranged for the same macros to be installed on the computers of the employee's coworkers so that they all worked faster.
- In helping restructure task assignments to accommodate a worker with a cognitive disability, an employment specialist helped the employer discover a more productive way to get work done in the entire department.
- After helping a company hire an individual he represents, an employment specialist offers to help the company's human resources director advertise additional openings to other employment agencies.
- An employment specialist stops by a company's office just to bring cookies for the coworkers of an employee she helped the company hire.
- An employment specialist gives each employer that hires a job seeker he represents a coffee mug with the employment agency's logo on it.

The gesture does not have to be grand or significant. It only matters that the customer gets more than is expected. This communicates that the employer has the clear interest, respect, and thoughtfulness of the employment specialist. This strategy is probably one of the most important to implement—it is customer service at its most effective, especially in a field that has often been guilty of overpromising and underdelivering. It is usually easy and inexpensive. Most important, it creates a lasting customer service impression, as illustrated in Table 12.1.

Table 12.1. Outcomes of levels of promise and delivery

	Deliver low	Deliver high
Promise low	So who cares?	I can't believe this is so good! (Customer tells 5 people.)
Promise high	This is a nightmare! (Customer tells 15 people.)	Keep it up!

MEASURING CUSTOMER SATISFACTION

Customer satisfaction—how well an organization's (or product's) performance meets the customer's expectations—is an important indicator of organizational success. Everyone in the employment service business is also in the customer service business. Whether you are operating as an individual employment specialist or as a member of an employment agency's team, continuously measuring customer satisfaction helps to:

- View your services through the eyes of your customers (both job seekers and employers)
- Understand your customers' perceptions of you and your organization's ability to address their needs and wants
- Learn whether your services meet your customers' expectations
- Learn what you are doing well and what improvements should be made in your services or processes
- Instill a customer-centered approach throughout the organization
- Prioritize quality improvement efforts

Sound decisions about how services are delivered to customers should be based on clear data, and gathering the right data means using the right measuring sticks. Also, measuring your efforts and outcomes should be an integral part of your work. It should be woven into everything you do to ensure customized and effective service to employer (and job seeker) customers. Before investing time, money, or effort in developing an organization's overall strategy for service improvement, it is important to revisit what your customers want and expect. Then, it is a matter of clarifying how well you are meeting—or exceeding—those expectations. Customer service measurement strategies determine how you gather this important information.

Some key questions to ask internally before conducting customer satisfaction measures are:

- What information do you want to get from your customers?
- What will you do with the information?
- How do you determine what your customers want, need, and expect?
- Have you demonstrated flexibility in meeting these demands?
- How easy do you make it for your customers to do business with you?

The following strategies are ways to not only get answers to these questions, but are guiding activities to map out customer service strategies.

Five Steps for Improving Your Measurement Efforts

Measuring customer satisfaction should be viewed as more than a one-time or periodic exercise to give yourself a pat on the back. Rather, this activity should be integrated into organizational processes and the findings used continuously to improve services and processes. The following steps are ways to improve customer service measurement efforts.

Step 1: Assess Your Current Customer Satisfaction Activities   Think about your current efforts to measure customer satisfaction. Ask yourself and others who are part of your organization:

- How important is customer satisfaction to the organization (not important, somewhat important, very important)?
- Do you regularly or periodically measure customer satisfaction? If so, how often?
- What methods and tools do you use to measure customer satisfaction? Do these methods and tools give you the kind of information you need in order to identify strengths and weaknesses and to improve your services and processes?
- How does your organization use customer satisfaction data to improve its services and processes?
- To whom do you report your customer satisfaction measurement findings?
- If you do not currently measure customer satisfaction, what barriers must be overcome to initiate a measurement process (e.g., lack of commitment by upper management, competing priorities, insufficient time or financial resources)? How might these barriers be overcome?

Customer satisfaction can be divided into two parts: the degrees to which your customers are satisfied with 1) how they are treated (i.e., the *process* of customer service) and 2) what happened as a result of your services or the extent to which they received what they expected from you (i.e., the *outcomes* of customer service). As a baseline, it is important to define the organization's customer service and satisfaction goals, set up procedures for meeting these goals, define specific behaviors that are expected from all employment service staff, and provide mechanisms for continuous feedback to and from staff. Goals ideally are associated with both the processes and the outcomes of service. For example, an organization may establish a goal of returning all telephone calls within 24 hours, an activity that improves the *process* of doing business with employment service organizations. A goal related to *outcomes* might be that 95% of all employers who hire job seekers represented by your organization will rate your service as good or excellent.

Step 2: Outline Reasons for Measuring Customer Satisfaction   It is often useful to describe your rationale and list your goals for measuring customers' satisfaction. The rationale should explain in broad terms why the organization would want to measure customer satisfaction and how the information will be used. Reasons for measuring satisfaction are related to specific goals you hope to achieve. For example, do you hope to increase employers' loyalty to your organization? Identify and resolve problems with internal processes? Better understand your customers' expectations? Identify gaps in your services? Improve frontline employees' ability to discern and meet customers' needs? Determine the usefulness of your printed materials or website?

Measuring customer satisfaction means more than simply gaining feedback from customers. It provides a basis for open, nonjudgmental, and constructive discussions about service weaknesses and strengths. It can also provide a benchmark measurement from which future progress can be evaluated. Such measurement can result in areas of strength being identified and highlighted through marketing and promotional efforts to other potential customers. But more important, areas of weakness can be identified so that specific action plans for improvement can be developed and topics for staff development can be expanded. In either case, customer satisfaction data are invaluable in helping employment specialists and employment service organizations shape their programs so that they are known for delivering stellar service. In the simplest of terms, you should be asking two questions of your customers: How are we doing? And how can we get better?

Step 3: Select Your Tools and Methods   Organizations can use a variety of tools and methods to infer their customers' levels of satisfaction. Be sure the tools you choose help you to achieve your measurement goals and that they are appropriate for the intended audience. Also, when choosing your tools, you must be sure to design processes and allot adequate resources to maximize their value. Organization may want to assign responsibility for customer satisfaction measurement activities to one staff member or a small team. That individual's or group's responsibilities might include preparing and sending out questionnaires; planning and administering formal surveys; organizing the repository of responses; entering, tabulating, and analyzing the data; and interpreting and reporting the results. Customer satisfaction tools might include customer feedback questionnaires, formal customer service surveys, a customer service feedback page on the agency's web site, a suggestion box, and informal feedback.

Customer Feedback Questionnaires   One of the most useful ways to gather feedback on an organization's services and processes is by having customers complete a questionnaire after it provides a service or during the course of service provision (see Figure 12.3). The questionnaire should ask customers to rate and provide open-ended feedback on their level of satisfaction during the job development process. To reduce the

---

Sample Customer Service Questionnaire for Employers

1. How would you rate your overall relationship with our organization?

   1 - Excellent   2 - Good   3 - Not very good   4 - Poor

   Suggestions/Comments:

2. How would you rate our ability to help you address your business needs?

   1 - Excellent   2 - Good   3 - Not very good   4 - Poor

   Suggestions/Comments:

3. How would you rate our ability to help you address your hiring/human resources needs?

   1 - Excellent   2 - Good   3 - Not very good   4 - Poor

   Suggestions/Comments

4. How would you rate your staff's willingness to listen to and respond to your interests and needs?

   1 - Excellent   2 - Good   3 - Not very good   4 - Poor

   Suggestions/Comments:

5. What aspect of our organization's services is most important to you?

6. What aspect of our services is least important to you?

7. What changes could we make to enhance our relationship with you or other employers?

8. Would you recommend our services to other employers in our community?

   Yes   No

   Why or why not?

9. Other comments:

Thank you for taking the time to share your thoughts with us.

Figure 12.3. Sample customer service questionnaire for employers.

burden on the respondent, keep the questionnaire simple and concise. Also, you may find that completing the survey orally will be more appropriate for some customers as a way to be respectful of their time and circumstances.

Formal Customer Satisfaction Surveys   Conduct formal, periodic surveys of employers with whom you have worked to learn how well you are helping them to meet their business and hiring needs, how you could serve them better, or why they have not continued their relationship with you. The surveys, which may be administered by mail, telephone, or e-mail, should be sent to all or a random sample of your employer contacts. Administering the survey periodically (e.g., quarterly) will help you monitor changes (positive or negative) in employers' satisfaction over time.

A Customer Feedback Web Page   Give customers an opportunity to provide feedback through your web site. For example, you could include your customer feedback questionnaires on your web site or include a "Tell Us What You Think" page with an e-mail link that website users can use to communicate complaints, concerns, and suggestions.

Focus Groups   Focus groups can be convened periodically (e.g., once or twice per year) or as needed to gain insight into any aspect of your services or processes. Unlike surveys or individual feedback methods, focus groups offer the advantage of dynamic interaction and conversation about a particular topic. For example, you might gather a group of employer partners to generate ideas about how to strengthen your relationships with them. When convening focus groups, be sure you have a well-defined purpose and have carefully designed the questions to be asked. Also, be sure that your moderator is objective and that your focus group report is not biased. Chapter 9 provides details on how to convene focus groups.

A Suggestion Box   Placing a suggestion box and comment cards in your office's reception area gives visitors the opportunity to voice suggestions and ideas. Although the users of this tool will be limited to those who physically come to your office, a suggestion box may provide useful input about your organization (e.g., suggestions for improving physical accessibility of your offices or the efficiency of your reception services). A suggestion box can also be used by employees, who may hesitate to communicate through other avenues.

Informal Feedback   Any customer satisfaction feedback your staff receives—whether through a formal survey method or in an informal conversation—is valuable information. All staff members should understand that any complaints or concerns voiced by your customers should be noted and addressed immediately, and the person voicing concern should be informed of changes or progress toward addressing the concern. Likewise, praise received from customers about the organization or individual employees should be communicated to the entire staff or the individuals.

Step 4: Analyze the Data to Improve Your Services and Processes   Customer satisfaction data are not gathered to sit on a shelf. Be sure to analyze and use your findings to improve your services and processes so that you can better meet your customers' expectations. Use the data to identify issues that have recently arisen and need immediate attention, as well as to track customer satisfaction trends and make adjustments over time.

Be sure to assign responsibilities and set timelines for resolving problems. View problem solving from a systemic perspective rather than placing blame on individuals or groups. Also, be sure to involve all of the organization's employees in designing and implementing improved customer service strategies. Well-considered, collected, and analyzed data from customers document and reinforce excellent service behavior (the process) and excellent service results (the outcomes), as well as identify improvements in the process and outcomes that are needed.

Setting up and maintaining a customer service and satisfaction measuring system can be a time-consuming and energy-consuming process. Thus, it often makes sense to assign a particular individual to the tasks or a particular time of the work week when these issues are examined. For example, a weekly staff meeting standing agenda might include customer service feedback and discussion. Also, it is important to use customer service feedback to design staff development activities. All staff benefit from training in customer service vision, goals, and procedures for obtaining customer feedback from the field.

Step 5: Share the Results   Customer satisfaction measurement efforts are reinforced and supported when the results are shared with others who have a stake in the organization. Thus, areas of strength can be celebrated and, when appropriate, so can communication about how problems have been resolved. Customer satisfaction results should be shared with the organization's chief executive officer and management staff, the board of directors, advisory committee members, all employees, job seekers, employer partners and prospective partners, funding organizations, and other partners in the community. Results can be shared through many channels, including one-to-one communication, e-mail, formal presentations to board and advisory committees, staff meeting presentations, special letters to partners and other stakeholders, reports to funding organizations, newsletters, web sites, and marketing materials.

A well-designed and high-quality employment service program is one that has a mechanism for gathering and using feedback from its customers. Well-gathered feedback is invaluable: It can inform, enlighten, and clearly pinpoint areas needing modification and improvement. It measures the customer's level of satisfaction at any point of contact with the service. Ultimately, the measurement and analysis of customer satisfaction will benefit staff competence, confidence, preparedness, ability to handle the unexpected, creativity in problem solving, rapport with employers, knowledge of the customer, and skill in tailoring services to meet the unique needs of each customer.

SUMMARY

This chapter presents time-honored customer service strategies that when adopted in the context of job development, result in successful relationships with employers. Attracting and retaining interested employer customers requires that the process of delivering service is characterized by attentive activity and that the outcomes for employers are quality-oriented, with value added. Many jobs and careers are launched for job seekers as a result.

Ten common customer service strategies are presented, along with illustrations in practice. Tips for achieving effectiveness with each strategy were also presented. Finally, a rationale and process of measuring customer satisfaction are detailed to help employment specialists and employment agencies gauge how employers feel about the service they receive. Such measurement enables employment specialists to continually improve the way they interact with and deliver service to employers.

III

New Directions for Employment Partnerships

13

Nontraditional Employment Through Customized Consultation

Richard G. Luecking and Sara Murphy

> *We have forgotten what creates a job:*
> *a problem to be solved or a benefit sought. We have forgotten*
> *that a job seeker is not hired on the basis of qualification, but rather for*
> *his or her ability to solve a particular problem or meet a specific need of the employer.*
>
> DENISE BISSONNETTE

Finding jobs that offer good pay and benefits is a challenge for anybody. For individuals who have unusual or extensive needs for support or accommodation, there are, of course, potentially many additional considerations. Employment specialists and employment agencies who are assisting these individuals often hit a brick wall when trying to come up with ideas and opportunities for employment. Part of the challenge is gaining access to companies where higher pay and more diverse work assignments are possible. Seemingly, for many job seekers who are represented by disability employment agencies, limited job histories and lack of specific employment skills make the entrée into such companies difficult. This challenge is often exacerbated because employment specialists often underestimate how their expertise can provide the entrée.

It is exactly such expertise, applied in uncommon ways, that can offer fresh direction for employment specialists. They can customize their work in such a way as to become effective business consultants who help solve business problems. This is really an enhanced

way of using the strategies and techniques described in Section II. Under the right circumstances and with the right approach, the concept of consultation to businesses represents a professional role for the employment specialist that not only elevates the profession
but opens doors and exposes many hidden opportunities for job seekers with disabilities.
This chapter provides a conceptual model for consultation as a job development tool, presents several case study examples of business consultation that resulted in partnerships and
jobs, and examines the implications of this tool for future business relationship building.

SETTING THE STAGE FOR CONSULTATION

Employment specialists can do many things to use more sophisticated techniques and to
set the stage for consultation. These strategies involve searching beyond traditional job advertisements and helping companies examine operational needs gaps in their work force
in order to create new jobs (as opposed to the more customary practice of trying to fill existing jobs with particular job seekers). The difference between conventional practices and
more innovative methods is often simply the approach to a task.

Search Beyond Conventional Job Advertisements

They call it "job development" for a reason. In the *What Color Is Your Parachute?* series,
Bolles (2003) encouraged job seekers with disabilities to not limit themselves to searching for traditional jobs or jobs that are available. How many jobs, for example, are advertised as having flexible schedules, resourceful supervisors, and co-workers who are skilled
at identifying and implementing all manner of accommodation? How many companies
even think about reorganizing work flow or restructuring job assignments so that workers who need such accommodations can be employed at their company? Of course, such
opportunities are rarely, if ever, advertised. They will not be found in want ads and they
especially will not be found by asking employers if they have any job openings. Resourceful and skilled employment specialists have to create them or at the very least, uncover them.

Whether a company is looking to fill a position or not, all kinds of possibilities are
available to the job seeker who can demonstrate that he or she has what an employer needs.
In any case, want ads and cold calling are less effective and less useful than solid partnership and relationship building. What better way to build a partnership than to directly
assist an employer to improve operations and even to profit from those changes. This is
job development from the demand side—create a demand for your service and then supply what the employer customer needs. From such thinking springs many opportunities.

Meeting Company Needs: Beyond Job Carving

One approach to job development that has been advanced by many researchers and practitioners in the disability employment arena has been to carve tasks from a company position or restructure jobs so that a narrower set of tasks are assigned to the worker with a disability (Nietupski & Hamre-Nietupski, 2000). Job carving is often seen as a way of at least getting a foot in the door of employment for people with significant support needs. It can also help individual job seekers develop their work skills and experience employment in spite of a limited work history or narrow set of skills. This approach has been a particularly useful tack for individuals who require unusual or complicated job accommodations (DiLeo, Luecking, & Hathaway, 1995; Nietupski & Hamre-Nietupski, 2001).

However, these benefits are not particularly important to employer customers. The employer may see these type of arrangements as fabricated jobs that seem more like charity than a way to restructure work flow that makes the operation more efficient. If the employer sees the job as charity, it will only last as long as the employer feels good about helping out and as long as the bottom line allows the luxury of such an add-on position. Also, if management or supervisors change, there is no guarantee that the new people in charge will feel as charitable. The job is therefore in continuous jeopardy.

However, when the employment specialist provides more careful consultation that has direct, obvious benefit to the company's operational processes, he or she creates the opportunity to create jobs for people that will endure bottom-line considerations and changes in company leadership. For example, employment specialists may assist the company to identify particular task assignments that, if restructured and assigned to an individual job seeker they represent, allow co-workers to more quickly perform other, more complicated or advanced assignments. (See again the discussion in Chapter 11 on job matches to modified job descriptions and through employment proposals.)

Although this approach offers a greater potential array of work opportunities for people with disabilities, the employer's interest—and ultimately the effectiveness of the approach—is dependent on how well such task assignments benefit the company's operation. Thus, it is less useful to go into a company seeking to carve jobs for particular individuals, although that may ultimately be what happens. The more effective approach is to begin by inquiring into and examining particular company challenges. In other words, approach the situation as any good business consultant would.

CONSULTATIVE JOB DEVELOPMENT

Consultative Selling (Hanan, 1995), a popular business publication, offers a useful process that has been adopted by many business consultants. Hanan's model certainly has many applications for employment programs wishing to add depth and effectiveness to their

Table 13.1.   Business consultation and job development comparison

Hanan's consultation steps	Corresponding job development concept
Examine the operating mix	Knowing the business customer
Supplant a component of the mix with the consultant's services	Job carving and matching
Manage the operating mix	Follow-up support and coaching

business relationships. In Hanan's view, a good consultant is able to show the business customer how to increase profit or improve operations by using the consultant's services. His model emphasizes optimization of what he called the consultant customer's "operating mix," which contains three basic steps:

1.   Examine the business's operating mix, the processes for getting things done
2.   Supplant one or more components of the operating mix with the consultant's services
3.   Help manage the new operating mix, or the new way of getting things done as a result of the consultant's help

This is not dissimilar to what any good job development approach should include. The difference is the intensity of the relationship that is implied by such an approach and the business savvy that is required. Table 13.1 illustrates this process as it relates to job development. The next subsections examine these steps in more detail, including their relevance to job development.

Examine the Company's Operating Mix

In the words of one employer, "Nothing beats showing me how you can help me meet my needs." This should sound familiar because it is what customer service to the employer is all about. Taking it to the next level, however, requires a comprehensive knowledge of the employer's operation that can only be obtained by being there and developing the kind of rapport that the most effective business consultants strive for.

An easy way to gain access is to simply express interest in the company and ask for a visit or a tour. Once inside, there are usually plenty of opportunities to observe the company's operation in order to determine how things get done, what parts of the operation run well, and what parts of the operation are problematic. Often, through conversation with key personnel, employment specialists can also learn what these insiders think are problem spots in the company operation. Job developers can thus discover and observe one or more company functions and begin to identify particular operational or human resource activities that can be altered or improved. Consider the following example.

One employment specialist contacted the manager of a large department store and asked if he could make a visit. He told the manager he wanted to visit in order to better learn the requirements of the retail business and thus better prepare students with whom he was working for retail occupations. Over the course of several visits, he noticed that whenever the daily delivery of new merchandise was delivered to the store, several sales associates from the clothing department were required to assist in the unloading and stacking of that incoming merchandise. They would subsequently remove the clothing from the boxes, strip off the cellophane covering individual articles, and rehang the articles on hangers for display in the store. During this process, the customers in the clothing department had no one to assist them. Sales were being lost. A better way of getting the clothes ready for display was needed, an observation that led the employment specialist to the second step.

Supplant Operational Components With Consultant's Services

Job developers are often in a position to suggest alternative methods of task completion that not only improve the operation but also result in an employment opportunity for a job seeker he or she represents. In some cases, assigning selected tasks to a new employee allows work to be accomplished faster, more precisely, and more efficiently. The employment specialist at the department store, for example, was working with a young woman who liked clothes and wanted to work in a store. He suggested to the manager that if someone could be assigned exclusively to the tasks in the receiving department, accepting the incoming clothing merchandise, then the sales associates could remain on the sales floor and attend to customers. He proposed that one of his students who loved clothes but did not have the verbal skills to be sales clerk be assigned the tasks in the receiving department. He suggested to the manager that the cost of hiring the young woman could be offset by an increase in sales that would result from more attention to the store's customers. After some negotiation, the manager was convinced to give it a try.

The employment specialist essentially supplanted the previous process—having the sales clerks receive and prepare new merchandise—with his service. A job seeker who wanted to work with clothes was taught the necessary tasks by the employment specialist and the employment specialist also coached the manager and co-workers how to prompt the young woman through her tasks and how to interact most effectively. A job was thus carved, but more important to the company, a business problem was solved through the help of a competent consultant.

Manage the Operating Mix

Managing the operating mix requires the abilities to analyze the work process in a company's operation and to apply the expertise of disability employment programs in a way that results in the company's benefit. This expertise can be in the form of job and task analysis, ways of presenting new tasks, or the introduction of a worker who will perform selected aspects of an operational process. When substituting one process for another, the employment specialist must ensure that the basis of the recommended change is that improved financial and performance benefits will accrue to the company if the process is altered.

In the department store example, the employment specialist made sure he was available to organize and oversee the newly identified arrangement. He thus helped manage the operational mix. He was also able to validate the benefits of his consultation: The additional sales generated did indeed exceed the cost of employing the job seeker he represented. It should be obvious also that the relationship was not based or focused on his technical expertise or on the fact that he was helping students in special education get jobs. Rather, it was based on responding to the company's needs. The beauty of the outcome from a job developer's perspective is that there was not a job opening at the store nor was there a job description for the work that the young woman was eventually hired to do—a hidden opportunity uncovered.

In the end, the employment specialist had to be what Hanan (1995) called process smart, application smart, and validation smart. That is, he had to learn and understand how things got done at the store, he had to know how to apply his expertise (in supporting a worker with a significant disability in the workplace) to solve a business problem, and he had to be able to suggest that the application of his expertise would make money for the store. This suggests an evolving and increasingly sophisticated role for job developers and employment specialists. If these professionals can market and apply their services in the cause of increased business profit or improved company operations, then the future of job development is bright indeed. Consider the following two examples and how they contributed to the solving of staffing issues at two companies.

Improving Company Assets

AMB Investments is a real estate investment trust company based in San Francisco, California. The company owns and operates office buildings and large industrial properties throughout the United States. After a period of rapid growth, many departments within the company have experienced difficulty dealing with ever-increasing workloads. This lack of efficiency created a problem for a privately held company that was planning to go public as a member of the stock exchange. It needed to maximize its expense-to-revenue ratio to enhance the attractiveness of its venture to potential stockholders.

An Example

A department responsible for consumer relations within a large federal department had been receiving hundreds of telephone calls per week. There were five employees who received telephone calls and responded to customer concerns. Each call had to be logged in and information on the calls entered into a large database. Although each customer service representative fielded calls randomly, each had a particular area of expertise. Consequently, some callers were on the telephone for shorter periods of time if they happened to get the right representative. Other calls took longer because the customer service representative had to seek out the answer. Callers were often on hold for extended periods, and calls got backed up, especially when the customer service representatives had to take time to log the information into the database. Ironically, the customer relations department was receiving many complaints about its lack of efficient customer response.

An employment specialist was introduced to this federal department through a mutual friend of the manager of the department. After observing the operation, the employment specialist introduced the idea of changing the process for handling the calls. In the same vein as Hanan's (1995) consultation model, she suggested supplanting two aspects of the operation with her service and a job seeker she represented. First, the new employee answered calls and redirected them to the most appropriate representative. Second, the same employee entered selected items in the database, thus saving time for the representatives. The employment specialist helped reorganize the change in procedure, instruct the new employee in the reassigned duties, and secure the assistive technology that enabled the employee to operate a one-handed keyboard and a hands-free telephone receiver. Within a month, the response time to a typical call was reduced by several minutes, much to the delight of the department manager, and a long-term federal job with accompanying benefits resulted for the new employee.

In looking to fill the continuing demand for clerical support, AMB came in contact with WorkLink, a San Francisco–based employment agency operated by TransCen. WorkLink's employment specialists met with human resources personnel to determine potential employment needs. During the course of several meetings, the employment specialists had the opportunity to examine AMB's operating procedures and identified a number of areas in which more centralized administrative support would improve efficiency and communication within the company. The acquisitions department, responsible for purchasing new properties for the trust, was the first area where WorkLink staff observed operational processes. As AMB's business grew, so did the volume of properties being submitted for review. Within this department, administrative assistants were having difficulty with organizing and tracking the high volume of property submissions. To complicate matters, acquisition managers typically received additional unsolicited submissions from AMB's regional transaction groups. Many times these errant submissions were misplaced and were not delivered to the correct manager's desk. Others took an unacceptably long time to get to the next department for processing.

Working closely with AMB's staff, WorkLink helped create an alternative process for handling submissions. An administrative support position was added to manage a central filing room for submissions. William, a job seeker supported by WorkLink, became the new assistant. He was responsible for collecting and filing all inactive submissions, sending old files to storage, and pulling files requested by managers. In addition, he was required to log in miscellaneous submissions, create folders with a tracking number for these properties, and deliver them to the appropriate acquisition manager. Accommodations were necessary for William to complete the newly assigned job duties, and these were facilitated by WorkLink staff. This more centralized process allowed administrative assistants to spend less time on organizing and screening properties. They could now devote their efforts to examining the properties AMB was potentially interested in purchasing. And they accomplished this work much faster, validating the worth of the new process.

Because of William's successful work in the acquisitions department, other departments at AMB that were experiencing work delays requested assistance from WorkLink. WorkLink's staff worked with department managers to determine how tasks could be reassigned. Ultimately, William's hours were increased to meet the needs of two other departments. A weekly schedule was developed, as well as a method of requesting assistance for random assignments (e.g., large copying projects, mailings, other tasks that occurred intermittently). Collating, basic data entry, and general clerical support tasks were also added to William's regular assignments. In 1 year, this clerical support position was increased from 20 to 40 hours per week, and William is now earning a full administrative assistant's salary, has full company benefits, and no longer needs the SSI that he received. More important to the company, the efficient handling of submissions and the assignment of other tasks to the supported employee have saved the company much more money than it spends on William's salary and fringe benefits. See Table 13.2 for a comparison of the mutual benefits achieved in this situation.

Table 13.2.   Mutual benefits of AMB consultation

AMB Investments' staffing issues and concerns	William's duties
Packages and faxes left in reception area	Delivers packages and faxes
Limited budget for administrative assistance	Creates files for property submissions
Property submissions not getting to correct account manager	Routes submissions to appropriate account manager
Privately held company going public	Shelves circulated periodicals Collates packets Files for three departments
Results for the company	**Results for William**
Speedier processing of property submissions from 4 weeks to 4 days	Full-time employment, with benefits
Multiple departments share cost of administrative assistance	No longer dependent on Supplemental Security Income and government benefits
Fewer packages misplaced, faxes delivered promptly	Career
Cost efficiencies lead to more profits and higher dividends for stockholders	

Stretching the Nonprofit Dollar

The American Conservatory Theater (ACT) is a nationally known nonprofit theater production company based in San Francisco. In addition to its production company, ACT operates a theatrical conservatory for both youth and adults. WorkLink staff contacted ACT on behalf of Rosita, a young woman who had a strong interest in theater. Indeed, it was her dream to be an actor. The employment specialist was informed that ACT is a nonprofit that generates all of its operation funds through ticket sales, tuitions, and fundraising activities. It operates under a very tight budget. Although the personnel manager did not think there was an opportunity for the young woman, they agreed to meet with the WorkLink staff.

When the employment specialist met with ACT's managers, she noticed that the organization had very small departments (one to three employees). In some instances, employees were responsible for duties in multiple departments. Another factor that added to the complexity of ACT's administrative situation was the seasonal fluctuations of ACT's work. The theater's production schedule and the school calendar affected all departments. Some of the smaller departments had trouble dealing with these seasonal fluctuations. For example, the human resources manager, who also serves as the organization's office manager, was responsible for hiring all employees. During production seasons, ACT hires actors, stage crews, and additional theater staff, growing from 35 employees year-round to 150 employees during production season. She had difficulty with managing these seasonal hires in addition to her other year-round responsibilities.

The marketing department had similar challenges. The beginning of the production season meant numerous mailings and media events to publicize upcoming shows. Their two-person department had a difficult time handling the time-consuming mailings as well as organizing events and interviews. In all departments, problems occurred when a staff person left the organization. In some instances, there was no one to manage the department's daily functions while the opening was filled and the new employee was trained.

ACT addressed these operational difficulties by pulling employees to work in departments that were overburdened or temporarily understaffed because of an opening. Often, employees had to work overtime, costing more money. The organization also relied heavily on temporary employees. To complicate matters, hiring temporary help also required that a staff person be available to train and supervise the temporary worker. For smaller departments, finding the time to orient a temporary worker was more trouble than it was worth. ACT began to realize that paying overtime, paying high temporary agency contracting fees, and using directors and managers to perform routine tasks, such as stuffing mailings, were not cost-effective solutions.

When WorkLink's employment specialist examined ACT's production cycle and each department's workload, she determined that the annual fluctuations were very consistent and that when one department was slow, another was busy. She proposed a floating position be created to address the seasonal needs of four different departments. A person could be assigned to do administrative tasks in the human resources department and marketing department during the production season and in the development department and the conservatory during the off season. This position would eliminate the need for pulling staff or bringing in temporary workers. WorkLink presented ACT with a list of potential tasks that could be restructured into a support position for the four departments. The list clearly demonstrated the benefits for each department and prompted discussion about creating a new position.

Initially, ACT agreed to hire Rosita for 3 days per week. The employment specialist worked closely with ACT's department managers to organize the new position. It included year-round administrative duties but also left flexibility to handle seasonal tasks. Rosita's initial responsibilities included filing tax forms and collating information packets for seasonal hires, processing mailings for the marketing department, and doing data entry for an ongoing customer satisfaction survey. She also filed student information for the conservatory and photocopied scripts and other classroom materials. Rosita proved to be so helpful that her hours were increased to 5 days per week.

Other departments also began to request Rosita's assistance to fill work needs. The theater staff had trouble finding ushers for matinee performances. Rosita was taught the theater's seating procedures and now handles the entire mezzanine level for every production. The costume shop could not keep up with entering rentals in their database. Without this information, they did not know when a costume was to be returned and when it could again be rented. Rosita is now responsible for this task.

Rosita's success and the department managers' enthusiasm for the new position was further reinforced by the cost savings that this arrangement created for ACT. ACT's managers are now able to concentrate on the critical aspects of their positions. The organization is no longer using highly paid staff to usher matinees or file student paper work. Temporary workers are now rarely used. ACT had effectively cut costs due to WorkLink's consultation. For her part, Rosita is not an actor, but she has still has the job of her dreams—she works in theater alongside of lots of other people who share that affinity! Table 13.3 illustrates the mutual benefits ACT and Rosita achieved through the effective consultation delivered by the employment specialist.

Business Consultation for Better Results

Successful consultation, as that in both of these case studies, relied on the ability of the employment agency to fully appreciate that satisfying the companies' operational needs was more important than the introduction of an employee with a disability. The employment specialists in each case were able to observe the operation, supplant an aspect of the operation with the agency's service, and help manage the changed operation through continued follow-up and support. In both cases, there was an improvement in company efficiency and profit. In the bargain, individuals with disabilities secured full-time employ-

Table 13.3.   Mutual benefits of ACT consultation

ACT's staffing issues and concerns	Rosita's duties
Seasonal fluctuations	Floats between departments seasonally
Nonprofit company with a very tight budget	Files employee information, time sheets, and so forth
Small departments	Invoices costume rentals
Used temporary workers for administrative needs	Collates media kits Enters new donor information in the database Photocopies and binds scripts Processes market mailings

Results for ACT	Results for Rosita
Lower administrative costs—no longer uses temporary workers, stays within budget	Dream job in theater
	Steady income
All departments share administrative assistance	New peer group
	Free theater tickets
Flexibility to meet seasonal activities	

ment in jobs of their choosing with the same benefits as those available to all employees at the company.

The job tasks and the work circumstances that these individuals experience have not traditionally been available to people with significant support and accommodation needs. However, with an eye toward employers' needs, the employment specialists in each of these cases ably performed the role of an effective business consultant. The companies, the job seekers, and the employment agencies all significantly benefited. Indeed, flourishing partnerships for all.

WHAT GOOD CONSULTANTS DO

The successful outcomes illustrated in the case studies were predicated on the technical competence and persistence of skilled, resourceful employment specialists. They essentially displayed the same type and range of skills that any good business consultant would have to demonstrate to perform well for business clients. The following is a list of commonly identified business consultant activities (DeBoer; 1995; Fabian, Luecking, & Tilson, 1994; Greenbaum, 1990; Shenson, 1990; Shenson & Nichols, 1993):

- *Instruct clients in new techniques.* Businesses spend billions of dollars per year on consultants who can teach employers what they need to know. In fact, human resource management training represents one of the most widely used types of business consultation.
- *Demonstrate new techniques.* Sometimes instruction must be coupled with demonstration, such as how to use a new computer software program or how to structure a product assembly sequence.

- *Facilitate decision making and planning.* Solving specific problems often requires intensive planning. Similarly, the launching of a new product line ultimately requires objective decision making that can best be facilitated by an outside consultant. Focus groups conducted by consultants are good examples of this.

- *Communicate new ideas or clarify old ones.* Communication is universally recognized as the single most important skill any consultant can have. It is also not surprising, then, that communication skills are high on the list of essential job developer competencies outlined in Chapter 7. Consultants may be asked to arbitrate disputes, negotiate agreements, handle difficult people, and even translate business's jargon. Also, written documents, such as reports, letters of agreement, and trade newsletters, represent important consultant tools for communicating with business clients.

- *Assess organizational needs.* Assessing relevant circumstances is a necessary preliminary to problem resolution (i.e., what is the problem and what can be done about it?). In addition, consultants are often asked to look at the needs of a company as a prelude to, or in conjunction with, training.

- *Prepare business clients to do for themselves.* The most effective consultants are those who provide consultation and subsequently step aside.

- *Conduct an inventory of internal expertise, skills, and interests.* If the consultant is to leave business clients able to do for themselves, then he or she often must find out who in the company is best suited to assume new or expanded responsibility.

- *Follow up after consultation is provided.* The best consultants, like the best businesses, are those who provide service after the sale. This not only contributes to long-term relationships—an essential ingredient of any successful business partnership—but also results in repeat business and strong referrals for new business.

The action verbs that begin each point above could easily be ascribed to any number of traditional job placement activities. Employment specialists are instructors, evaluators, facilitators, mentors, communicators and listeners, demonstrators, and educators, just to name a few. Good employment specialists use these skills in their interactions with job seekers with disabilities. Outstanding employment specialists also apply these skills in the context of employers' needs and the unique aspects of each workplace, as in the case studies. These consultant activities can be applied in efforts to promote employment for people with disabilities.

Instruction

Instruction is a critical element of almost all job placement programs, and job placement professionals, for the most part, are very good at it. Unfortunately, this highly developed skill is most often applied only to job seekers with disabilities, teaching them job search skills or actual job skills. However, it can become a valuable tool for providing service to employers and businesses as well.

For example, the authors trained one company's personnel manager how to instruct store managers and supervisors how to train, accommodate, and supervise workers with learning disabilities (Fabian et al., 1994). As a result, more than 40 individuals with learning disabilities were hired by this company during the 2-year course of consultation. Instruction as a consultation tool can take many forms, such as disability awareness training. How to prompt a new employee through a series of work tasks is another example.

Demonstration

When working with employers, it is often necessary to demonstrate specific job accommodations. For example, one young man was hired as an assistant store clerk. Among other responsibilities, he was required to inventory and stock shelves. However, every time he was given more than two instructions at a time, he would act as if he understood but would invariably make critical mistakes. He needed one-step oral directions accompanied by written instructions. Once the store manager used this supervisory approach demonstrated by an experienced job placement professional, he had no further problem with the employee.

In another case, a supervisor called the employment specialist who helped him hire an individual in his company. This individual was performing so poorly that he would be fired if he did not improve. However, when the supervisor was shown how to rearrange the presentation of the work material—simply reversing the direction of a circuit board on an assembly table so that it was easier to grasp by the employee—he noted an immediate improvement in the employee's performance. The employee was retained. Scenarios like these occur each day. Many jobs have been saved and many employers have improved their supervisory approach as a result of such effective demonstrations by employment specialists.

Facilitation

One manufacturing company was having problems with employee hiring and retention in a tight labor market. Employment specialists facilitated a series of focus groups with employees and managers on different shifts. A common theme was the need for mentors and coaches for new employees to help them manage the new job and the fast pace expected of the manufacturing line. The employment specialists recommended a coaching program for all new employees using experienced line workers as the designated coaches. This not only helped reduce turnover for the company, but it also created new opportunities for workers with disabilities because the coaching provided by this new arrangement became a built-in accommodation for some applicants (Verstegen, 2000).

Communication

Using communication skills in consultation with employers is very important. Indeed, it is one of the cornerstones of employment specialist competencies, as this example illustrates. An employment specialist assisted a young adult in getting a job at a microfiche company. From the very beginning, the employment specialist began teaching the company's staff how to structure assignments, how to provide feedback and what to say when the young adult went off task. The interaction occurred primarily between the specialist and the employer in the context not only of communicating (i.e., educating and demonstrating) to the employer how to interact with the young adult but also of listening to how the employer wanted to get the job done. Essentially, the specialist's communication skills were used to help the employer learn how to train, supervise, and accommodate the employee.

Assessment

Assessment of the skills, interests, and aptitudes of job seekers with disabilities has been one of the most widely applied job placement practices. Vocational evaluation, assistive technology assessments, and work adjustment training have traditionally received a great deal of emphasis in job preparation and job development. Their accompanying bodies of knowledge and skills, applied more directly on the employer's environment, can also be utilized as consultant tools when working with employers. Consider this example.

Bertha is a 20-year-old graduate of special education who uses a motorized wheelchair. As part of her educational experience prior to graduation, Bertha was spending part of her school day as a part-time package courier for a local company. It was determined that job modifications and assistive technology would be necessary in order for her to perform the requirements of the job. Her teacher videotaped her daily routine and sent a copy of the videotape to be reviewed by a rehabilitation technology team.

A telephone conference was scheduled at the worksite. Bertha, her employer, and her teacher subsequently were connected to the rehabilitation technology team via telephone, and both groups simultaneously viewed and discussed Bertha's work and possible modifications. During the conference, the rehabilitation technology team made specific recommendations for modifications and technology. Each suggestion was discussed in detail with all parties involved; a plan was developed to make modifications to Bertha's wheelchair and to restructure her office environment (i.e., applying Velcro to the package carrying case for stabilization, lowering shelves, moving document slots to a lower position, and rearranging Bertha's workspace for greater accessibility). As a result of this assessment and the subsequent modifications and applications of technology, Bertha's performance increased and she was offered a permanent position with the company.

This was a great benefit to the employee, and her employer was a direct recipient of such valuable consultation as well. This assessment was provided at the place of employment with the input of the employer. Bertha did not have to travel to a specially equipped center, nor was the employer forced to wait until a specially trained team of technologists could travel to the worksite. Thus, technology brought the consultation directly to the employer—a problem of logistics was solved for the employer as well.

It is useful to consider assessment as a consultation tool best used in the direct context of employers and their workplaces. For example, William's employment specialist helped AMB Investments assess the workflow of the organization. When considering the process, she was able to subsequently suggest task reassignment that both resulted in a job for William and a faster and more effective way to get the company's work done.

Preparation

An example of preparation as a consultation tool in action for employment of people with disabilities is the example of Cincinnati Children's Hospital Medical Center, cited in Chapter 6. The hospital wanted to initiate a program that would enable it to hire more people with disabilities to fill support positions. In order to do so, it needed the help and consultation of organizations expert in accommodations and instructional techniques. Two such organizations helped the hospital organize a hiring and training process that eventually helped the hospital hire more than 100 employees with disabilities. These organizations essentially prepared the hospital not only to hire and train employees with disabilities but also to hire and train its own job coaches.

Conducting Inventory

We assisted Marriott Corporation in piloting an internally operated supported employment project. The pilot called for establishing a mechanism for Marriott to hire, train, and provide ongoing support to employees with disabilities who required considerable training and supervisory support. This approach required the identification of an available Marriott employee to perform the functions of a job trainer. The idea was that an employee who knew the needs and expectations of the company would be better equipped than an outside job placement professional to ensure job success for applicants with disabilities.

To identify such a person essentially required that a consultant assist Marriott in conducting an inventory of staff who had served in various capacities within the company and had the aptitude to be an effective job trainer for people with disabilities. After interviewing several Marriott personnel, reviewing work histories, and spending time observing various corporate operations, a person was identified. She had worked in hotels, food service, and personnel recruiting, and most important, she had no preconceived notions about people with disabilities. The inventory thus yielded a person who made the pilot successful and has subsequently received several promotions.

In a more formal sense, accessibility surveys conducted through the use of computer software such as ADAAG Express (Kokomo Software, 1993) are a means by which companies can be assisted in taking an inventory of physical environments so as to both comply with Title III of the ADA and enhance their ability to provide a more friendly environment for present and future employees with disabilities. As job placement agencies and professionals offer such services to employers, they are providing consultation that facilitates expanded capabilities in accommodating employees with disabilities.

Follow Up

Consider the following scenario: An employment specialist checks back in to see if in fact the company has improved its sales as a result of the restructured task assignments. Upon talking to the employer and observing the situation, she discovers that the employee is taking too much time doing his work. She worked for a few minutes to reinstruct the employee and checked back later to re-enforce the new task completion procedure. The employee improved, and the employer was grateful. This was definitely good consultant follow-up service.

The best employment specialists understand the importance of responsive follow up. They often call on employers after contact, after training, and after hiring someone new in order to determine when retraining is necessary, when an additional accommodation must be identified, or whether more help is needed in any way. Indeed, the value of this follow-up service is as important to the employer as it is to the employee with a disability, and as discussed in Chapter 12, it is a hallmark of outstanding customer service.

SUMMARY

This chapter presents a framework for employment specialists and employment agencies to provide consultation to employers in such a way that results in job opportunities for people with disabilities. As the case studies illustrate, the key to the success of such consultation is making sure that there are specific positive results for the employer. This framework is borrowed from proven business consultation models that are used daily in business environments. Such approaches, as suggested by this framework, offer promise for future directions for the management of relationships with employers. Strong, enduring partnerships between employers and employment specialists are the intended result.

There seems to be endless possibility for partnerships engendered through professional consultation provided by employment specialists who can customize their expertise to meet the needs of each employer. Employment specialists and employment programs have at their disposal a wealth of knowledge and expertise that businesses can use. The key will be for the job placement field to show businesses that by using the consultation services of employment specialists, there will be a return on investment that merits future partnerships.

14

Organization Change

BUILDING EMPLOYER-FRIENDLY SERVICES

Debra Martin Luecking and Richard G. Luecking

*Small, well-focused actions can sometimes produce
significant and enduring improvements if they are in the right place.*

PETER SENGE

We hope that employment service programs and employment specialists who follow this book's advice are well on their way to establishing durable, effective partnerships with employers that are built on trust and mutuality. However, we fear that the field will only get so far if it is only individual employment specialists who digest and adopt many of the strategies outlined throughout this book. Employment service programs and organizations often need to bolster their organizational structures and processes so that these organizations, and the employment specialists affiliated with these organizations, can really develop dynamic and successful partnerships with businesses.

Employment service organizations, in order to thrive, must present themselves as credible partners to employers. It is therefore often necessary for employment service programs to first re-examine many of their organizational processes that complement credible delivery of services to employers and those that do not. As discussed in other chapters, there are typically distinct, unconnected, and often incompatible perspectives held by employment service providers and by employers. From the employer's point of view, it is not sufficient for an employment specialist or an employment service organization *to do good* by finding jobs for people with disabilities. The specialist and the organization also have *to be good* by competently providing good service.

Thus, this chapter discusses the importance for organizations to move from internally driven processes and outcomes to external focus on the employer customer. It is meant to be of primary interest to managers and administrators of employment service programs, but individual employment specialists may derive important perspectives that will help in their work and in their relationships within their organizations. It presents a framework for transforming internal organizational structures and processes to create services that are friendly to employer partners; that is, they are conducted in a professional, customer-oriented manner, they are convenient, and they are understandable to employers.

WHY BECOME MORE BUSINESS FRIENDLY?

Employer perceptions of employment agencies could use improvement. Instead of altruistic motives, employers view employment and hiring from a business perspective. Thus, they expect their partners to behave like businesses, not charity organizations. They are accustomed to working with others who make decisions on the basis of business practices and use the language of business. Partnerships develop when employers feel confident that the relationship will benefit them and that they will receive a return on their investment of time and resources when working with employment service organizations and the applicants they represent. Ultimately, then, the most successful employment service programs will be those that have employers who need them at least as much as they need the employers.

For some employment service providers, becoming more business friendly means improving specific aspects of their operation, such as upgrading their written marketing materials or instituting procedures for following up more regularly with employers. For other providers, becoming business friendly means reinventing entire aspects of their organizations, including carefully analyzing employer's needs, retraining staff, and deploying staff in different ways. Most of all, it means continuously upgrading the internal and external service quality of the organization.

Figure 14.1 represents a quick tool for assessing the business friendliness of employment service organizations and individual employment specialists. We use this tool in many of our training seminars and consultations to disability employment agencies as a way to help participants think about how ready they and their organizations are to begin partnering with business.

If the organization or individual employment specialist cannot check off most of the items in Figure 14.1, then it is necessary to consider organization development interventions and strategies that can address these gaps. Before examining the specifics of such interventions, it is useful to re-examine the importance of both internal operational

How Business Friendly Are You?

Use this quick tool to assess how business friendly you and your organization are.

My organization . . .

☐ Makes customer service a priority

☐ States its commitment to business friendliness in its mission and values

☐ Has top-level management and board commitment to a business-friendly, customer service philosophy

☐ Involves businesses in its operations through an active business advisory group that works with employment staff

☐ Communicates the importance of customer service to staff at all levels

☐ Devotes adequate resources to tracking trends and developing business relationships

☐ Belongs to local business organizations

☐ Has a written plan to make its operations more business friendly

☐ Is committed to staff development and offers training opportunities

☐ Communicates its expectations for employee performance and customer service

☐ Seeks input from the staff about customer service opportunities and barriers

☐ Has systems in place to address quickly any problems with customer service

☐ Encourages all staff members to seek out possible job opportunities and business partners

☐ Makes its services convenient and understandable to employers

☐ Maintains a database that captures information about job development opportunities and employer contacts

☐ Has standards for dress, office appearance, and courtesy

☐ Has professional-looking promotional materials

☐ Solicits continuous feedback from employers

As an employment specialist, I . . .

☐ Make customer service a personal priority

☐ Am aware of and try to fulfill my organization's mission and values

☐ Look for ways to be business friendly in my everyday work

☐ Continuously look for ways to make and maintain contacts in a variety of industries

☐ Communicate, through my words and actions, the importance of customer service

☐ Devote time to becoming more knowledgeable about business trends and employers in my community

☐ Am active in local business organizations

☐ Look for ways to make my daily actions more business friendly

☐ Actively and enthusiastically participate in staff development and training activities

☐ Understand and live up to my organization's expectations for performance and customer service

☐ Communicate ideas about how to improve customer service

☐ Am willing to find ways to resolve problems with customer service

☐ Am always looking out for possible job opportunities and business partners

☐ Look for ways to make my services convenient and understandable to employers

☐ Keep detailed records and use information gathered about job development opportunities and employer contacts

☐ Dress professionally; keep my work space organized; and always try to be helpful and courteous to co-workers, clients, and employers

☐ Suggest ways to improve my organization's promotional materials

☐ Solicit continuous feedback from employers

Figure 14.1.   Sample tool for assessing business friendliness.

processes (e.g., how things get done and how staff members are selected, prepared, and supported) and the perceptions of external customers (i.e., job seekers and employers).

INTERNAL VERSUS EXTERNAL FOCUS TO SHAPE CUSTOMER DEMAND

The economy and the world of human resources development are driven by a balance between supply and demand. Traditionally, the field of disability employment services has paid the most attention to the supply side of human resources development. That is, processes for linking job seekers with employers have tended to focus primarily and sometimes almost exclusively on the development and preparation of the job seeker, rather than also on labor market or employer demands. The focus of employment service agencies thus often tends to be on internal issues and complexities, such as reporting requirements, service hours, staff turnover, transportation, regulation compliance, and so forth. External factors, such as local labor market demands, typically do not shape the way in which services are delivered, and consequently employment service providers generally have difficulty with shaping employer demands for their service. Too often, employment specialists and employers have little information about one another, and therefore employers often have difficulty seeing how job placement services can be beneficial to business.

This type of internally driven focus is characteristic not only of employment service agencies but also of other human service agencies (Albin, 1992). The key force driving these agencies is often internal performance, not external forces such as customer satisfaction or a changing economy. Thus, the relationship between process and outcome—between the delivery of services and the successful acquisition of jobs by people with disabilities—is often obscured. The benefits of services are realized in their actual delivery (e.g., funding provided for number of hours of service), not in outcomes subsequently achieved (i.e., reimbursement based on jobs obtained). In addition, many agencies must adhere to accreditation measures or reporting expectations of funding entities that accentuate internally focused procedures and processes. It is not surprising, then, that employment service agencies develop an overemphasis on internal issues, processes, and operations, to the exclusion of external approaches and activities to improve outcomes. Under such conditions, it is easy to lose sight of the external environmental demands of the labor market and employer customers.

One of the frustrating aspects of an internally focused employment service agency is that the failure to find sufficient or appropriate job opportunities for job seekers frequently results in a quest for more internal resources, not toward improving their understanding of external environmental and customer demands. In other words, agencies often search for solutions internally in order to explain and improve poor job development outcomes (Fabian, Luecking, & Tilson, 1994). They look for more staff, money, time, and help. Although this search is not inherently misguided, the overlying problem of poor employment outcomes is not resolved. If employment outcomes are poor, how often do agencies ask job seekers and employers how they can improve services? How much time is spent examining the impressions that services and procedures create on the external environment? Conversely, how much time is spent trying to find ways to increase internal resources as the sole response to poor outcomes?

There is strong support for the focus to shift to external evaluation of services through customer feedback for improving internal processes. For example, the federal government is beginning to examine how to get a better return on investment by setting policy that emphasizes evidence-based practice ("Model Demonstration Projects," 2002). In effect, the government would like to begin saying in so many words, "Show me that it works first, and then we'll fund it." The accreditation field has continually evolved its measures to be more oriented to outcomes and customer satisfaction rather than to merely process compliance (Gardner, 1999). And finally, there are efforts to introduce employment service agencies to organization development theory and practice that have been used extensively in business, education, and human services to improve effectiveness and outcomes (Petty, Brickey, & Verstegen, 1999). It is the latter development that has implications for employer partnership development.

ORGANIZATION DEVELOPMENT AND CHANGE

For any organization, better outcomes and higher-quality service cannot be achieved without undergoing organizational self-analysis and change. Similarly, it is often necessary for employment service organizations to engage in major shifts in how they are structured and how they approach their missions. Otherwise, business as usual will yield the same unsatisfactory employment outcomes for the job seekers they serve. This section outlines basic organization development approaches and strategies that lead to service improvement.

Defining Organization Development

Prior to exploring the concept of organization development and its application to disability employment service delivery, it is important to note how it is defined. Leading professionals define *organization development (OD)* as a top-supported, long-range effort to improve an organization's effectiveness. The effort may include a series of planned processes by which staff are identified, utilized, and developed in ways that strengthen organizational capabilities by increasing problem solving and renewal processes (French & Bell, 1990). According to Rothwell, Sullivan, and McLean, there are several points that are key to understanding this definition of organization development:

> First, OD is long-range in perspective. It is not a "quick fix" strategy for solving short-term performance problems, as employee training is often inappropriately perceived to be. OD is a means to bring about complex change.
>
> Second, OD should be supported by top managers. They are usually the chief power brokers, change agents, and they control the organization's resources and reward systems. OD is less likely to succeed if it does not have at least tacit approval from—or better yet, participation of—top management.
>
> Third, OD effects change through education. Through this effort people's ideas, beliefs, and behaviors are expanded so that they can apply new approaches to old problems. OD change efforts go beyond employee-training interventions and concentrate on the work group or organization in which new ideas, beliefs, or behaviors are applied.
>
> Fourth, OD emphasizes employee participation in diagnosing problems, considering solutions, selecting a solution, identifying change objectives, implementing planned change, and evaluating results. In this sense OD differs from other methods that hold managers or consultants responsible for the success or failure of a change effort.
>
> In OD, everyone in an organization who is affected by change should have an opportunity to contribute to, and accept responsibility for, the continuous-improvement process. Empowering employees gives them a say in decision making and creates open communication which promotes a culture of collaboration, inquiry, and continuous learning. (1995, pp. 7–8)

These conditions and circumstances characterizing organization development apply directly to the operation of employment service programs that seek to change organizational processes and therefore improve program outcomes. Organizations that take on the challenge of recrafting their process to become more effective partnering with employers, for example, typically do so out of dissatisfaction with their present performance and a strong desire to improve. This impetus to improve may come from top management or from an employment specialist. Or an organization may be stimulated by external forces (e.g., federal or state initiatives, employer feedback). Organizations may choose to improve through self-directed efforts or by using external OD consultants to guide them through a performance improvement process.

Through our practice as organizational consultants, we have utilized a performance improvement process model that has yielded a systematic approach that is long range, is supported by top management, brings about change through education, is highly interactive, and engages employees in diagnosing problems, considering solutions, selecting solutions, implementing planned change, and evaluating results. We have found that Rothwell's (1996) six steps to performance improvement form a useful process for managing change, as illustrated in Figure 14.2.

| Performance analysis | Cause analysis | Intervention | Implementation | Change management | Evaluation and measurement |

Figure 14.2. Six steps to performance improvement. (*Source:* Rothwell, 1996.)

Implementing the Organization Improvement Process

Prior to beginning the improvement process, it is critical to build interest and gain commitment from staff. Everyone in an organization who is affected by change should have an opportunity to contribute to and accept responsibility for improvement. Providing information and the opportunity to have a say in decision making empowers employees and promotes a culture of collaboration, inquiry, and continuous learning. A means to this end is to form a team that will guide the performance improvement process. Key members of this team are representatives from top management, middle management, employment specialists and other related direct service staff, board of directors, employers, and job seekers with disabilities. Important to keep in mind is the selection of members who have the motivation and skills to design a plan that will move the organization to offering employer-friendly services.

Because members are coming into the team with their own mental picture, training and education may be needed on effective practices in employment—such as those presented throughout this book—and common elements that have emerged from organizations that have recreated themselves, such as those examples included in this chapter. Especially useful is to review studies that reveal what employers value in services provided by employment service programs (see Chapter 4).

Once the guidance team determines its direction, what typically emerges is the desire to get the information they have received to everyone in the organization. The executive director plays a key role here in communicating to everyone in the organization that he or she is committed to this new direction. This proclamation should be followed by small-group meetings facilitated by guidance team members to send the message that this new focus is a top priority for the organization and to glean feedback from employees about their concerns and commitment. Keeping everyone in the organization informed and involved throughout the process is critical to the organization effectively changing directions. Proclaiming that it is everyone's responsibility to job develop has been viewed as a means of stimulating the workforce by provoking questions, excitement, and even concerns. The steps frequently taken to focus on and improve performance are detailed as follows.

Business Partnership Institute

The Business Partnership Institute (BPI) is an organizational change process we have been using for the past several years that is designed to improve the employment outcomes for customers of disability employment service agencies. The BPI features three major activities:

1. On-site training and facilitated strategic action planning, usually conducted over the course of two consecutive days with a team of key agency representatives. The intervention begins with a introductory training on effective business partnership strategies, such as those featured in Section II of this book, with the majority of the remaining time spent constructing an action plan for service improvement.
2. Follow-up technical assistance to help implement the action plan and to incorporate strategies into regular agency operations to make the process more business friendly and ultimately more successful in helping more job seeker customers secure employment.
3. Annual networking meetings with other agencies participating in the BPI process.

Typical action plans developed through the BPI are provided in Figure 14.3.

Step 1: Performance Analysis   The process begins with collecting information that describes past and present efforts, desired performance, and perceived customer requirements. Using an interview or focus group format, information is gleaned from a guidance team that is composed of employees representing all tiers of the organization (i.e., board of directors, top managers, middle managers, employment specialists, direct service staff from all service areas) and from customers (i.e., employers and job seekers with disabilities). Questions to answer may include:

-   What is the desired performance (e.g., how many job seekers should you help to obtain employment)?
-   What is the actual performance (e.g., how many do you help now)?
-   What do employers want from your employment service program? Have you asked them?
-   How satisfied are employers with your present services? Have you asked them?
-   What do job seekers want from your employment service program? Have you asked them?
-   How satisfied are job seekers with your present services? Have you asked them?
-   What is the performance gap between the desired performance and actual performance (e.g., the difference between how many job seekers you want to assist in getting jobs minus the number who actually get them, what employers want from you versus what you are delivering)?
-   How has the gap been affecting the organization (e.g., are you losing funding, referrals)?
-   How much has the gap cost the organization? How can the tangible economic impact of the gap best be calculated (e.g., loss in revenue due to resources to meet demand)? How

can the intangible impact of the gap be calculated in lost customer goodwill or worker morale (e.g., job seekers no longer ask for employment service, limited support throughout the organization)?

The outcome of the performance analysis should be a clear description of the existing and desired conditions surrounding performance.

Step 2: Cause Analysis   At this point, the root causes of the past, present, and future performance gaps are identified. The overarching question to be answered is "Why does the performance gap exist?" The following issues should be considered:

- How well do the employment specialists and other staff see the results or consequences of what they do? How do they see their work helping to meet the desired performance?
- Are employment specialists and other staff given the data, information, or feedback they need in order to perform on a timely basis?
- Do all employees have the ability, time, and other resources necessary to perform?
- How well are employment specialists and other staff supported in what they do by appropriate environmental support, resources, equipment, or tools?
- How well do employment specialists' knowledge and skills match up to performance demands?
- Do employment specialists want to achieve desired results? What payoffs do they expect? How realistic are their expectations?
- How well are employment specialists and other staff rewarded or provided with incentives for performing as desired?

The outcome of the cause analysis should be a clear description of the cause(s) of the performance gap.

Externally Driven by Customers

A consortium of employment service providers formed to solicit input from local businesses to learn what services employers wanted from them and their perceptions of their present performance toward providing job development and supports for job seekers with disabilities. The results have led to a set of standards, generated by the employers, for providers to abide by.

The Problem Belongs to the Whole Organization

An employment service provider uncovered through a case analysis that human resources were inadequate to meet the demand on their time to assist job seekers in obtaining employment. Through an analysis of the steps necessary to be taken by an employment specialist to achieve an employment agreement with an employer, management became alarmingly aware that the employment program must have qualified and trained staff to provide service to their employment customers. Before this analysis, the lead employment specialist had been voicing a concern. The concern, under these circumstances, became that of the entire agency. Moving through the cause analysis allowed the guidance team to work together to recognize and resolve the problem.

Clarifying Roles and Service Process

A large organization that provided an array of services to people with disabilities—including service coordination, community residential services, and employment services—sought out external consultant services to assist them in improving the performance of its employment service program. The performance problem identified was that it did not have the present capacity to meet the demands of job seekers and employers. Not enough people were getting jobs. The process began with the formation of a guidance team. The team in turn identified job seekers who wanted employment services. Early into the process, however, it became clear that not all of the team members understood how employment services were delivered or what it took to make it happen. Thus, it was difficult for the team to think strategically about staff roles and responsibilities. To address this issue, the team went through a process of clarifying roles in relation to desired employment services to be delivered by 1) developing a list of employment services, 2) defining the services, 3) determining who had primary roles in delivering the services, and 4) providing new training and support for staff. This exercise also resulted in the development of a service and staff deployment schedule that is used by the whole organization as a communication and management tool.

Step 3: Intervention   By addressing the root causes of the gap between desired and actual performance, interventions should be selected that will have the greatest chance of producing significant improvements. Interventions to consider that will support improvement include:

- Team building focused on uniting around the desired performance
- Coaching to develop strategic direction to get to the desired performance
- Facilitation of cultural change to occur throughout the organization
- Training and education
- Leadership coaching that will support cultural change
- Performance support
- Analysis of desired performance and staffing needs
- Clarification of roles and work processes developed

These are the types of interventions that typically appear on an action plan.

Step 4: Implementation   This step engages the organization in preparing to install the desired performance of becoming an employer-friendly organization through the strategic development of an action plan. A guidance team, composed of key stakeholders that have been cultivated throughout this process, are the natural group to develop the plan. The plan should include the details for reaching the desired performance: 1) vision, 2) guiding principles, 3) mission, 4) goals and tasks, 5) timeline, and 6) responsible parties for each task. During plan development, the guidance team should examine answers or solutions to issues or questions that may have resulted from the cause analysis prior to plan development such as:

- What is the organization currently doing to address the causes of the performance gap (e.g., is it developing more tools for the staff to use)?
- What should the organization do in the future to address the causes of the performance gap (e.g., staff reinforcement for delivery of customer service)?
- What internal or external forces may affect the organization's ability to reach its desired performance (e.g., regulations, funding sources, training, consultation)?
- How will the strategic plan help the organization meet its desired performance?
- What are the best sources of talent and resources to implement the strategic plan?

This step usually results in a clear sense of desired outcomes to be achieved, an action plan that has commitment from the guidance team, and the assembly of talent and skills necessary to implement the plan. To enjoy continued effectiveness requires long-term commitment and oversight by stakeholders and decision makers. Figure 14.3 represents sample action plans developed by an organization that have provided it with a unified strategic direction.

Step 5: Change Management   The guidance team should review the strategic plan on a frequent and regular basis to determine the organization's effectiveness and to determine any obstacles that may hinder progress. Frequent discussion and plan review prove to be productive in maintaining unity of purpose by providing opportunity to clarify roles and to modify action so as to be in step with internal and external changes. The strategic action plan can become an effective communication tool for all concerned. Anxiety may result among a few team members as the organization moves to actually managing the changes called for in the plan. It is a very natural course for a team to go through stages of development: 1) forming a team and feeling a sense of excitement or anxiousness, 2) experiencing a storming stage in which the members begin to open up more and express their personal positive or negative feelings, 3) actually coming to agreement and standardizing the process, and 4) learning to perform together as a unified group. The team should consider answering the following questions as they manage the change that is called for in the organization's strategic action plan:

- How well do the strategic plan and other interventions assist the organization in reaching its desired performance?
- What measurable improvements can be shown?
- How much ownership have the stakeholders vested in implementing the strategic plan? What step can be taken to improve that ownership?
- How are changing conditions inside and outside the organization affecting the implementation of the plan?

Action Plan			
Team/Organization: _Valley Rehabilitation Services (VRS)_			
Challenge area: _Marketing message mixed with different parts of organization_			
Goal	**Activity**	**Leadership**	**Timeline**
All materials associated with employment service will be customer focused.	1. Review current materials. 2 Conduct features to benefits analysis to revise materials. 3. Produce new materials with a focus on business language instead of rehab language.	Employment service team Staff Director	2/1 3/1 6/1
The message will no longer be confusing because of the association with the larger organization.	1. Change the name of the community employment program.	Director and board	4/1
We will continually evaluate the effectiveness of the marketing message.	1. Survey employers. 2. Revise current survey materials: How did you hear about us? What made you call?	Employment service team Director	Start on 5/1 and monthly thereafter Every 6 months
All staff will use materials in an effective way.	1. Train staff on the use of marketing materials and delivery of the message. 2. Incorporate business terminology in the message and opening lines to employers.	Director Director	3/1 and then ongoing 3/1
Resources available: _Examples of materials used by other agencies, survey forms_			
Resources needed: _Change of rehab language to business language, script samples_			

Figure 14.3. Sample action plans.

Action Plan			
Team/Organization: *Valley Rehabilitation Services (VRS)*			
Challenge area: *Refining VRS's customer service techniques for employers*			
Goal	**Activity**	**Leadership**	**Timeline**
We will solicit feedback from employers.	1. Develop employer survey for new placements.	Director	10/1
	2 Send and analyze surveys for new placements.	Team	Weekly and ongoing
	3. Revise annual surveys to better gain feedback.	Team	Ongoing
	4. Train staff to use the survey.	Director	Ongoing
We will reorient the focus of customer service to a business and employer focus.	1. Identify the material format.	Team leaders	11/1
	2. Identify who receives it.	All staff	Ongoing
	3. Identify when they get it.	Director	Ongoing
	4. Make customer service discussion a regular agenda item for staff meetings.	Team leaders	Weekly
Resources available: *Sample customer service surveys from consultants*			
Resources needed: *Good customer service training modules*			
Challenge area: *We are not viewed as a viable contact for meeting human resources needs of area employers*			
Goal	**Activity**	**Leadership**	**Timeline**
We will increase the number of employer relationships by 10 each quarter.	1. Meet with business associations.	Director and team	3/1
	2. Submit articles to local papers.	Team	5/1
	3. Attend two job fairs.	P.R. Department	6/1
	4. Develop employer recognition notification process (e.g., letters, silk ties).	Team	10/1
Resources available: *Names of local business associations and groups*			
Resources needed: *Examples of good templates for letters to employers*			

Step 6: Evaluation and Measurement   Important to this entire process are the abilities to evaluate achievements, to measure impact, and to use the information gleaned in order to continuously improve the performance process. Questions to consider are:

- Were desired outcomes and measurable results achieved?
- What were the positive and negative side effects?
- What were the best practices or lessons learned that could be applied to the future?
- How well has the organization adopted the vision of a business-friendly organization?
- Did results match intentions?
- What value was added in economic and noneconomic terms?

Organizational Change in Practice

One employment service provider that we worked with exemplified the organization development approach to change to become a more business friendly operation. With the help of external facilitators, this organization went through the six steps toward performance improvement. After forming a team—consisting of the executive director, the employment program manager, employment specialists, a development manager, and two job seekers served by the organization—it began the performance analysis (Step 1). The team members agreed that they wanted to assist at least 20 more individuals currently served by the organization in moving from sheltered to community employment. This focus was motivated by funding opportunities that would be tied to more job outcomes and by their job seeker customers who expressed a desire for achieving employment. At the start of the process, only about 25% of the individuals the agency served worked in regular community jobs. They also realized that they really had no idea what their job seeker customers and the employers they worked with thought of their service. This later found its way into the action plan.

Analyzing the possible causes of the organization's performance gap (Step 2), the team realized several painfully obvious contributors to the gap, including the lack of clear set of job duties or performance expectations of the employment program staff, no organized staff training in job development and job matching, no mechanisms to support and reinforce employment staff who tried to help job seekers get jobs, and the fact that there was really only one person who had specified responsibility for job development and he was also assigned to get contracts for the sheltered workshop, so he had split duties and loyalties.

Several interventions were identified to address these circumstances (Step 3). Training was a major need. But before training could have an impact, the group had to address staff assignments and expectations. So the team decided that the action plan had to include the development of new job descriptions, a re-organization of staff assignments so that job development and postplacement support was shared by a number of staff, and new structures for regular employment program staff.

As a prelude to developing and implementing the action plan (Step 4) to accomplish improved performance, the team agreed on a unifying vision for the employment programs: to be known as a premier deliverer of good job candidates and good service to the community's employers. The action plan then began to take shape. It featured many activities designed to improve its image in the employer community, such as new marketing material, and to improve the staff efficiency, such as training and support for delivering customer service to employers. Also, as a way of getting meaningful feedback from employers and job seekers, a questionnaire was developed, along with a process for administering it. Another major decision was to form a business advisory council (see Chapter 9) as a vehicle to obtain regular employer input and feedback on the program's activities. Finally, key among several other activities, the agency renamed its employment services program Career Solutions to distinguish this department from the rest of the agency, which was highly visible in the community as a human service program that provided an array of other services to people with disabilities.

The organization's team then made sure that they continually monitored the plan's implementation (Step 5). In fact, a review of the plan and the status of the outcomes became a regular agenda item for the agency's board of directors and the business advisory council meetings. This ensured continuing top-level support for the plan and a continuing opportunity to get outside input from the very constituent group, employers, from which the agency was attempting to solicit more job opportunities and which it was attempting to better serve. The board of directors was especially interested in getting reports on the outcomes that were obtained as a result of the action plan (Step 6). Within a year, this agency achieved a dramatic increase in business partners along with an accompanying increase in job acquisition for job seekers served by the organization.

SUSTAINING THE MOMENTUM

Implementing business-friendly strategies and beginning an organization change process are, of course, just a beginning. The effort must be sustained if the employment agency is to cultivate its employer partnerships, make them last, and ultimately help job seekers attain the employment outcomes they desire. It is often helpful for organizations to take frequent and continuous assessment of how well they reflect the values and practices of business friendliness. Some ongoing guiding questions may include:

- Do the organization's mission and value statements and policies continue to reflect a commitment to its external customers?
- Do the organization's procedures and practices help or hinder employer relationships?
- Are the organization's staff continuously reinforced or rewarded for good service to its external customers?

- Does the organization make it easy for the staff to adhere to business-friendly practices?
- Are the organization's job descriptions and duties written to reflect attention to external customers?
- Do staff development efforts and staff training programs feature external customer service strategies?
- Do employers come back to the organization asking for more employees?
- Are the organization's funders referring more job seekers or asking the organization to expand its services?
- Ultimately, is the organization helping the job seekers it represents achieve jobs and careers they desire?

One way to conceptualize how organizations can continually address internal and external quality for continuous improvement of services that are effective and business friendly is depicted in the chart in Figure 14.4 (Heskett, Jones, Loveman, Sasser, & Schles-

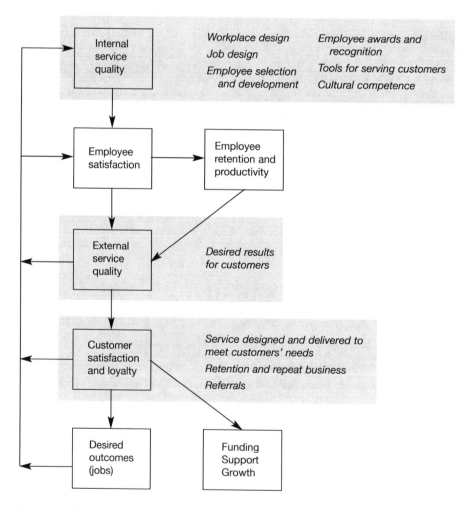

Figure 14.4.   Links in the service–outcome chain. (*Source:* Heskett, Jones, Loveman, Sasser, & Schlesinger, 1996.)

inger, 1996). The links in the service–outcome chain are sequentially ordered to show that internal service quality (i.e., workplace design, job design, employee selection, employee rewards, and cultural competence) leads to employee satisfaction, retention, and productivity. Employee satisfaction and productivity leads to value for the job seekers and employers, which leads to customer satisfaction and loyalty. Customer satisfaction and loyalty in turn lead to desired outcomes (i.e., jobs for job seekers, value for employers) and potentially more funding support due to successful outcomes.

Where there are weaknesses in the links, the desired outcomes decrease. Organizations must then re-evaluate each of the links, continuously asking the important questions and taking any necessary corrective action. They must also continuously solicit and use external customer feedback to shore up each link so as to ensure desired outcomes. Chapter 12 provides ideas, strategies, and tools for measuring and using customer feedback.

SUMMARY

In spite of the purported intent to produce employment outcomes for job seekers served by employment service programs, there has been a tendency for these programs to use processes that impede that very objective. Focus on internal concerns, regulatory and funding requirements, and naiveté related to business views often creates ineffective processes and consequently poor employment outcomes. It is therefore important for employment service programs to develop procedures that are more employer friendly (i.e., convenient, helpful, and understandable to employers). A tool to examine individual and organizational employer friendliness is often a helpful place to begin comparing how things are now done with more ideal processes. This chapter provides such a tool.

This chapter introduces the concept of organization development and change as a way to develop and implement processes that are friendlier to prospective and current employer partners. A six-step strategic approach to helping organizations adopt more employer-friendly processes is adapted from the Human Performance Improvement Process Model of the American Society for Training and Development and includes performance analysis, cause analysis, intervention, implementation, change management, and evaluation and measurement. Case studies of organizations who adapted this process are presented, along with sample action plans that one agency developed to improve its relationships with employers.

It is important to continue to address both internal and external circumstances that might influence effectiveness in developing employer relationships and jobs for people with disabilities. Continuous organization improvement can be conceptualized along a chain of linked activities, each of which require attention in order to sustain performance and keep employer and job seeker customers happy. Sustained partnerships and improved employment outcomes are the likely results.

15

Job Retention and Career Growth

*The greatest thing in this world is not
so much where we are, but in which direction we are moving.*

OLIVER WENDELL HOLMES

Up to this point, the book covers information about linking job seekers and employers so that the job seeker gets a job. Effective job development strategies and marketing practices help ensure that individuals with disabilities secure employment that is consistent with their interests and goals. The success of these strategies has been demonstrated throughout the earlier chapters of the book. Of course, getting a job is a critical, but only a first step in terms of promoting long-term attachment to the labor market for individuals with disabilities. One of the major issues that has emerged recently is how people with disabilities can be assisted to move beyond merely getting a job to genuine career advancement (Hope & Rice, 1995; Rumrill & Roessler, 1999).

Career advancement refers to a positive trajectory or pattern of jobs over time. Although the totality of an individual's career path throughout the life span may reflect the ups and downs associated with specific choices (e.g., returning to school), environmental factors (e.g., the economy), and life stage (e.g., having children), generally, a trajectory suggests a dynamic, positive movement. This positive movement can be reflected in a variety of indicators, such as higher wages, more job benefits, more diverse or interesting job

tasks, increasing job responsibilities, and eventually more rewards in terms of self- and career satisfaction. Unfortunately, many individuals with disabilities, particularly those with
significant disabilities, evidence job patterns that are just the opposite of career advancement (Rumrill & Roessler, 1999; Walls & Fullmer, 1997). In other words, their work histories are characterized by a number of entry-level positions held for a relatively brief period of time, and resulting in negative or no career growth (Fabian, 1999; Pumpian,
Fisher, Certo, & Smalley, 1997). This "serial jobs" pattern can actually be deleterious to
long-term labor market attachment, as it may decrease vocational self-efficacy and depress
positive expectations of career outcomes (Fabian, 2000; Romoser, 2000). The future of
employment services for individuals with disabilities will surely include a sharper focus
on career direction. The purpose of this chapter is to review some of the barriers to career
advancement for individuals with disabilities and to suggest some strategies or practices
for addressing them.

BARRIERS TO CAREER ADVANCEMENT

The changes in the nature of employment and work that have been described earlier in the
text have implications not only for assisting people to get jobs but also for career advancement. Today's economic context includes demands for part-time and contract workers, heightened job mobility, and more emphasis on advanced technical skills. These factors have changed the concept of career advancement. When workers no longer have a job
for life, then career no longer means moving up within one company or even in one industry. Instead, career advancement in this new work world suggests an individual's progression of learning and working throughout life. Old concepts such as job retention are
replaced with strategies that encourage long-term attachment to the labor market, pro-
jecting a more flexible notion of a progression of jobs and the accompanying need for lifelong access to career counseling and career support services (Rumrill & Roessler, 1999).
That is, career counseling is no longer conceived as being offered at a specific life point,
such as when a young adult first enters the world of work. Instead, career services need
to be viewed as an ongoing, flexible system of career assessment and support, available
through numerous outlets, including educational institutions, businesses, and public employment centers such as the federal One-Stop Career Centers, authorized through the enactment of the Workforce Investment Act (WIA) of 1998 (PL 105-220).

For individuals with disabilities, access to the types of career support services that
support advancement and progression throughout life are available through public systems, such as vocational rehabilitation, as well as through private agencies, such as

community-based rehabilitation or supported employment services. Even though these types of services are theoretically available to support the career needs of individuals with disabilities, the concept of life planning or lifelong career planning has not been as popular in the job development and placement literature targeted at individuals with disabilities as it is in general career planning literature (Szymanski et al., 2003). This may be for a couple of reasons. One reason is that the emphasis in rehabilitation has historically been on getting a job, as opposed to keeping it, primarily in response to the traditional administrative structure that is geared toward time-limited services (e.g., Noble, Honberg, Hall, & Flynn, 1997). A second and more important reason for the neglect of the concept of career advancement is the barriers that individuals with disabilities encounter as they progress through their work lives. The following four represent some of the major obstacles to career advancement for employees with disabilities.

Social Security Disincentives

This is frequently mentioned as the most entrenched and perhaps strongest disincentive to both getting and keeping a job for individuals with disabilities who receive income support and health care benefits from the two major disability entitlement programs of the Social Security Administration (SSA): Social Security Disability Insurance (SSDI) and Supplemental Security Insurance (SSI) (Drew et al., 2001). Loss of health care benefits is a particularly acute issue for the eight million or so social security disability beneficiaries who often fear that returning to work or enlarging the scope of their work will result in denial of the health benefits provided through either federal Medicare or Medicaid insurance programs. That this issue represents a substantial return to work barrier is supported by the fact that fewer than 1% of disabled people who are Social Security disability beneficiaries leave the rolls each year, despite their expressed desires to work (Kornfield & Rupp, 2000). Furthermore, of those who do leave, about one third are unsuccessful and return within 1 year. Although the Ticket to Work and Work Incentives Improvement Act of 1999 (PL 106-170) was designed to mitigate these disincentives to work, it is too early to determine how successful these new provisions will be, particularly in addressing entrenched consumer anxieties associated with losing access to health care. Moreover, Social Security benefits provisions require understanding of complex regulations that are often beyond the expertise of employees and service providers. Employment specialists, or even the agencies they work for, may not have access to benefits counselors or expert advisors to help them understand how these new regulations change the scope of requirements regarding employment and, in particular, how they affect access to health insurance.

Real and Perceived Workplace Discrimination

Even with the passage of the Americans with Disabilities Act (ADA) of 1990 (PL 101-336) and the changing political landscape, negative attitudes in the workplace toward specific disabilities persist (Unger, 2002a). This is particularly true for people with emotional and mental disabilities, for whom stereotypes and biases not only affect hiring decisions but also may negatively influence work retention as employees are reluctant to request workplace accommodations for fear of evoking negative reactions from supervisors and co-workers (Corrigan, 1998). More insidiously, anxiety associated with negative attitudes may exacerbate symptoms of the impairment for some individuals with disabilities, thus decreasing their performance. For example, an employee with a less apparent disability, such as multiple sclerosis, may avoid asking for an accommodation to a work schedule because of fears that knowledge of the condition may affect employer decisions regarding promotion. As a result, the heightened fatigue and increased stress will, of course, eventually affect many of the behaviors required for effective work performance—both physical and mental—and possibly lead to job loss. When an employee does disclose a disability or impairment, such as severe depression, he or she risks evoking employer stereotypes regarding perceived limitations that might interfere with job promotion.

Lack of Postemployment Services

Although state vocational rehabilitation agencies have the capacity to fund postemployment services for eligible individuals with disabilities, indications are that individuals rehabilitated through the state federal program do not receive adequate postemployment services that would help sustain employment (Hope & Rice, 1995; Noble et al., 1997). Supported employment programs, designed specifically to provide continuous or ongoing job support are obviously the alternative, but studies indicate that even these services fail to promote long-term job tenure for those individuals with severe disabilities served by these programs (Bond et al., 2001). Moreover, it is clear that not enough supported employment programs are available to serve the number of individuals with disabilities who need them (Podmostko, 2000), thus access to the kind of continuous job support available through these programs is limited by the number of slots that can be funded.

People with disabilities who are Social Security beneficiaries may use special funds to purchase employment support services. These funds are available through a program called the Plan for Achieving Self-Sufficiency (PASS), and studies have shown that individuals with disabilities have used PASS funds to purchase employment-related services, such as transportation (West, Wehman, & Revell, 1996). Despite the increased use of PASS funds in the 1990s, many advocates for people with disabilities know little about the program (West et al., 1996). However, PASS funds do present an opportunity for SSA beneficiaries to purchase postemployment services in order to achieve financial independence.

Career Choice and Self-Determination

Career choice and self-determination have been addressed in earlier chapters as critical components of the job search and job acquisition process. Career choice is also related to job tenure, as employees are much more likely to leave jobs that provide few rewards and little satisfaction. In other words, for job retention to occur, the job or position the individual occupies must satisfy at least some of his or her basic interests and values (Lofquist & Dawis, 1984).

Labor market and other studies suggest that individuals with disabilities who work tend to have jobs that might be described as part of the secondary labor market, meaning that they are entry-level jobs with poor hourly wages that provide few or limited benefits (Hagner, 2000). For example, a study of job outcomes of state vocational rehabilitation customers in 1998 indicated that only 18% of them were in professional or managerial positions, while more than 60% of them were in clerical sales, service, and benchwork (Walls, Misra, & Majumder, 2002). The problem with this is not the nature of the jobs themselves but the fact that in the general labor market, average job tenure for these types of positions is about 6 months. Without adequate access to ongoing career counseling services, then, workers with disabilities have no assistance with finding different or better jobs after this initial step, thus contributing to the pattern of serial jobs.

PROGRAMMATIC COMPONENTS TO STIMULATE WORK RETENTION

Although there is voluminous literature regarding developing strategies to help people find jobs, much less literature regarding helping people to keep them is available. Although indications are that there is a renewed political and economic interest in job retention for people with disabilities evidenced by changes to social security laws and modifications to vocational rehabilitation services, there is certainly insufficient data available regarding what types of interventions and services might work best. This section summarizes some of the basic programmatic interventions that are associated with job retention and career advancement.

Workplace Support

Workplace support is, of course, the hallmark feature of supported employment programs since it was initially defined in the Rehabilitation Act Amendments of 1986 (PL 99-506). In supported employment programs, ongoing support is frequently provided by an employment specialist or job coach, either at the job site or off, depending on the nature of the individual's disability (Hanley-Maxwell, Owens-Johnson, & Fabian, 2003). Recent studies of supported employment programs have indicated that jobsite interventions are required even 18 months after job stabilization (West, Wehman, & Revell, 2002). In addition to the employment specialist or the job coach providing direct jobsite intervention, other supported employment programs have demonstrated the utility of training co-workers to be the primary source of support (Mank, 1996), a strategy that only works if the employee has disclosed his or her disability to the employer. Community-rehabilitation and other treatment programs also provide other valuable types of workplace supports, including individual and group counseling, work retention groups, substance abuse prevention, and assistive technology. Career counseling and job support services may be available through the network of One-Stop Career Centers, established through the WIA. However, intensive and individualized job support required by individuals with disabilities, even if the need is only intermittent or short-term, may be beyond the scope of the services typically available through such centers, unless the capacity to do so is established with the help of disability experts.

Employers and businesses may also offer workplace supports to employees with disabilities. For example, mid-size and large companies may have employee assistance programs available to workers. These programs provide time-limited intervention services designed to assist employees whose personal or other psychological problems are interfering with their job performance. Although employee assistance programs can be a valuable resource for early intervention and stabilization, access to these types of benefits may be limited, particularly for employees who work in smaller businesses or at lower-level or part-time jobs. Employers might also provide transportation assistance to employees, a support feature that is frequently needed by individuals with disabilities who may lack access to personal transportation or may need financial or other assistance in getting to work.

Social Supports

Social supports outside the work environment can also be important buffers in mitigating stress and improving functioning. The voluminous literature on social support suggests that it is a key factor in promoting adjustment and in assisting people to cope with stress (Sarason, Pierce, & Sarason, 1990; Weiss, 1974). Moreover, at least one study of work adjustment in a sample of individuals with mental illness (Hammen, Gitlin, & Altshculer, 2000) found that it was the quality of relationships outside of work that was most important in sustaining vocational performance. Personal or social supports outside of the work environment may be particularly important for employees who are reluctant to disclose their disabilities.

Substantial evidence has pointed to the importance of social networks and social support in sustaining positive behaviors and reducing stress for all individuals, not just those with disabilities. Moreover, the benefits of personal networks and social support systems may be particularly important for employees with disabilities, who may have less access to or ability to form the types of social networks that create a buffer to reduce stress and assist in coping and self-management. Personal support networks can be provided through formal means, such as personal care attendants or residential counselors, or informal means, such as family, religious groups, spouses, and friends. The increased use of the Internet as a supportive intervention may also benefit employees with disabilities, who can link to online support groups that are either peer-facilitated or conducted more formally by employment programs or other service providers.

Sustaining personal supports outside of work is also important in career advancement, as finding better jobs is more successfully done via personal networks than through any other means (Granovetter, 1995). Chapter 5 describes some of the strategies for assisting individuals with disabilities to develop such social support networks, using, for example, religious or social groups or centers and volunteer or recreational activities and participating in formal business groups such as the Chamber of Commerce. Many employees enhance their social support networks through participation in educational and training activities, such as taking courses at community colleges or other adult education settings. Work retention groups and ongoing job clubs—in both real time and virtual time—also represent opportunities for maintaining and enhancing social support networks.

Lifelong Learning and Training

As described in earlier chapters, America's occupational structure has been transformed from an industrial to a postindustrial society, one that is based on information instead of manufacturing. It follows that in order to succeed in this postindustrial world, employees need to constantly upgrade their skills and sustain the kinds of basic skills and behaviors that are associated with success in this evolving world of work, such as the ability to work as a member of a team, to demonstrate problem-solving capacities on the job, and to work creatively. These basic skills are viewed as necessary, but they are not sufficient to succeed in the world of work, suggesting that today's workers need to constantly update their skills and acquire new ones if they are to move beyond the secondary labor market into good jobs (Hoyt, 1996). The need for acquiring new skills is especially important for workers without advanced or postsecondary education. For example, the U.S. Department of Labor's (2003) *Occupational Outlook Handbook* stated that employment in occupations requiring less than a college degree with additional vocational training will increase by 32% by 2013, more than for any other level of education reported. This means, of course, that workers with disabilities, particularly those who may lack formal educational credentials, will need to have access to ongoing opportunities to acquire new skills in order to adapt to new occupational demands. The consequence of not retooling skills is, of course, to remain stuck in the secondary labor market of low-paying, entry-level service jobs.

CAREER ADVANCEMENT STRATEGIES

Given these issues, what can employment specialists and employment agencies do in terms of facilitating interventions to improve work retention and career advancement for employees with disabilities? The following list of recommendations and practices includes both activities that employment specialists can incorporate immediately into their work, as well as strategies that likely require additional resources and planning.

1. Identify support aspects in the work environment. Even for the worker who does not disclose his or her disability to the employer, having a colleague or co-worker who can help problem-solve during times of stress or who can just serve as a social connection may have beneficial effects on sustaining performance.

2. Work with employees to locate off-site supports. Assist workers to identify supports in their larger environments. Because of social skills deficits and lack of access to social support networks, employment specialists may need to assist employees in getting involved in supportive networks, both real and virtual, such as support groups connected to their disability, or being involved in social activities that are not related to their disability but where they can find social resources.

3. Encourage employees to use electronic methods to obtain support at work. The increased acceptance of electronic communication—such as e-mail, cell phones, and personal digital assistants (PDAs)—multiply opportunities for counselors to directly, yet nonintrusively, intervene in the worksite. Having e-mail check-ins may be an effective work retention intervention that can reduce intervention costs.

4. Maintain positive expectations of future outcome. One of the most empowering ways to do this is by assisting individuals to set meaningful and achievable goals and then having them incorporate these goals into their daily functioning (Bandura, 1986). For

example, encourage employees to enter their goals on their PDAs, both as a constant source of reminder and as a means of tracking their progress.

5. Make connections with local social service agencies for counseling and job-related support services. These connections can be beneficial in terms of assisting employment specialists to problem-solve around how specific accommodation needs may manifest themselves as functional work limitations in the work environment so that they may be anticipated and more effectively accommodated. Some local resources, such as the public vocational rehabilitation program, may be able to provide specific assistance in purchasing necessary accommodations and assistive technology. Linking workers with disabilities to SSA staff who can provide benefits counseling, either live or on the Internet, addresses one of the paramount obstacles to job retention.

6. Increase collaborations and partnerships with businesses in the community as a career advancement strategy. Collaborative activities, such as those discussed in detail in Section II of this book, not only increase the odds that employment specialists can serve as resources to employees and businesses but also increase the opportunities to educate local businesses about important aspects of career advancement, such as reasonable accommodations and the ADA. The more connections in the community the employment specialist has, the more likely it is that employers will seek out advice and consultation on managing disability issues in the workplace.

7. Ensure that all job seekers have a career goal, not just a job goal. Even if the longer-term goal is a year or more away, the fact that the individual is already planning for it before he or she starts back to work helps ensure its success. Identify resources in the community environment, such as training or education, that can assist the individual to continue to work toward the goal.

8. Develop and conduct a postemployment service, such as a work retention or career advancement group that has face-to-face meetings, as well as virtual meetings. Maintaining contact and brainstorming with peers is a powerful intervention strategy in and of itself. In addition, the types of problems and challenges that each employee encounters on the job presents an opportunity for vicarious learning and problem solving for other employees.

9. Empower individuals to acquire the types of job development skills that will enable them to self-manage their careers. Although some individuals with the most severe disabilities may always need intervention and assistance to achieve desirable employment outcomes, many others can benefit from learning skills associated with networking, information interviewing, and job preparation to progress through their own career lives.

SUMMARY

The concept of getting and retaining a single job for individuals with disabilities is being replaced with notions of long-term attachment to the labor market and career advancement. These concepts present a more optimistic perspective by describing a dynamic trajectory of progress and growth. It also reframes the perspective on job loss in terms of viewing it as an opportunity to learn new skills, develop new interests, and acquire more experiences. It is a much more empowering perspective than one that features simply getting and keeping a single job.

Career counseling and career development services should be accessible to individuals throughout their working lives. This is particularly important for individuals with disabilities, who may otherwise be relegated to the secondary labor market without access to the types of resources and services that can help them to explore different options, understand the labor market within their local economies, and equip themselves with the necessary knowledge and skills to attain new goals. This chapter provides a few basic strategies to provide this assistance.

16

Into the Future

CHALLENGES AND ISSUES AFFECTING
JOB AND PARTNERSHIP DEVELOPMENT

Even if you're on the right track, you'll get run over if you just sit there.

WILL ROGERS

Many circumstances that are in the offing will affect the future of the important work this book has highlighted—promoting and facilitating the linking of people with disabilities with employers. In spite of, and in some cases because of, economic fluctuations, global events, shifting political priorities, legislative developments, and advancing technology, there is much to be optimistic about. The field has become more and more aware of the value of choice and self-determination, for example. Paternalism of employment and vocational programs toward job seekers with disabilities is quickly becoming a practice of the past. Due to the ADA, more and more employers have not only become careful not to discriminate against applicants and employees with disabilities, but hundreds of companies have taken affirmative steps to recruit, hire, and accommodate workers with disabilities. In addition, assistive technology and other technologies have changed the way people can do their work and the way work generally gets done. All of these developments bode well for people with disabilities who will seek to become employed or to advance their careers. We have discussed these in many contexts in the preceding chapters.

However, vigilance and flexibility will be necessary no matter how adeptly or effectively the strategies we have presented are implemented: vigilance to monitor economic, political, and cultural shifts and the flexibility to react to these shifts. The framework pre-

245

sented in Chapter 2 suggests the important influence of these fluctuations on the employment process. In fact, legislative and policy considerations are continually under review
and new directions in these arenas will likely have far-reaching implications for disability
employment initiatives. Significant among these are the future reauthorizations of the
Rehabilitation Act, WIA, and any new legislation that affects the nation's workforce investment activity. There may be continual restructuring of these two federal legislative
pieces that together fund and regulate much of the employment service activity that intends to benefit job seekers with disabilities. The Individuals with Disabilities Education
Act (IDEA) Amendments of 1997 (PL 105-17) is also subject to considerable transforma-
tion in future reauthorizations, which will affect how well students with disabilities are
situated for transition from school to an adult working life. Regardless of the direction of
these legislative actions, a host of legislative and policy directions will bear constant
watching.

Business trends are also looming that have implications for employment programs.
Since the 1990s, for example, as a result of constant restructuring to adapt to economic
fluctuations, outsourcing of specific jobs or projects to other companies has been a common practice in companies who want to permanently reduce the size of their workforces
(Corbett, 2002). This, of course, influences where the jobs are and what types of jobs
are available. Another trend that affects the labor market is the proliferation of small
employers—virtually all new jobs are being created in small business (Donohoe, 2003). In
addition, rapid changes in technology affect not only the landscape of companies within
every industry sector but also how work gets done in all workplaces.

Education reform movements are also underway. There are, of course, considerations
related to future authorizations of IDEA that might affect how well students who receive
special education services are prepared for jobs and careers. There are also ongoing and
often unpredictable general education reforms that may affect the future direction of employment services. For all students, important unanswered questions include: How well
will they respond to competency testing as a high school graduation requirement? How
much help will future job seekers need as they exit school? How closely will schools and
educators be able to collaborate with employers and employment service programs? How
well prepared will students be to pursue postsecondary education and training that will
lead to good paying jobs?

This chapter presents issues and trends that are likely to influence the success of
future partnerships between disability employment initiatives and business and therefore employment opportunities for job seekers with disabilities. The issues covered in this
chapter are not necessarily in order of significance and do not necessarily constitute an all-
inclusive list. They are based on our ongoing conversations with job seekers, employers,
policy makers, advocates, educators, and employment specialist colleagues. They all bear
watching as the field refines activities that link job seekers with employers.

TRENDS AND ISSUES AFFECTING
FUTURE EMPLOYMENT PRACTICE

Issue 1: Access to Generic Workforce Development Programs

As discussed in Chapter 1, WIA represents a significant attempt at reform of the delivery of national employment and training services by consolidating separate and disconnected services previously organized according to categories of service recipients, such as for workers who lose their jobs, welfare recipients, offenders, veterans, and people with disabilities. This has many implications for job seekers with disabilities, not the least of which are new avenues for employment acquisition assistance that are not defined as a special disability-only service. People with disabilities can theoretically obtain employment assistance that is available to the general population. Indeed, WIA has provisions that the One-Stop Career Centers it funds are to be universally accessible to any job seeker, including those with disabilities, and provisions that the state vocational rehabilitation agency be a partner in the operation of the One-Stop Career Centers so that disability expertise is available.

Subsequent reauthorizations of WIA—or any new workforce investment legislation—may shift many of these basic features, but in the main the legislation represents a definite trend toward generically accessible and coordinated services for multiple categories of job seekers. Indeed, if the long-time rhetoric of disability advocates for inclusion and integration of people with disabilities into their communities is to be actually realized, then this is a very important trend. Already there has been significant federal investment in making One-Stop Career Centers physically and programmatically accessible for customers with disabilities as well as investment in projects that demonstrate how people with disabilities can receive comprehensive and coordinated employment services through these centers.

Potential Effects on Partnership Practice   Will One-Stop Career Centers replace long-standing disability employment organizations? The disability employment organizations' expertise will not likely completely be replaced in the near future by One-Stop Career Centers or similarly constructed generally available employment service. However, the immediate effect of this trend toward more generically available services will be the opportunity for employment specialists and employment programs to work more closely in concert with new and different partners. Partnerships with and access to One-Stop Career Centers funded by WIA potentially will allow a broader range of job seeking service options for people with disabilities, broader employer partnerships that will lead to more job opportunities, and more resources that can be mutually leveraged by different One-Stop partners to accomplish their respective missions. As a result, some of the potential benefits that such a direction offers job seekers with disabilities include:

- *Additional and convenient sources of career development information.* Among the core services available through One-Stop Career Centers are labor market information, information on the area's economy and employers, Internet access to career development information, résumé development, and a host of other services that may provide useful adjuncts to job seekers and the employment specialists who assist them.
- *Indefinite, lifelong access to career development assistance.* Core services of the One-Stop Career Centers are available to everyone at any time in their career. This opportunity allows individuals to return for career and job search assistance without waiting for eligibility determination or designated program referrals. This also represents an avenue for addressing the issues of career advancement discussed in the previous chapter.
- *Reduction of stigma.* The intended coordinated service approach of WIA reduces the need for categorical labels in workforce development systems, and the emphasis on universal access means that disclosure of disability is dependent on individual preference.

Issue 2: Streamlining Employer Contacts through Cooperating Workforce Programs

Employers have typically been puzzled by the fragmentation of employer recruitment initiatives because there are so many disparate programs that represent various categories of job seekers. It remains a common practice for multiple agencies, representing distinct categories of job seekers, to compete for employer attention. This frustrates and confuses employers and often creates unnecessary duplication on the part of workforce development programs and professionals (Luecking, 2003). It is unrealistic for employers to know the differences and distinctions between one disability employment program or another, or one disability category or another, much less the distinctions between other job seeker categories, such as welfare recipients, unemployment benefits recipients, youth who are at risk, and so forth. However, in the competition among employment service entities to gain employer attention, employers are frequently left to sort out the nuances of these various programs on their own.

One trend, given impetus by the WIA, presents some new possibilities for streamlining employer contacts and relationships. As mentioned, the WIA provides the incentive and opportunity for previously disparate categorical programs to work together as co-located partners in One-Stop Career Centers to serve diverse job seekers. The WIA also offers new opportunities to broker employer engagement by unifying and streamlining the manner in which employers are recruited for workforce development initiatives. Co-located One-Stop Career Center partners, for example, might come together to share employer contacts and use a common protocol for recruiting and serving employers.

One particularly effective example of this type of approach to employer recruitment is the Employer Service Network (ESN) in Rhode Island. It features a formal affiliation of workforce and economic development entities and professionals who strive to offer an array of services to employers. Its purpose is to add value, reduce waste, and continuously improve Rhode Island's capacity to connect people, employers, jobs, education, and services. The ESN membership comprises more than 150 local and state organizations. The majority of these organizations are direct providers of workforce development services. They represent an array of constituent customers, including welfare recipients, dislocated workers, youth, people with various disabilities, and other groups of job seekers. Care was taken to develop a protocol that includes well-defined procedures for all members to follow and to which all members are expected to adhere. The protocol includes specific procedures for establishing and designating a lead point of contact for each employer, as well as procedures for staff training, employer follow-up, and record keeping.

Another example of this approach is in Montgomery County, Maryland, where disability employment providers have cooperated since 1987 in what is called the Coordinating Council of Employment Service Providers for People with Disabilities. Although not as comprehensively organized as the Rhode Island ESN, the Coordinating Council meets on a regular basis to share job leads, meet and talk to employers, and receive joint training. A job line is also maintained that lists current job openings by area employers. Employers have a convenient way to broadcast job openings and employment service providers have the opportunity to expand their employer contacts by using the job line as a source of job possibilities for the job seekers they represent.

Potential Effects on Partnership Practice   Both of these examples illustrate how cooperation among potential competitors might benefit everyone involved in the employment process. For employers, the ease of dealing with agencies through a consolidated effort makes great sense. They also benefit from a much larger pool of workers than what might be available to them when working with an organization representing a single category of job seekers. Cooperating employment agencies benefit from a much-expanded universe of employer contacts. They also have more to offer their employer customers. For example, if the employer has recruitment needs that cannot be filled by one agency, that agency can connect the employer to an entire network of employment service providers—a clear value that employment programs can add to their employer relationships. And finally, they benefit by pooling their resources for staff training. Their training budgets go farther and their staffs receive high-quality professional development opportunities.

Ultimately, the job seekers benefit from being served by organizations that have numerous employer contacts at their disposal and well-trained staff to assist them in their job search. They also are less likely to have to rely on single, category-based employment programs because the cooperating employment service programs can market their services to employers with a more broad-based appeal that is not dependent on selling particular, often stigmatized, categories of job seekers. Such activities are not likely to catch on everywhere due to entrenched competition for job seeker customers and for funding, but where enterprising and cooperating employment specialists and agencies can orchestrate such collaborative efforts, it is likely that employer partnerships will flourish.

Issue 3: Partnership Incentives for Business

Tax credits and incentives have long been the cornerstone of marketing disability employment to business—to mixed effect (Blessing & Jamieson, 1999; Culver, Spencer, & Gliner, 2001). On the one hand, marketing such incentives sends a message that extraordinary efforts and considerations are necessary in order for employers to be willing to give job seekers with disabilities a chance. This certainly contradicts the message of competency and value that must be communicated in any kind of marketing campaign for any kind of service or product. On the other hand, a few businesses have taken good advantage of these credits to generate bottom-line revenue. Mostly, however, they are not extensively used, and employers complain that they are more trouble than they are worth due to cumbersome administration requirements and that they have not been that effective in promoting hiring of people with disabilities (General Accounting Office, 2002).

Some of these credits may indeed be useful, especially for employers who go beyond legal requirements for reasonable accommodations. However, the trend, it seems, is to move away from such incentives as primary aspects of disability marketing campaigns. Indeed, many employers are calling for a more business-focused means of giving incentives to employers who create partnerships with disability employment initiatives. According to Katherine McCary (personal communication, May 29, 2003), Vice President of Sun-Trust Bank and a leader in the Business Leadership Network movement, these include identifying people with disabilities as a large group from which future workforce needs of employers can be addressed, identifying how this can link to larger diversity initiatives of companies, making it simple and convenient for businesses to get connected to disability employment programs (e.g., through single points of contact), and identifying how such involvement creates a larger customer base for the company (i.e., people with disabilities buying their products and services). If tax credits continue to be available, they will have to be easier for employers to gain access to.

Potential Effects on Partnership Practice   Employment specialists may want to add the availability of tax credits and the means for obtaining them to their repertoire of services to employers, perhaps at the back end of hiring to use them to sweeten the pot, so to speak, when they are negotiating a final placement arrangement. On the whole, however, the best incentive to present employers is a straightforward exchange of value between employment agencies and employers, such as that which this book has highlighted throughout Section II. In any marketing initiative, there is no magic bullet. Even with the most attractive buyer incentive, a good product or service must be rendered in order to satisfy the customer. Converting the features of the employment program to benefits for employers, as discussed in Chapter 10, will ultimately provide one of the clearest and most effective incentives for employers to consider in the hiring of job seekers with disabilities.

Issue 4: Accountability and Performance-Based Funding

This issue is thorny. On the one hand, both the public vocational rehabilitation system and the workforce investment system have attempted to improve the way they pay for people getting and keeping jobs. Both systems have always put a premium on rewarding their vendors for getting these results. In addition, under WIA and its predecessor, the Job Training and Partnership Act, workforce programs have been given a set of performance standards that must be met to get both formula-based funding and performance bonuses.

On the other hand, this has often created a situation in which the easiest individuals to serve are often the only ones assisted in order for programs to meet their performance goals. Consequently, people with more complicated or extensive support needs are not always served very well (Hoff, 2003). This problem is also common in the developmental disabilities and mental health systems, in which supported employment programs funded by these systems—intended to enable people with significant support needs to receive that support for the long term in order to get and keep jobs—will choose to serve the people who need the least support because that is the easiest way to achieve employment goals. In addition, some state systems have few outcome requirements as funding requisites (Conley, 2002). In effect, policy makers are still struggling with determining a truly effective way to fund employment programs of all kinds.

Complicating this issue is the economic and political realities of funding employment services. Fluctuations in the economy affect available tax revenue that funds these services. In harder times, public and community-based entities face budget cuts that create ripple effects throughout the system of employment service delivery. During such times, state vocational rehabilitation agencies, for example, often implement "order of selection" procedures that dictate the number and category of clients who can be served. Political will to fund these programs also fluctuates with the priorities of political leadership at national and state levels.

Regardless of the challenges, more and more attention is being placed on performance-based funding. This makes intuitive sense—why should the government pay for something unless it gets results? It also makes policy sense: If it is desirable for people with disabilities to be employed, then the mechanisms for funding those programs that assist job seekers with disabilities ought to reward those programs that are effective and cease funding those that are not.

Potential Effects on Partnership Practice   The image, purpose, and performances of human service programs will be under scrutiny as budgets tighten, federal priorities continually shift, and private sector interests favor partnerships that deliver returns on investment. Current circumstances already suggest that performance will be more important than having a good cause. First, there are funding initiatives in the offing that will put more control in the hands of the job seekers to choose who will help them find employment. These initiatives include, among others, the Ticket to Work and Work Incentives Improvement Act of 1999 (PL 106-170), which gives job seekers vouchers to be used to purchase job seeking assistance from self-selected providers. It is too early to tell if this legislative initiative will fulfill its promise for providing incentives for people to relinquish income entitlements such as Supplemental Security Income and Social Security Disability Insurance in favor of employment, but the trend for more individual control of service is definitely well underway.

Second, as available government funding is shifting to more accountability for outcomes, organizations that are merely able to claim having a good cause will see more and more of their funding support slipping. Funding support will favor those organizations that are able to directly assist people in getting jobs. These organizations will also be more likely to adopt strategies that are proven to work and are supported by evidence. Evidenced-based practices are likely to be given more and more attention in the arena of employment services for all population of job seekers, especially those with disabilities.

Third, the very success of the relationships that employment programs and employment specialists have with employers will be determined by delivering good service, as discussed in Chapter 12. Past appeals to employer altruism have not resonated with the business community to the extent needed for more people with disabilities to achieve employment. Ultimately, jobs opportunities are created when employers get what they need, not simply when employers meet someone else's need to have a job.

Issue 5: Education Reform

How will education reform at both the secondary and postsecondary levels affect job seekers with disabilities? Unfortunately, the best answer may be "it depends." As IDEA undergoes future reauthorizations, it will likely offer many new opportunities and challenges for youth with disabilities as they prepare for postsecondary life. On the one hand, the requirements for transition planning that have been in place since 1990 will likely be given even stronger emphasis. This bodes well for helping students, with the support of their families, get ready for jobs and careers. On the other hand, transition education and services are still lagging well behind where the original legislation intended them to be (Sitlington, Clark, & Kolstoe, 2000). In addition, a great deal of disconcerting data suggests that youth with disabilities are still not faring well as they exit school, in terms of employment status (Wagner, Cameto, & Newman, 2003).

Aside from IDEA's influence on postsecondary employment outcomes, there is growing attention to the implementation of minimum competency testing and standards as a means of reforming general education. Now required in almost half the states (Council of Chief State School Officers, 2002), these standards are requiring that minimum competency be exhibited by students as a condition for graduation. Minimum standards attached to receiving a high school diploma suggest that it has more meaning. Yet, such a requirement can be highly problematic for students with disabilities, who then have fewer or no alternative performance outcomes for which to achieve a regular diploma. This means that more and more students with disabilities will receive some sort of alternative exit certificate or worse, that they will drop out of school at rates that are even higher than the current unacceptable rate as they become frustrated with the difficulties of diploma requirements (Johnson et al., 2002).

The bottom line is that 22% of people with disabilities do not complete high school, compared with 9% of people without disabilities (Taylor, 2000). In addition, people with disabilities are also far less likely to attend and graduate from college than those without disabilities (Johnson et al., 2002). The broad implications of these circumstances require far more elaboration than can be provided here, but the general subtext for youth who will be exiting special education programs, and young adults with disabilities in general, is that they will be fighting an uphill battle to gain access to the types of jobs and careers that will allow them to earn a good income.

Implications for Partnership Practice   There is strong evidence that work experiences in secondary school are critical factors in subsequent adult employment success for youth with disabilities, regardless of their level of special education support or primary disability label (Colley & Jameson, 1998; Luecking & Fabian, 2000; National Council on Disability, 2000). Given the issues surrounding education reform, it will become imperative for such experiences to be available to youth in secondary education. The most effective transition programs, then, will be those that incorporate these experiences into the curriculum and individualized education programs. This also means that special educators will have an increasing role in facilitating the kinds of relationships that link students with employers for these important experiences. Work experiences are necessarily reliant on available and willing employers. Thus, as educators, transition specialists, family members, and youth organize and establish work experiences, it is essential to understand employers' needs, circumstances, and perspectives. It will be especially important that pre- and in-service preparation for transition educators include job development and work experience facilitation as integral to that preparation.

Moreover, students with the most significant support needs will only succeed in adult employment if there is direct collaboration and linkages with postschool employment services in order for the necessary support to continue after exit from public education. Teachers and adult agency employment specialists will find themselves working together in job development and job support with students well before they exit school in order to assist these students in achieving employment, preferably *before* they enter the adult employment system (Luecking & Certo, 2003). Finally, it will be even more important to attend to the issues of skill development during secondary school, postsecondary training, and indeed throughout the working lives of individuals with disabilities. The next issue expands on this need.

Issue 6: Changing Occupational and Skill Demands

In a technology-driven work world that is changing rapidly, there will be an increasing need for all job seekers to upgrade their skills in order to be attractive to employers and to compete in the workplace. This is important for three reasons. First, the idea of long-term job security is continually being challenged by company downsizing when the economy shifts. The resultant personnel layoffs create a domino effect of workers moving to new companies. This, of course, increases the competition for jobs, with those who have the highest level of skills having a distinct advantage. Second, the idea of lifelong employment using narrow, specialized skills is changing in favor of the ability to generalize skills across job tasks. This is especially relevant to people with disabilities, who are often hard pressed to maintain continuous attachment to the workplace due to low skills and over-reliance on entry-level jobs. Finally, skills become obsolete much more quickly than ever before. As business expert Warren Bennis said, "No job is safe. Never will be. The half-life of any particular skill set is, at most, five years" (Levy, 2003, p. 58).

Potential Effects on Partnership Practice   How can job and career seekers keep pace with the constant necessity to upgrade skills? What does this mean for the employment specialists who are integral in assisting individuals navigate these changes? For job seekers, it is more and more important not only to be connected to postsecondary training and education opportunities but also to pursue retraining opportunities throughout their careers. Apprenticeships, internships, and postsecondary training will only become more important for people with disabilities working to gain access to good jobs.

For employment specialists, it means that refined partnerships with employers will be even more critical: to learn of employment needs and trends, to identify on-the-job training opportunities, and to look creatively—as good business consultants (see Chapter 13)—at particular operational needs in a company that can provide a niche for job seekers who have a more narrow range of skills. It also means helping job seekers obtain basic or targeted work skills and also attending to the development of those soft skills that employers look for in all employees: punctuality, attendance, ability to accept supervision, ability to work as a member of a work team, and the willingness to learn new skills and take on new assignments.

Finally, people with disabilities will need assistance in accessing and completing the types of technical coursework that will make them attractive to employers in the ever-evolving technological demands of the workplace. Intermediary entities that assist job seekers prepare for their careers, including secondary and postsecondary schools, will need to expand their capacity to support this access.

Issue 7: Public–Private Partnerships

This book is about partnerships between publicly and tax-supported employment initiatives for people with disabilities and employers, most of whom are from the private sector and are profit oriented. However, one emerging trend is leading to more formal iterations of this notion of partnership. It is the result of two rapidly converging developments. The first is an impending and potentially serious labor shortage. The Society of Human Resources Managers predicted that labor force growth will continue to drop through 2020 (Sinclair, 2002). Fewer and fewer new people will join the workforce. To illustrate the effect this will have on the workplace, Sinclair reported that the jobs that employers will have to fill will exceed the projected workforce by more than 10 million nationally in just a few years, regardless of the economy's vibrancy. This projection is based on the combination of an aging workforce that will be retiring, a slowing growth of the population of working-age people, and an anticipated continuing rise in jobs in all industries except manufacturing.

The second development is the emergence of a renewed emphasis on the employer as a distinctly courted customer of the public rehabilitation system. Vocational rehabilitation systems in several states have recently implemented highly visible and concentrated initiatives to create partnerships with employer customers (Brooke & Healy, 2003). These initiatives feature support from the leadership level, specific marketing activities focused on employer needs, and the deployment of designated account representatives who call on and offer services to employer customers by identifying their human resource needs, referring candidates from the vocational rehabilitation system, and providing ongoing support to the relationship. Thus, the bottom-line needs of employers for more workers to get the work done and the increased focus of the public vocational rehabilitation system on the employer customer will likely lead to more and more formally developed public–private partnerships.

Potential Impact on Partnership Practice   Such public–private partnerships have the potential to create additional conduits through which contacts with employers can be made. Consequently, more and more employment specialists will want to affiliate themselves with these partnership initiatives. On an even broader scale, activities and developments will proliferate that have the potential to expand partnerships and increase their resultant benefit:

- Events that are jointly sponsored by business and disability employment programs that enable business people, employment specialists, and job seekers to meet each other
- Shared human resources. The staffs of companies and employment specialists will work together on employment initiatives, as in the case of Cincinnati Children's Hospital Medical Center, described in Chapter 6.
- Employer-friendly processes and language. As employment program leadership interacts more regularly with employers, processes that are more convenient to employers (e.g., single points of contact), and less jargon (e.g., "account representatives" rather than "rehabilitation specialists") are likely to be identified and adopted, making joint partnerships easier to initiate.
- Expanded knowledge of employee management and accommodation. Companies will add to their ability to manage diversity and thus to their comfort in hiring candidates represented by employment programs.
- Expanded knowledge of human resources. Disability employment specialists and employment programs will gain a better and a more useful understanding about how businesses operate, what they need for the development in their workforce, and what they expect in participating in partnerships with employment programs.

When all is said and done, the bottom line for companies is the bottom line. Employee management and profitability are deeply intertwined. As long as these partnerships result in better use of human resources for employers, and thus profit, such partnerships will flourish.

Issue 8: Personnel Development and Support

We saved this issue for last, not because it is the least important but because it is the issue that perhaps should be the one that lingers in your memory. This work of linking job seekers and employers depends on the skill, knowledge, and efficiency of high-quality and high-performing employment specialists. Without more emphasis on developing and supporting the human resources of this field, the effort to develop and maintain business partnerships will be a continuing challenge. The consequences will be disinterested—or worse, disgruntled—employers whom the field of employment services for people with disabilities will be forever struggling to engage. Ultimately, job seekers' success at gaining access to employment opportunities will depend on well-prepared and supported staff.

In Chapter 7, we discuss that although there is a set of fundamental skills that are needed by employment specialists, there is no one set of universally agreed-upon or applied professional standards in this area. This represents, perhaps, the difficulty in organizing such an effort with so many diverse programs and organizations that champion this work. But it might also represent the unfortunately low level of significance that is sometimes given to job development activities and to the people who engage in these activities. In either case, the fact remains that the workforce of employment specialists are provided far too little formal training on how to do their jobs, far too little support to do their jobs, and far too few formal rewards—financial and otherwise—for doing their jobs well.

Potential Impact on Partnership Practice
Whether or not the field or related professional organizations ever develop universally accepted standards for employment specialists, there will always be the need to upgrade and support the performance of these professionals who are so critical to this work. Important directions for partnership practice that may address this need include:

- *Reconsidering staffing patterns:* In disability employment programs of all types, there should be consideration for putting more human resources in the position and with the responsibility to directly link with employers.
- *Training and development:* More resources are necessary to make sure that partnership and job development skill sets are taught to all professionals involved in assisting job seekers connect with employers and job opportunities, whether that involvement is direct, as in the case of designated job developers, for example, or whether that involvement is indirect, as is the case for everyone else in disability employment programs.
- *Refined rewards systems:* The ways in which employment service agencies reinforce employment specialists have an important influence on whether specialists meet outcome expectations by helping people get jobs or merely try to do so. Reward systems in the most successful companies and in the most successful employment programs reward results rather than merely effort.
- *Performance support:* Training, supervision, mentoring, and reward systems all act to support the performance of employment specialists.
- *Internal performance standards:* We are not referring here to a rigidly defined set of standards or accreditation on a national scale. Rather we are suggesting that disability employment organizations develop and adhere to a set of internal performance standards for their staffs so that they are properly trained, supported, and rewarded. The Job Development Efficacy Scale presented in Chapter 7 is offered to the reader as a place to start the thinking about what areas of professional development are important for the development and support effective employment specialists. The organization development strategies in Chapter 14 are suggested as a means of implementing staff development and support improvements.
- *Compensation:* Professional-level salaries for skilled employment specialists, commensurate with higher performance expectations, has been a long-standing need in this field. Funding levels will always ultimately influence how well this can be addressed. Thus

employment organizations and funding sources will continually need to take serious looks at restructuring operational budgets as well as funding priorities and allocations.

Disability employment programs that want seriously to undertake the mission to help individuals obtain high-quality jobs and careers will focus strongly on personnel development and support. Advocates, policy makers, and funders who want to ensure that real employment is achieved for individuals with disabilities will focus on this issue. And job seekers who are poised to enter the workforce and to improve career prospects will demand that the individuals who assist them in this effort will be well trained and supported.

SUMMARY

This chapter presented several trends that are likely to affect both the manner in which job seekers with disabilities link with employers and their success at doing so. We see legislative, economic, business, and educational trends for which employment specialists should be alert and to which they should be ready to react. Some of these trends will likely challenge the system of workforce investment as it assists job seekers with disabilities. Some will likely enhance the system. To one degree or another, all will likely be continuously in flux, necessitating vigilance and flexibility on the part of employment specialists, employment service programs, and indeed anyone interested in the policy and practice of employment of people with disabilities. We have attempted to outline some of the potential impacts on job development and business partnership practice for each of these issues and trends. One thing is sure: Employment specialists and employment programs will need to update their knowledge and skills to maintain the ability to make the right connections for job seekers and for employers. This is important work and it deserves the best we all can give it.

References

Albin, J.M. (1992). *Quality improvement in employment and other human service: Managing for quality through change.* Baltimore: Paul H. Brookes Publishing Co.

Alea, P., & Mullins, P. (1998). *The best work of your life.* New York: Penguin Putnam.

American Youth Policy Forum (AYPF) & Center on Education Policy (CEP). (2001). *Twenty-five years of educating children with disabilities: The good news and the work ahead.* Washington, DC: Author.

Americans with Disabilities Act (ADA) of 1990, PL 101-336, 42 U.S.C. §§ 12101 *et seq.*

Armstrong, T. (1993). *Seven kinds of smart: Identifying and developing your many intelligences.* New York: Penguin Books.

Atkinson, D., Morten, G., & Sue, D.W. (1989). *Counseling American minorities: A cross cultural perspective* (3rd ed.). Dubuque, IA: William C. Brown.

Bandura, A. (1986). *Social foundations of thought and action: A social cognitive theory.* Englewood Cliffs, NJ: Prentice Hall.

Bandura, A. (1994). Self-efficacy. In *Encyclopedia of human behavior* (Vol. 4). San Diego: Academic Press.

Banks, A. (2000). Learn to brag. In I. Misner & D. Morgan (Eds.), *Masters of networking: Building relationships for your pocketbook and soul* (pp. 101–103). Marietta, GA: Bard Press.

Bell, C. (2002). *Managers as mentors: Building partnerships for learning.* San Francisco: Barrett-Koehler Publishers.

Benz, M., Doren, B., & Yavanoff, P. (1998). Crossing the great divide: Predicting productive engagement for young women with disabilities. *Career Development for Exceptional Individuals, 21,* 3–16.

Benz, M., Yavanoff, P., & Doren, B. (1997). School to work components that predict postschool success for students with and without disabilities. *Exceptional Children, 63,* 151–165.

Bissonnette, D. (1994). *Beyond traditional job development: The heart of creative opportunity.* Chatsworth, CA: Milt Wright & Associates.

Blackorby, J., & Wagner, M. (1996). Longitudinal outcomes for youth with disabilities: Findings from the National Longitudinal Transition Study. *Exceptional Children, 62,* 399–419.

Blanck, P.D. (1998). *The Americans with Disabilities Act and emerging workforce: Employment of people with mental retardation.* Washington, DC: American Association on Mental Retardation.

Blessing, L., & Jamieson, J. (1999, Summer). Employing persons with a developmental disability: Effects of previous experience. *Canadian Journal of Rehabilitation, 12*(4), 211–215.

Bloch, D. (2002). *How to get your first job and keep it.* Chicago: VGM Career Books.

Boldt, L. (1999). *Zen and the art of making a living.* New York: Penguin Putnam.

Bolles, R.N. (2003). *What color is your parachute? 2004.* Berkeley, CA: Ten Speed Press.

Bolles, R.N., & Brown, D.S. (2001). *Job hunting for the so-called handicapped or people with disabilities* (2nd ed.). Berkeley, CA: Ten Speed Press.

Bolton, B. (1982). Vocational adjustment and rehabilitation. In B. Bolton (Ed.), *Vocational adjustment of disabled persons* (pp. 1–20). Baltimore: University Park Press.

Bond, G.R., Becker, D.R., Drake, R.E., Rapp, C.A., Meisler, N., Lehman, A.F., Bell, M.D., & Blyler, C.R. (2001). Implementing supported employment as an evidence-based practice. *Psychiatric Services, 52,* 313–322.

Boyle, M. (1997). Social barriers to successful reentry into mainstream organizational culture: Perceptions of people with disabilities. *Human Resource Development Quarterly 8*(3), 259–268.

Brooke, V., & Healy, D. (2003, May). *Fast facts: Public/private partnerships.* Retrieved June 5, 2003, from http://www.dtra.mil/jb/jb_fastfact.html

Brown, D.W. (2000). *Learning a living: A guide to planning your career and finding a job for people with learning disabilities, attention deficit disorder, and dyslexia.* Bethesda, MD: Woodbine House.

Brown, D.W., & Konrad, A.M. (2001). Granovetter was right. The importance of weak ties to a contemporary job search. *Group & Organization Management, 26,* 434–462.

Burkhead, E.J., & Wilson, L.M. (1995). The family as a developmental system: Impact on the career development of individuals with disabilities. *Journal of Career Development, 2*(3). 187–199.

Butterworth, J., & Pitt-Catsouphes, M. (1997). Employees with disabilities: What managers, supervisors, and co-workers have to say. *Employment in the Mainstream, 22,* 5–15.

Career Services, University of Waterloo. (2001–2002). *Career Development eManual.* Retrieved from http://www.cdm.uwaterloo.ca/

Cincinnati Children's Hospital Medical Center. (2003). *Corporate information: Vision and mission.* Retrieved May 8, 2003, from http://www.cincinnatichildrens.org/about/corporate/mission.htm

Civil Rights Act of 1964, PL 88-352, 20 U.S.C. §§ 241 *et seq.*

Colley, D., & Jamison, D. (1998). Post-school results for youth with disabilities: Key indicators and policy implications. *Career Development for Exceptional Individuals, 21*(2), 145–160.

Conley, R. (2002). *Supported employment in Maryland: A report of the Maryland Chapter of the Association of Persons in Supported Employment.* Columbia: Maryland Association for Persons in Supported Employment (APSE).

Connellan, T., & Zemke, R. (1993). *Sustaining knock your socks off service.* New York: AMACON.

Cook, J.A., & Razzano, L.A. (1994). Cultivation and maintenance of relationships with employers of people with psychiatric disabilities. *Psychosocial Rehabilitation Journal, 17*(3), 103–117.

Corbett, M. (2002, June). *The global outsourcing market—2002.* Available from Michael F. Corbett & Associates, Ltd., 845-452-0600.

Corey, M.S., & Corey, G. (1997). *Group process and practice.* Pacific Grove, CA: Brooks/Cole.

Corrigan, P.W. (1998). The impact of stigma on severe mental illness. *Cognitive and Behavioral Practice, 5,* 201–222.

Council of Chief State School Officers. (2002). *Key state education policy on K-12 education.* Washington, DC: Author.

Csikszentmihalyi, M. (1990). *Flow: The psychology of optimal experience.* New York: Harper & Row.

Culver, J., Spencer, K., & Gliner, J. (1990). Prediction of supported employment placements for job developers. *Education and Training in Mental Retardation, 25*(3), 237–242.

Dawis, R.V. (1996). Vocational psychology, vocational adjustment, and the workforce: Some familiar and unanticipated consequences. *Psychology, Public Policy, and Law, 2*(2), 229–248.

DeBoer, A. (1995). *Working together: The art of consulting and communicating.* Longmont, CO: Sopris West.

DiLeo, D., & Langton, D. (1993). *Get the marketing edge! A job developer's toolkit for people with disabilities.* St. Augustine, FL: Training Resource Network.

DiLeo, D., Luecking, R., & Hathaway, S. (1995). *Natural supports in action: Strategies to facilitate em-*

ployer supports of people with disabilities. St. Augustine, FL: Training Resource Network.

Diska, E., & Rogers, S. (1996). Employer concerns about hiring persons with psychiatric disability: Results of the Employer Attitudes Questionnaire. *Rehabilitation Counseling Bulletin, 40,* 31–44.

Donohoe, T. (2003, August). *Congress finally gets the message: Small business drive our economy. U.S. Chamber of Commerce commentary.* Retrieved November 5, 2003, from http://www.uschamber.com/sb/analysis/commentary/0308.htm

Drehmer, D.E. (1985). Hiring decisions for disabled workers: The hidden bias. *Rehabilitation Psychology, 30,* 157–164.

Drew, D., Drebing, C.E., Ormer, A.V., Losardo, M., Krebs, C., Penk, W., & Rosenheck, R. (2001). Effects of disability compensation on participation in and outcomes of vocational rehabilitation. *Psychiatric Services, 52,* 1479–1484.

E.I. du Pont de Nemours and Company. (1993, May). *Equal to the Task II: 1990 DuPont Survey of Employment of People with Disabilities.* Wilmington, DE: Author.

Enright, M.S. (1996). The relationship between disability status, career beliefs, and career indecision. *Rehabilitation Counseling Bulletin, 40*(2), 134–152.

Fabian, E.S. (1999). Rethinking work: The example of consumers with mental health disorders. *Rehabilitation Counseling Bulletin, 42,* 302–316.

Fabian, E.S. (2000). Applying social cognitive career theory to individuals with psychiatric disorders. *Psychiatric Rehabilitation Journal, 23,* 262–269.

Fabian, E.S., Luecking, R., & Tilson, G. (1994). *A working relationship: The job development specialist's guide to successful partnerships with business.* Baltimore: Paul H. Brookes Publishing Co.

Fabian, E.S., Luecking, R., & Tilson, G. (1995). Employer and rehabilitation personnel views on hiring persons with disabilities: Implications for job development. *Journal of Applied Rehabilitation Counseling, 61,* 42–49.

Fabian, E.S., & Waugh, C. (2001). A job development efficacy scale for rehabilitation professionals. *Journal of Rehabilitation, 67,* 42–47.

Fesko, S., & Temelini, D. (1997). What consumers and staff tell us about effective job search strategies. In W. Kiernan & R. Schalock (Eds.), *Integrated employment* (pp. 67–81). Washington, DC: American Association on Mental Retardation.

Fletcher, J. (1993). *Patterns of high performance.* San Francisco: Berrett-Koehler Publishers.

Fox, J. (2000). *How to become a marketing superstar.* New York: Hyperion Books.

Fox, M. (1994). *The reinvention of work.* New York: HarperCollins.

French, W., & Bell, C. (1990). *Organization development: Behavioral science interventions for organization improvement* (4th ed.). Englewood Cliffs, NJ: Prentice Hall.

Fuqua, D., Rathburn, M., & Gade, E. (1984). A comparison of employer attitudes toward the worker problems of eight types of disabilities. *Vocational Evaluation and Work Adjustment Bulletin, 15,* 40–43.

Gardner, J.F. (1999). Quality in services for people with disabilities. In J.F. Gardner & S. Nudler (Eds.), *Quality performance in human services: Leadership, values, and vision* (pp. 21–42). Baltimore: Paul H. Brooks Publishing Co.

General Accounting Office. (2002). *Business tax incentives: Incentives to employ workers with disabilities receive limited use and have an uncertain impact.* Washington, DC: Author.

Gerber, P., & Brown, D. (1997). *Learning disabilities and employment.* Austin, TX: PRO-ED.

Gilbride, D., & Stensrud, R. (1999). Demand-side job development and system change. *Rehabilitation Counseling Bulletin, 42,* 329–342.

Gilley, J., & Boughton, N. (1996). *Stop managing, start coaching.* New York: McGraw-Hill.

Gitomer, J. (1998). *Customer satisfaction is worthless, customer loyalty is priceless: How to make customers love you, keep them coming back, and tell everyone they know.* New York: Bard Press.

Gladwell, M. (1999, January 11). Six degrees of Lois Weisberg. *The New Yorker,* 52–63.

Goleman, D. (1998). *Working with emotional intelligence.* New York: Bantam Books.

Granovetter, M. (1974). *Getting a job.* Chicago: The University of Chicago Press.

Granovetter, M. (1979). *Placement as brokerage: Information problems in the labor market for rehabilitated workers.* In D. Vandergoot & J.D. Worrall (Eds.), Placement in rehabilitation (pp. 83–101). Baltimore: University Park Press.

Granovetter, M. (1985). Economic action and social structure: The problem of embeddedness. *American Journal of Sociology, 91,* 481–510.

Granovetter, M. (1995). *Getting a job* (2nd ed.) Chicago: The University of Chicago Press.

Greenbaum, R. (1994). *The handbook for focus group research* (2nd ed). New York: Lexington.

Greenbaum, T. (1990). *The consultant's manual: The complete guide to building a successful consulting practice.* New York: John Wiley & Sons.

Greenleigh & Associates. (1975). *The role of sheltered workshops in the rehabilitation of the severely disabled.* New York: Department of Health, Education, and Welfare.

Griffin, C., & Hammis, D. (2003). *Making self employment work for people with disabilities.* Baltimore: Paul H. Brookes Publishing Co.

Hackett, G., & Lent, R.W. (1992). Theoretical advances and current inquiry in career psychology. In S.D. Brown & R.W. Lent (Eds.), *Handbook of counseling psychology* (2nd ed., pp. 419–451). New York: John Wiley & Sons.

Hagner, D. (2000). Primary and secondary labor markets: Implications for vocational rehabilitation. *Rehabilitation Counseling Bulletin, 44*(1), 22–29.

Hagner, D. (2003). Job development and job search assistance. In E.M. Szymanski & R.M. Parker (Eds.), *Work and disability: Issues and strategies in career development and job placement* (2nd ed., pp. 343–373). Austin, TX: PRO-ED.

Hahn, H. (1985). Disability policy and the problem of discrimination. *American Behavioral Scientist, 8,* 293–318.

Hahn, H. (1993). The political implications of disability definitions and data. *Journal of Disability Policy Studies, 4,* 41–52.

Hammen, C., Gitlin, M., & Altschuler, L. (2000). Predictors of work adjustment in Bipolar I patients: A naturalistic longitudinal follow-up. *Journal of Consulting and Clinical psychology, 68,* 220–225.

Hanan, M. (1995). *Consultative selling.* New York: AMACOM.

Hanley-Maxwell, C., Owens-Johnson, L., & Fabian, E. (2003). Supported employment. In E.M. Szymanski & R.M. Parker (Eds.), *Work and disability: Issues and strategies in career development and job placement* (pp. 373–404). Austin, TX: PRO-ED.

Hansen, L.S. (1976). *Toward an expanded concept of career education: An examination of the definitions and concepts of career development.* Washington, DC: National Advisory Council for Career Education.

Harris, C.C., Lee, R.M., & Brown, P. (1987). The fate of the redundant in the market. In C.C. Harris, P. Brown, R. Fevre, G. Leaver, R.M. Lee, & L.D. Morris (Eds.), *Redundancy and recession in South Wales* (pp. 177–194). Oxford: Blackwell.

Hearne, P. (1991). Employment strategies for people with disabilities: A prescription for change. In J. West (Ed.), *The Americans with Disabilities Act: From policy to practice* (pp. 111–128). New York: Milbank Memorial Fund.

Hernandez, B. (2000). Employer attitudes towards disability and their ADA employment rights: A literature review. *Journal of Rehabilitation, 16,* 83–88.

Hershenson, D.B. (1996). Work adjustment: A neglected area in career counseling. *Journal of Counseling & Development, 74,* 442–446.

Heskett, J.L., Jones, T.O., Loveman, G.W., Sasser, W.E., & Schlesinger, L.A. (1996). *Putting the service-profit chain to work.* Cambridge, MA: Harvard Business School Publishing Corporation.

Hoff, D. (2003). *A report on the use of One Stop Centers by people with disabilities.* Boston: Institute on Community Inclusion.

Hoff, D., Gandolfo, C., Gold, M., & Jordan, M. (2000). *Demystifying job development: Field-based approaches to job development for people with disabilities.* St. Augustine, FL: Training Resource Network.

Holland, J.L. (1973). *Making vocational choices: A theory of careers.* Englewood Cliffs, NJ: Prentice Hall.

Hope, R.C., & Rice, B.D. (1995). *Report from the study group on strategies to enhance job retention and career advancement in rehabilitation.* Fayetteville: Arkansas Research and Training Center in Vocational Rehabilitation, University of Arkansas, and Arkansas Rehabilitation Services.

Houtenville, A.J. (2001a). Estimates of employment rates for persons with disabilities in the United States by state, 1980–1990. Ithaca, NY: Cornell University, Rehabilitation Research and Training Center for Economic Research on Employment Policy for Persons with Disabilities. Retrieved November 3, 2003, from http://www.ilr.cornell.edu/ped

Houtenville, A.J. (2001b). Estimates of median household size-adjusted income for persons with disabilities in the United States by state, 1980–1990. Ithaca, NY: Cornell University, Rehabilitation Research and Training Center for Economic Research on Employment Policy for Persons with Disabilities. Retrieved November 3, 2003, from http://www.ilr.cornell.edu/ped

Hoyt, K. (1996). Preparing the "high skills" workforce. In R. Feller & G. Walz (Eds.), *Career transitions in turbulent times* (pp. 163–174). Washington, DC: U.S. Department of Education, ERIC/CASS Publication #RR93002004.

Individuals with Disabilities Education Act (IDEA) of 1990, PL 101-476, 20 U.S.C. §§ 1400 *et seq.*

Job Training and Partnership Act (JTPA) of 1992, PL 97-300, 29 U.S.C. 801 *et seq.*

Johnson, D., Stodden, R., Emanuel, E., Luecking, R., & Mack, M. (2002). Current challenges facing secondary education and transition services: What research tells us. *Exceptional Children, 68*(4), 519–531.

Johnson, V.A., Greenwood, R., & Schriner, K.F. (1988). Work performance and work personality: Employer concerns about workers with disabilities. *Rehabilitation Counseling Bulletin, 32,* 50–57.

King, A. (1993). Doing the right thing for employees with disabilities. *Training and Development, 47, 44–47.*

Kleiman, C. (1994). *The career coach.* Chicago: Dearborn Financial Publishing.

Kleiman, C. (2002). *Winning the job game: The new rules for finding and keeping the job you want.* New York: John Wiley & Sons.

Kokomo Software. (1993). *ADAAG Express* [computer program]. Salt Lake City, UT: Author.

Kornfield, R., & Rupp, K. (2000). The net effects of the project NetWork return to work case management experiment of participant earnings, benefit receipt, and other outcomes. *Social Security Bulletin, 63*(1), 12–33.

Kotler, P. (2003). *Marketing insights from A to Z: Concepts every manager needs to know.* New York: John Wiley & Sons.

Kregel, J., & Unger, D. (1993). Employer perceptions of the work potential of individuals with disabilities. *Journal of Vocational Rehabilitation, 3,* 17–25.

Krueger, R. (1993). *Focus groups: A practical guide for applied research.* Newbury Park, CA: Sage Publications.

Krumboltz, J.D. (1991). *The career beliefs inventory.* Palo Alto, CA: Consulting Psychologists.

LaPlante, M.P., Kennedy, J., Kaye, H.S., & Wenger, B.L. (1996). *Disability and employment* (Disability Statistics Abstracts, 11). Washington, DC: National Institute on Disability and Rehabilitation Research, U.S. Department of Education. (ERIC Document Reproduction Service No. ED427472).

Lent, R.W., Brown, S.D., & Hackett, G. (1994). Toward a unifying social cognitive theory of career and academic interest, choice, and performance. *Journal of Vocational Behavior, 45,* 79–122.

Levinson, J. (1993). *Guerrilla marketing: Secrets for making big profits from your small business.* New York: Houghton Mifflin.

Levinson, J. (1999). *Mastering guerrilla marketing: 100 profit-producing insights that you can take to the bank.* New York: Houghton Mifflin.

Levy, J.M., Jessop, D.J., Rimmerman, A., Francis, F., & Levy, P.H. (1993). Determinants of attitudes of New York state employers towards the employment of persons with severe handicaps. *Journal of Rehabilitation, 59,* 49–54.

Levy, S. (2003, April 28). Next frontier: For successful businesses, it's all about the right community. *Newsweek, 40–58.*

Lin, N., & Dumin, M. (1986). Access to occupations through social ties. *Social Networks, 8,* 365–383.

Liptak, J.J. (1992). *The career exploration inventory: A guide for exploring work, leisure, and learning.* Indianapolis: Jist Works.

Locklin, D. (1997, Fall). *Community exchange.* Knoxville, TN: Regional Continuing Education Program for Community Rehabilitation Providers.

Lofquist, L.H., & Dawis, R.V. (1984). Research on work adjustment and satisfaction: Implications for career counseling. In S. Brown & R. Lent (Eds.), *Handbook of counseling psychology* (pp. 216–237). New York: John Wiley & Sons.

Louis Harris & Associates (1998). *The ICD Survey III: Employing disabled Americans.* Washington, DC: National Organization on Disability.

Luecking, R. (1997). Persuading employers to hire people with learning disabilities. In P. Gerber & D. Brown (Eds.), *Learning disabilities and employment* (pp. 215–233). Austin, TX: PRO-ED.

Luecking, R. (2000). *Analyzing work outcomes for youth with disabilities participating in a standardized internship program.* Unpublished doctoral dissertation, George Washington University.

Luecking, R. (2000, Fall). What employers are saying about recruitment and retention. In *The National Supported Employment Consortium* (pp. 2–3). Richmond: Virginia Commonwealth University.

Luecking, R. (2003). *Doing it the company way: Employer perspectives of workplace supports. HEATH Resources.* Washington, DC: The George Washington University.

Luecking, R. (in press). *Voices from the field: Employer perspectives of youth with disability in the workplace.* Minneapolis, MN: National Center on Secondary Education and Transition.

Luecking, R., & Certo, N. (2003). Integrating service systems at the point of transition for youth with significant support needs: A model that works. *American Rehabilitation, 27,* 2–9.

Luecking, R., & Fabian, E.S. (2000). Paid internships and employment success for youth in transition. *Career Development for Exceptional Individuals, 23*(2), 205–221.

Luecking, R., & Tilson, G. (2002). *A practical introduction to customized employment.* (Available from TransCen, Inc., 451 Hungerford Dr., Suite 700, Rockville, MD 20850).

Mank, D. (1996). Evolving roles for employers and support personnel in the employment of people with disabilities. *Journal of Vocational Rehabilitation, 6,* 83–88.

Mank, D., O'Neill, C.T., & Jensen, R. (1998). Quality in supported employment: A new demonstration of the capabilities of people with severe disabilities. *Journal of Vocational Rehabilitation, 11*(1), 83–95.

Mast, M., Sweeney, J., & West, M. (2002). Presentation portfolios. *Job Training & Placement Report, 26,* 1–3.

Maxwell, J. (2002). *Your roadmap for success.* Nashville, TN: Thomas Nelson Publishers.

McDaniels, C. (1984). Work and leisure in the career span. In N. Gysbers & Associates (Eds.), *Designing careers* (pp. 558–590). San Francisco: Jossey-Bass.

McNeil, J.M. (1997). *Current population rep. No p70-61, Americans with disabilities: 1994–95 at 7, table 2.* Washington, DC: U.S. Department of Commerce.

Metcalf, C.W. (1992). *Lighten up.* Reading, MA: Addison-Wesley.

Minskoff, E.H., Sautter, S.W., Hoffmann, F.J., & Hawks, R. (1987). Employer attitudes toward hiring the learning disabled. *Journal of Learning Disabilities, 20*(1), 53–57.

Misner, I., & Morgan, D. (2000). *Masters of networking: Building relationships for your pocketbook and soul.* Marietta, GA: Bard Press.

Mitchell, L.K., & Krumboltz, J.D. (1990). Social learning approach to career decision making: Krumboltz's theory. In D. Brown, L. Brooks, & Associates (Eds.), *Career choice and development* (2nd ed., pp. 145–196). San Francisco: Jossey-Bass.

Model demonstration projects, 84.324M, 67 Fed. Reg. 78,428–78,438 (2002). Retrieved May 16, 2003 from http://www.ed.gov/legislation/FedRegister/announcements/2002-4/122402d.html

Morgan, D. (1991). *Focus groups as qualitative research.* Newbury Park, CA: Sage Publications.

Morgan, D. (1993). *Successful focus groups: Advancing the state of the art.* Newbury Park, CA: Sage Publications.

Morris, T. (1997). *If Aristotle ran General Motors.* New York: Henry Holt and Company.

Muller, L.S. (1992). Disability beneficiaries who work and their experience under program work incentives. *Social Security Bulletin, 55,* 2–19.

Murnane, R., & Levy, F. (1996). *Teaching the new basic skills: Principles for educating children to thrive in a changing economy.* New York: The Free Press.

Naisbitt, J. (2000). What is a network? In I. Misner & D. Morgan (Eds.) *Masters of networking: Building relationships for your pocketbook and soul* (pp. 13–16). Marietta, GA: Bard Press.

National Career Development Association. (2001). *Consumers and job seekers: Frequently asked questions.* Retrieved from www.ncda.org

National Council on Disability (NCD). (2000). *Transition and post-school outcomes for youth with disabilities: Closing the gaps to post-secondary education and employment.* Washington, DC: Author.

Nemko, M., Edwards, P., & Edwards, S. (1998). *Cool careers.* Foster City, CA: IDG Books Worldwide.

Nichols, M. (1989). *Demonstration study of supported employment program for persons with severe mental illness: Benefits, costs and outcomes.* Indianapolis: Indiana University and Purdue University.

Nietupski, J., & Hamre-Nietupski, S. (2000). A systematic process for carving supported employment positions for people with severe disabilities. *Journal of Developmental and Physical Disabilities, 12,* 103–119.

Nietupski, J., & Hamre-Nietupski, S. (2001). A business approach to finding and restructuring supported employment opportunities. In P. Wehman (Ed.), *Supported employment in business* (pp. 59–73). St. Augustine, FL: Training Resources Network.

Nietupski, J., Hamre-Nietupski, S., & DiLeo, D. (1997). *Employer perceptions of workers with disabilities: Marketing benefits, responding to concerns.* St. Augustine, FL: Training Resources Network.

Nietupski, J., Hamre-Nietupski, S., VanderHart, N., & Fishback, K. (1996). Employer perceptions of the benefits and concerns of supported employment. *Education and Training in Mental Retardation and Developmental Disabilities, 31,* 310–323.

Noble, J.H. (1998). Policy reform dilemmas in promoting employment of persons with severe mental illness. *Psychiatric Services, 49,* 775–782.

Noble, J.H., Honberg, R., Hall, L.L., & Flynn, L. (1997). *A legacy of failure: The inability of the federal-state vocational rehabilitation system to serve people with severe mental illness.* Arlington, VA: National Alliance for the Mentally Ill.

Occupational outlook handbook. (2003). U.S. Department of Labor, Bureau of Labor Statistics. Retrieved October 30, 2003, from http://www.bls.gov/oco/oco2003.htm

Olshansky, S., Grob, S., & Malamud, I. (1958). Employers' attitudes and practices in the hiring of ex-mental patients. *Mental Hygiene, 42,* 331–342.

Olson, L. (1997). *The school-to-work revolution: How employers and educators are joining forces to prepare tomorrow's skilled workforce.* Reading, MA: Addison-Wesley.

Parent, W., Hill, M., & Wehman, P. (1989). From sheltered to supported employment outcomes: Challenges for rehabilitation facilities. *Journal of Rehabilitation, 55*(4), 120–125.

Peters, T. (1987). *Thriving on chaos.* New York: Alfred A. Knopf.

Peters, T. (1993). *The new manager and the new organization* (recording). Boulder, CO: CareerTrack Publications.

Peters, T., & Waterman, R. (1982). *In search of excellence.* New York: Harper & Row.

Petty, D.M., Brickey, J., & Verstegen D. (1999). *Breaking out of the box: A descriptive account of community rehabilitation providers engaged in transformational change.* Knoxville: The University of Tennessee.

Pimental, R., Baker, L., & Tilson, G. (1991). *The Americans with Disabilities Act: Making the ADA work for you.* Northridge, CA: Milt Wright and Associates.

Podmostko, M. (2000). *Issues and trends in the employment of people with disabilities.* Washington, DC: Community Options.

Polloway, E.A., Smith, J.D., Patton, J.R., & Smith, T.E. (1996). Historic changes in mental retardation and developmental disabilities. *Education and Training in Mental Retardation and Developmental Disabilities, 31*(1), 3–12.

Pumpian, I., Fisher, D., Certo, N., & Smalley, K. (1997). Changing jobs: An essential part of career development. *Mental Retardation, 35,* 49–48.

Rehabilitation Act Amendments of 1986, PL 99-506, 29 U.S.C. §§ 701 et seq.

Rehabilitation Act of 1973, PL 93-112, 29 U.S.C. §§ 701 et seq.

Research Triangle International. (2003). *Longitudinal study of the Vocational Rehabilitation Services Program.* Retrieved June 23, 2003, from http://www.als.uiuc.edu/dir

Romoser, M. (2000). Mal-employment in autism. *Focus on Autism and Other Developmental Disabilities, 14*(4), 246–247.

Rosenbaum, J.E., Kariya, T., Settersten, R., & Maier, T. (1990). Market and network theories of the transition from high school to work: Their application to industrialized societies. *Annual Review of Sociology, 16,* 263–299.

Rosenbluth, H., & Peters, D. (1992). *The customer comes second: And other secrets of exceptional service.* New York: William Morrow Company.

Rothwell, W.J. (1996). *ASTD models for human performance improvement: Roles, competencies, and outputs.* Alexandria, VA: ASTD.

Rothwell, W.J., Sullivan, R., & McLean, G.N. (1995). *Practicing organization development.* San Diego: Pfeiffer & Company.

Rubin, S.E., & Roessler, R.T. (1995). *Foundations of the vocational rehabilitation process.* Austin, TX: PRO-ED.

Rumrill, P., & Roessler, R. (1999). New direction in vocational rehabilitation: A "career development" perspective on "closure." *Journal of Rehabilitation, 65,* 26–30.

Salzman, M. (2003). *Buzz: Harness the power of influence and create demand.* New York: John Wiley & Sons.

Sarason, I.G., Pierce, G.R., & Sarason, B.R. (1990). Social support and interactional processes: A triadic hypothesis. *Journal of Social and Personal Relationships, 7,* 495–506.

Schwochau, S., & Blanck, P.D. (1999). The economics of the Americans with Disabilities Act, Part III: Does the ADA disable the disabled? *Berkeley Journal of Employment & Labor Law, 2,* 271–313.

Senge, P. (1994). *The fifth discipline.* New York: Currency/Doubleday.

Sharf, R. (1997). *Applying career development theory to counseling.* Pacific Grove, CA: Brooks/Cole.

Shenson, H. (1990). *Shenson on consulting.* New York: John Wiley & Sons.

Shenson, H., & Nichols, T. (1993). *The complete guide to consulting success.* Chicago: Enterprise Dearborn.

Silverstein, R. (2000). *Emerging disability policy framework: A guidepost for analyzing public policy.* Law, Health Policy & Disability Center, Iowa City, IA. Retrieved November 3, 2003, from http://disability.law.uiowa.edu/lhpdc/rrtc/documents/silverstein/IA_LAW_REVIEW_BOOK_AUG_2000.txt

Sinclair, M. (2002, November 4). *Forging the partnership: Using all of your resources in recruiting.* Presented at the National Business Leadership Summit, Washington, DC.

Sitlington, P., Clark, G., & Kolstoe, O. (2000). *Transition education: Services for adolescents with disabilities* (3rd ed.). Boston, MA: Allyn & Bacon.

Sitlington, P., Neubert, D., Begun, W., Lombard, R., & Leconte, P. (1996). *Assess for success.* Reston, VA: The Council for Exceptional Children.

State of California, Department of Finance. (1998). *County population projections with age, sex, and race/ethnic detail: July 1, 1990–2040 in 10-year increments.* Sacramento, CA: Author. Retrieved November 3, 2003, from http://www.dof.ca.gov/ HTML/DEMOGRAP/Proj_age.htm

Stigler, G. (1962). Information in the labor market. *Journal of Political Economics, 70,* 94–105.

Super, D.E. (1976). *Career education and the meaning of work: Monographs on career education.* Washington, DC: The Office of Career Education, U.S. Office of Education.

Super, D.E. (1990). A life-span, life-space approach to career development. In D. Brown, L. Brooks, & Associates (Eds.), *Career choice and development: Applying contemporary theories to practice* (2nd ed., pp. 197–261). San Francisco: Jossey-Bass.

Szymanski, E.M., & Hanley-Maxwell, C. (1996, Jan/Feb/Mar). Career development of people with developmental disabilities: An ecological model. *Journal of Rehabilitation,* 48–55.

Szymanski, E.M., Hershenson, D.B., Enright, M.S., & Ettinger, J. (1996). Career development theories, constructs, and research: Implications for people with disabilities. In E.M. Szymanski & R.M. Parker (Eds.), *Work and disability: Issues and strategies in career development and job placement* (pp. 79–126). Austin, TX: PRO-ED.

Szymanski, E.M., & Parker, R.M. (1996). Work and disability: Introduction. In E.M. Szymanski & R.M. Parker (Eds.). *Work and disability: Issues and strategies in career development and job placement* (1st ed., pp. 1–7). Austin, TX: PRO-ED.

Szymanski, E.M., Parker, R.M., Ryan, C., Merz, M.A., Trevino-Espinoza, B., & Johnston-Rodriguez, S.J. (2003). Work and disability: Basic constructs. In E.M. Szymanski & R.M. Parker (Eds.), *Work and disability: Issues and strategies in career development and job placement* (2nd ed., pp. 7–25). Austin, TX: PRO-ED.

Szymanski, E.M., Trevino, B., & Fernandez, D. (1996). Rehabilitation career planning with minorities. *Journal of Applied Rehabilitation Counseling, 27*(4), 45–49.

Taylor, H. (2000). *Conflicting trends in employment of people with disabilities 1986–2000.* Retrieved November 5, 2003, from http://www.harrisinteractive.com/harris_poll/index.asp? PID=121

Thakker, D. (1997). Employers and the Americans with Disabilities Act: Factors influencing manager adherence with the ADA, with specific reference to individuals with psychiatric disabilities. *Dissertation Abstracts International, 58-03A,* 1116.

The ticket to work and self-sufficiency program: Final rules, 20 C.F.R. § 411 (2001).

Ticket to Work and Work Incentives Improvement Act of 1999, PL 106-170, 42 U.S.C. §§ 1305 et seq.

Tieger, P., & Barron-Tieger, B. (2001). *Do what you are.* Boston: Little, Brown and Co.

Tilson, G., & Cuozzo, L. (2001). *Positive personal profile.* (Available from TransCen, Inc., 451 Hungerford Drive, Suite 700, Rockville, MD 20850).

Tschopp, M.K., Bishop, M., & Mulvihill, M. (2001). Career development of individuals with psychiatric disabilities: An ecological perspective of barriers and interventions. *Journal of Applied Rehabilitation Counseling, 32*(2), 25–30.

U.S. Department of Labor. (2003). *Labor force statistics from the Current Population Survey.* Retrieved November 3, 2003, from http://data.bls.gov

Unger, D.D. (2002a). Employers' attitudes towards people with disabilities in the workforce: Myth or realities? In D.D. Unger, J. Kregel, P. Wehman, & V. Brooke (Eds.), *Employers' views of workplace supports: Virginia Commonwealth University Charter Business Roundtable's national study of employer's experiences with workers with disabilities* (pp. 1–12). Richmond: Virginia Commonwealth University.

Unger, D.D. (2002b). Workplace supports: A view from employers who have hired supported employees. In D.D. Unger, J. Kregel, P. Wehman, & V. Brooke (Eds.), *Employers' views of workplace supports: Virginia Commonwealth University Charter Business Roundtable's national study of employer's experiences with workers with disabilities* (pp. 67–80). Richmond: Virginia Commonwealth University.

Unger, D.D., Wehman, P., Yasuda, S., Campbell, L., & Green, H. (2002). Human resource professionals and the employment of people with disabilities: A business perspective. In D.D. Unger, J. Kregel, P. Wehman, & V. Brooke (Eds.), *Employers' views of workplace supports: Virginia Commonwealth University Charter Business Roundtable's national study of employer's experiences with workers with disabilities* (pp. 13–31) Richmond: Virginia Commonwealth University.

Ury, W. (1991). *Getting past no: Negotiating with difficult people.* New York: Penguin Books.

Vandergoot, D. (1987). Review of placement research literature: Implications for research and practice. *Rehabilitation Counseling Bulletin, 31,* 243–272.

Verstegen, D. (2000, Fall). Corporate coaching for recruitment and retention. In *National Supported Employment Consortium.* Richmond: Virginia Commonwealth University.

Wagner, M., Cameto, R., & Newman, L. (2003). *Youth with disabilities: A changing population. A report of the findings of the National Longitudinal Transition Study (NLTS) and the National Longitu-*

dinal Transition Study 2 (NLTS2). Menlo Park, CA: SRI International.

Walls, R., & Fullmer, S. (1997). Competitive employment: Occupations after vocational rehabilitation. *Rehabilitation Counseling Bulletin, 41,* 15–25.

Walls, R.T., Misra, S., & Majumder, R.K. (2002). Trends in vocational rehabilitation: 1978, 1988, 1998. *Journal of Rehabilitation, 68*(3), 4–10.

Walters, S., & Baker, C. (1995). Title I of the Americans with Disabilities Act: Employer and recruiter attitudes toward people with disabilities. *Journal of Rehabilitation Administration, 20,* 15–23.

Wehman, P. (2001). *Supported employment in business.* St. Augustine, FL: Training Resources Network.

Wehman, P., & Kregel, J. (1985). A supported work approach to competitive employment of individuals with moderate and severe handicaps. In P. Wehman & J. Hill (Eds.), *Competitive employment for persons with mental retardation* (pp. 20–45). Richmond: Virginia Commonwealth University.

Weinstein, D. (2000). Practitioner competencies. In R. Huges & D. Weinstein (Eds.), *Best practices in psychosocial rehabilitation* (pp. 113–144). Columbia, MD: International Association of Psychosocial Rehabilitation Services.

Weiss, R. (1974). The provisions of social relationships. In Z. Rubin (Ed.), *Doing unto others* (pp. 17–26). Englewood Cliffs, NJ: Prentice Hall.

West, M.D., Wehman, P., & Revell, G. (2002). *Extended services in supported employment: What are providers doing? Are customers satisfied?* Richmond: Rehabilitation Research and Training Center on Workplace Supports, Virginia Commonwealth University.

West, M.D., Wehman, P., & Revell, G. (1996). Use of social security work incentives by supported employment agencies and consumers: Findings from a national survey. *Journal of Vocational Rehabilitation, 7,* 117–123.

Wilson, K.B., Alston, R.J., Harley, D.A., & Mitchell, N.A. (2002). Predicting VR acceptance based on race, gender, education, work status at application and primary source of support. *Rehabilitation Counseling Bulletin, 45,* 132–142.

Wittenburg, D., & Stapleton, D. (2000). *Review of longitudinal data on the school to work transition for youth with disabilities. Final report submitted to the Department of Education, National Institute on Disability & Rehabilitation Research.* Retrieved July 23, 2003, from http://www.ilr.cornell.edu/nte/papers.html

Workforce Investment Act (WIA) of 1998, PL 105-220, 29 U.S.C. 701 *et seq.*

Zander, R., & Zander, B. (2000). *The art of possibility: Transforming professional and personal life.* Boston: Harvard Business School Press.

Zemke, R., & Anderson, K. (2002). *Delivering knock your socks off service.* New York: AMACOM.

Zufelt, J. (2002). *The DNA of success: Know what you want . . . to get what you want.* New York: HarperCollins.

Index

Page numbers followed by f indicate figures; those followed by t indicate tables.